HAMMER
OF THE
GODS

HAMMER
OF THE
GODS

THE LED ZEPPELIN SAGA

STEPHEN DAVIS

William Morrow and Company, Inc.
New York

Library of Congress Cataloging in Publication Data

Davis, Stephen, 1947–
  Hammer of the gods.

  Bibliography: p.
  1. Led Zeppelin (Musical group)   2. Rock
musicians—England—Biography.   I. Title.
ML421.L4D4   1985   784.5'4'00922 [B]   84-24776
ISBN 0-688-04507-3

10

Dedicated to my brother C.B.D.
"Where'er I roam, whatever realms to see,
My heart untravel'd fondly turns to thee."
OLIVER GOLDSMITH

ACKNOWLEDGMENTS

In March 1975, while on a magazine assignment, I was a guest of Led Zeppelin aboard their *Starship* as they flew between concerts in southern California. For their generosity in those days, thanks to Jimmy Page, Robert Plant, John Paul Jones, and Peter Grant. Thanks also to the late John Bonham, a warm and funny man when I met him.

Thanks also to all those who helped with this book: Kenneth Anger, Ron Bernstein, Ron Bertelucci, David Bieber, Bebe Buell, William S. Burroughs, Chris Charlesworth, Richard Cole, Christopher Davis, Michael des Barres, Joshua Feigenbaum, Benoit Gautier, William Glasser, Danny Goldberg, James Grauerholz, Jake Holmes, James Isaacs, Andy Kent, Eddie Kramer, Darton John Lee, Lori Maddox, Tom Maxey, Doc Miller, Miss Pamela, Roy Pace, Neal Preston,

Ellen Sander, Peter Simon, Chris Welch, Phyllis Wiseman, the Michael Ochs Archive, the *Atlantic Monthly*, Atlantic Records, Regent Air, and the proprietors of the Standish Inn, Hammersmith.

Special thanks to Jim Landis.

Special thanks to Sidi Hamid Sherq.

CONTENTS

CONTENTS

PART
ONE

around the world bad trip for everyone
no more the man of paradise or the celt of
Albion. They queue like burning moths to
spread the old-time vicious lie, you christians
destroyed our tribe I fight you till I die

—ROY HARPER

OVERTURE

The maledicta, infamous libels, and annoying rumors concerning Led Zeppelin began to circulate like poisoned blood during the British rock quartet's third tour of America in 1969. Awful tales were whispered from one groupie clique to another, as Led Zeppelin raided their cities and moved quietly on. Devon and Emaretta might have heard them first in New York; they rang up the beautiful Miss Pamela and the other GTOs in Los Angeles, and then maybe the Plaster Casters in Chicago, and soon all the rock courtesans from the Tea Party to the Whiskey were telling each other *these stories* . . . about how Led Zeppelin sustained itself on the road by drinking vaginal secretions direct from the source; about Led Zeppelin eating women and throwing the bones out the window; about tumescent girls immersed in tubs of warm baked beans before coitus. In Los Angeles the girls staggered out of Sunset Strip hotels by first light of morning and carried preposterous lore back to Hollywood and the Valley, lurid accounts of invocations and gyromancy in candle-lit hotel suites, of maidens publicly banged on tabletops in raunchy rock scene nightclubs, of the beating of women, of sex magic and endless orgies. They talked about the drunken girl in the seaside hotel in Seattle who let Led Zeppelin drub her with a dead shark while Vanilla Fudge's super-8 camera rolled. In New Orleans there were improbable yarns of Led Zeppelin's dalliances with the French Quarter's flamboyant drag queen population. In a documentary called *Groupie*, one girl raved dementedly about the guitarist's prowess with a whip.

The groupies told their little sisters. Word spread to the high schools. Led Zeppelin had a sweet tooth. Led Zeppelin was *dangerous*.

And these rumors weren't even so bad, considering the times: America, especially Southern California, 1969. Nixon in the White House; genocide in Vietnam; Charles Manson out in Death Valley, frustrated by the music business, waiting to send one of his rat patrols of field hippies into Beverly Hills to kill record producers and chop them up. These were *witchy* times. Led Zeppelin's antics were merely the sadistic little games of young English artists loose in the United States with dirty minds and unlimited resources. They set an unattainable standard of depravity, mystique, luxury, and excess for the rock bands that tried to follow them, but by the cold light of day they were all really quite nice, even gentlemen.

But there was always something else whispered about Led Zeppelin, something more sinister than a rock group's after-hours vices. The worst rumor was the one that all the girls had heard, coast to coast. Don't quote me, the girls said (and still say), but Led Zeppelin sold their souls to the Devil in exchange for their instant success, their addictive charisma, their unbelievable wealth. The girls *devoutly* believed this, Led Zeppelin's purported Faustian bargain with Satan. Just *look*, they said. During their decade-long prime in the 1970s, Led

Zeppelin *was* the biggest band in the world, representing the booming record business at its peak as its biggest act. Now they *couldn't* have done this by themselves, it was said.

There was also a catch to this absurd fable. One of the four Zeppelin musicians, the girls insisted, wouldn't sell his soul to the Devil. One of them said no, and refused to sign in blood. And, the girls pointed out, look what happened (or *didn't* happen) to the one who sat out the deal. He was the band's outsider, and avoided the spotlight. He didn't even travel with the band when he could avoid it. He wouldn't let himself be . . . *manipulated*. And, years later, after all the deaths and disasters had befallen Led Zeppelin and the group had dissolved in shame and remorse, he was the only one to survive, almost unscathed.

But the story about Led Zeppelin's supposed deal with the Devil has a strong basis in popular musical tradition, especially considering that the group started out playing the blues. In fact all the young English musicians to flood America in the wake of the Beatles—the Rolling Stones, Animals, Yardbirds, and Kinks in the first wave; Cream, Jeff Beck, and Led Zeppelin in the second—considered themselves blues scholars. Before most of them ever set foot onstage, they had spent months and years locked in bedrooms playing old records, absorbing the classic U.S. blues of Blind Lemon Jefferson, Big Bill Broonzy, Skip James, Leadbelly, and Muddy Waters. Later they discovered Elmore James, Sonny Boy Williamson, and Robert Johnson, king of the Delta blues singers, the possessed and demonic musician who embodied the folkish idea of the blues as the Devil's music. In the Delta of the Mississippi River, where Robert Johnson was born, they said that if an aspiring bluesman waited by the side of a deserted country crossroad in the dark of a moonless night, then Satan himself might come and tune his guitar, sealing a pact for the bluesman's soul and guaranteeing a lifetime of easy money, women, and fame. To this day, the blues singer is somewhat taboo in his community in the American South.

Robert Johnson was the most crucial blues musician who

ever lived, and people murmured that he *must* have waited by the crossroad and gotten his guitar fine-tuned. Born in Robinsonville, Mississippi (about forty miles south of Memphis), about 1911, Robert grew up listening to the original country blues minstrels—Charley Patton, Son House, and Willie Brown. By the time he was twenty, Robert had learned to make his guitar cry and moan by sliding the broken neck of a glass bottle along the strings. By 1935 the enigmatic and secretive young musician had invented a ringing, percussive guitar style and wrote or collected a cycle.of songs that later became the raw material for rhythm and blues, rock and roll, and rock music. He cut violent love songs like "32–20 Blues" and "Kindhearted Woman" and bitter songs of loss like "Love in Vain." There were lighter tunes of punning sexual imagery, like "Terraplane Blues" and "Travelling Riverside Blues," where Robert commands his paramour to squeeze his lemon till the juice runs down his leg, a lyric trademark of Robert Plant forty years down the road. But Robert Johnson's trademark was the desperate sense of conviction in his harrowing songs of diabolic pursuit. In "Me and the Devil Blues" he confesses: "Me and the Devil were walking side by side/I'm going to beat my woman till I get satisfied." And anyone who listens to even the scratchy, fifty-year-old recording of "Hellhound on My Trail" can experience the panicky strain through which Robert Johnson delivered his most chilling lines: "I've got to keep on moving/blues falling down like hail/I can't keep no money/Hellhound on my trail."

By 1938 the recordings of this young genius began to filter north. In New York producer John Hammond was preparing his famous From Spirituals to Swing concert, which would present the greatest Afro-American musicians to the rarefied atmosphere of Carnegie Hall. Hammond had heard "Terraplane Blues" and "Last Fair Deal Gone Down" and wanted Robert Johnson to perform at the concert. But word that Robert had been murdered began to circulate around the Delta. He had been poisoned by a jealous husband near Greenwood,

Mississippi. His mother and brother buried him in an unmarked grave behind the Zion church near Morgan City. His guitar had vanished. And Hammond had to hire Big Bill Broonzy to play at Carnegie Hall instead.

"Hello Satan, I believe it's time to go," sang Robert Johnson, and although he may have kept his crossroad bargain, he didn't really die. In fact, he just grew. Legend has him already working with a small band in the months between his last recording and his death. His passionate style and intense rhythms were copied in the Delta as his records began to circulate, and "Terraplane Blues" was a minor hit in the South. The only musician ever taught by Robert was the son of one of his girl friends, who himself became a bluesman, working as Robert Jr. Lockwood. Two years after Robert's death, Lockwood was playing in Johnson's style with a partner, a singer and harmonica player named Rice Miller, whose *nom de bleus* was Sonny Boy Williamson. By 1941 Lockwood and Williamson were the stars of the King Biscuit Time on KFFA in Helena, Arkansas. By then Lockwood was playing the electric guitar; these broadcasts were the first on which many Delta musicians ever heard the sound of this relatively new instrument. Within a few years Muddy Waters, John Lee Hooker, Howlin' Wolf, B. B. King, and Elmore James plugged in and played Robert's music in Chicago, Memphis, and Detroit. By then it wasn't the blues anymore; it was called R&B. Ten years later Elvis Presley and Chuck Berry turned it into rock and roll. If Robert Johnson had lived another twenty years, he could've played Chuck Berry's guitar intro to "Maybelline." And Elvis and Chuck Berry were censored and banned all over the Blues Belt and the Midwest. It was called "Devil's music." Baptist preachers held torchlight rallies to burn records like witches.

There has always been something about music and the lives of virtuoso musicians that carries with it the whiff of brimstone. There's an aura of sadness, of melancholy, that pervades their world; all great performers know it and have their own methods of dealing with it. "Music," wrote Georges Bizet, "what a splendid art! And what a sad profession!"

The greater the skill of the musician, the higher the price paid for maintaining it. Consider the life of the Genoese violinist Nicolò Paganini (1782–1840), whose career has been compared to Led Zeppelin's. Paganini was the first great virtuoso and superstar within modern memory. In an era when operatic singers were the only musicians to gain substantial acclaim and fortune in Europe, Paganini performed as an instrumental virtuoso *in excelsis*. Appearing at sold-out concerts in tight pants and very long hair, he caused women to scream and faint as he produced mysterious original effects on his violin. He invented the use of harmonics on the violin, perfected double and triple stops, and revived the ancient practice of *scordatura*, the varied retuning of the strings. He was by far the richest musician of his era.

But Paganini was also cursed by annoying rumors and infamous libels throughout his career. His fame was so wide and his power over his instrument and women so legendary that every European peasant knew for a fact that Nicolò Paganini had sold his soul to the Devil. He was accused in the press of being incurably dissipated and a maniacal gambler. It was said that he was selfish, cruel, morbid, and greedy. He is supposed, in the popular imagination, to have led a band of brigands and to have killed the husbands of his noble patronesses. In one contemporary account, Paganini "secured his mastery over mankind and his pre-eminence in his art from the devil in exchange for a soul already sufficiently blasted and damned." Eyewitnesses in Italy soberly related having seen Satan guide Paganini's hands during a concert in Milan, while in France supposedly creditable witnesses swore that they saw emissaries from hell driving away from the concert hall along a road that was not even there. And when Paganini died in France in 1840, the Catholic church denied him burial in consecrated ground, despite pleas from Rome, because local peasants were too frightened. He remained unburied for three years until he was brought back to Italy.

The Devil appears, as Mephistopheles, with violin and bow in Goethe's *Faust*. The Devil's a fiddler in Charlie Daniels's "The Devil Went Down to Georgia." It's an old image.

In April 1982 a committee of the California state assembly convened to listen to a Led Zeppelin record played backward. Irate baptist preachers had complained that when Led Zeppelin records were played that way, satanic messages could be understood, via an obscure recording process called "backward masking," thus exposing upstanding American Christian youth to subliminal satanism and Devil worship. Sure enough, when the committee listened to "Stairway to Heaven" in reverse, some members said they could clearly hear the ominous, slurry, bone-chilling words:

"Here's to my sweet Satan."

ONE

THE TRAIN
KEPT A-ROLLIN'

You can still see the shadow from when the
Zeppelin floated over America: it took like Islam in
the desert . . .

—MICHAEL HERR

The Led Zeppelin saga begins in 1943, in the blacked-out, heavily rationed England of the war years. A clerk in an aircraft works named James Page married Patricia Elizabeth Gaffikin, who worked as a doctor's secretary. On January 9, 1944, she bore her only child, James Patrick Page, in Heston, Middlesex. After the war the father found work as an industrial personnel officer, and the Page family lived in Feltham, near Heathrow Airport west of London. In the mid-

1950s the Page family settled in Epsom, Surrey, a quiet ex-urb of country landscapes and horse races.

Jimmy grew up almost alone in the Pages' comfortable house on Miles Road. He doesn't remember having any playmates until he was five. "That early isolation probably had a lot to do with the way I turned out," he said years later. "A loner. A lot of people can't be on their own. They get frightened, but isolation doesn't bother me at all. It gives me a sense of security."

But Jimmy Page found his best friend when he was about fifteen. It was a Spanish-style guitar with steel strings. Jimmy didn't know what to do with the guitar, so he took it to school and a friend showed him how to tune it. He saw a crowd of kids surrounding a student who was playing some skiffle song, and later he went up to the boy and asked him to tune his guitar.

But Jimmy Page got beyond skiffle in a hurry. After he heard American rock and roll like Elvis's 'Baby Let's Play House" and Chuck Berry's "No Money Down," as he said, "the ex-citement and energy just grabbed me, and I wanted to be part of it." Jimmy took a few lessons from a teacher in Kingston-on-Thames before turning to the overseas radio and records for inspiration. "Solos which affected me could send a shiver up my spine," he remembered later, "and I'd spend hours and in some cases days trying to get them off." At first he worked on the chorded solos on Buddy Holly records, but then he began to concentrate on James Burton, the creative bent-note guitarist who played on most of Ricky Nelson's hits. The bending-string style of guitar solo drove Jimmy mad; trying to play them from scratch proved extremely frustrating. Finally someone told him the secret, replacing the usual coated third string with a much lighter, uncoated string. Otherwise the bent-notes were almost impossible to duplicate. Soon the guitar was the consuming passion of Jimmy Page's life, and he began immersing himself in west London's fledgling circle of young guitarists, record collectors, and blues scholars. One of his friends was a boy about Jimmy's age named Jeff Beck. Jeff had built his own guitar and had been playing for a year when he and his sister took the bus over to Jimmy's house in Epsom one weekend afternoon. Jeff played the James Burton solo from Ricky Nelson's "My Babe." "We were immediately like blood brothers," Jimmy recalled.

The Spanish acoustic guitar didn't last long. To duplicate the jangling guitar sound of Burton, Chuck Berry, or Cliff Gallup (who played with Gene Vincent), Jimmy had to have an electric guitar. So he delivered newspapers and bought a Hoffman Senator guitar with an electric pickup. But since the Senator didn't have a solid body, Jimmy didn't consider it a proper electric guitar. He convinced his father to cosign a hire/purchase agreement so that he could buy a cheap electric guitar called a Grazioso, a British copy of the classic rock and roll guitar, the Fender Stratocaster.

By 1960 Jimmy Page was an adept of the electric guitar. Tall, very thin, bright and alert, he was the hurdles champion of his school and a good student. His teachers confiscated his guitar every day as he arrived in school and kept it locked up until four in the afternoon. "The good thing about the guitar," Jimmy maintains, "was that they *didn't* teach it in school. Teaching myself was the first and most important part of my education. I know that Jeff Beck and I enjoyed pure music because we didn't *have* to."

By the time he was sixteen, Jimmy Page had played in local bands around Epsom. In 1960, playing acoustic guitar, he accompanied the beat poet Royston Ellis at a poetry reading at the Mermaid Theater in London. He had regained an interest in the acoustic instrument after hearing guitarist Bert Jansch. But Jimmy soon acquired an orange Chet Atkins Country Gentleman guitar, one of the very few in England at the time, and was playing with bands around western London. One night in 1961 Jimmy was working in the support band at the Epsom dance hall, warming up the dancers for the big southern bands of the day, Chris Farlowe and the

Thunderbirds and Johnny Kidd and the Pirates. Jimmy started to tear the place up with his unique, natural, dancing guitar rhythm, and a London singer/manager named Neil Christian happened to be there. After the show he offered Jimmy the job of lead guitar in his band, Neil Christian and the Crusaders. Since Jimmy had passed his exams, his parents gave their permission.

The Crusaders played Chuck Berry and Bo Diddley to disinterested audiences at least two years ahead of their time. But in London, seventeen-year-old Jimmy Page began to carve out a legend as *the* new English guitar ace. He was definitely the star of the Crusaders and a real raver, with all the most flash, up-to-date equipment that all the other young guitarists could never afford. He was making twenty pounds a week in an era when a bus driver was doing well to make ten. He was one of the first guitarists around London to play with a foot pedal, and it was *de rigueur* for every aspiring guitarist in London to check Jimmy Page out regularly. A young guitarist from south London named John Baldwin later told an interviewer, "Even in 1962 I can remember people saying, 'You've got to go hear Neil Christian and the Crusaders, they've got this unbelievable young guitarist.' I'd heard of Pagey before I'd heard of Clapton or Beck."

The Crusaders played all over southern England, but after a few months the strain began to debilitate Jimmy. As the star of the show, they had him arching over backward till his head touched the stage, and all the other corny moves that bands of that era had to deploy. Jimmy's health began to deteriorate. The Crusaders were practically living in their van, driving all over England in the damp, suffering the usual breakdowns on the M1. One night, at a gig in Sheffield, Jimmy was walking around outside and collapsed. He woke up on the floor of the dressing room. The doctors diagnosed glandular fever, complicated by exhaustion and fatigue. He was undernourished and emaciated, and had a bronchial cough. Faced with a continuing routine of stage acrobatics, desultory audiences, and almost no food or sleep, Jimmy packed it in. Reluctantly, he left the Crusaders and enrolled in art school in Sutton, intending to study painting.

While Jimmy was learning to draw and mix colors, a cultural whirlwind was brewing in England that would change popular music in Europe and America. In the northern port of Liverpool the Beatles had exploded behind the simple melodies of John Lennon and Paul McCartney.

But it was the 1963 British blues craze that brought a new generation of musicians and fans into the pop mainstream of the day. It had really started back in 1958, when Muddy Waters roared through an English tour with his slicked-down Chicago R&B band, complete with tight black suits, greasy pompadours and loud, rude amplifiers. British audiences had been expecting "authentic" country blues elders from the Delta; instead Muddy blew them away with his mojo working in overdrive and blues falling down like hail. Muddy on this tour converted two key English musicians—Alexis Korner and Cyril Davies—to lifelong disciples of the blues. Two years later bandleader Chris Barber was converted to Chess-style city blues while touring in America. When he returned to England he hired blues fanatics Korner and Davies to appear with his Trad orchestra, and featured them on his Saturday night show on BBC television, *Trad Tavern*. This led to the formation of the first blues band in England, Alexis Korner and Cyril Davies' Blues Incorporated. By May 1962 its members included blues neophytes Mick Jagger on vocals, Charlie Watts on drums, and Jack Bruce on bass; they jammed every weekend to packed houses at the Marquee, an old-line jazz club in Oxford Street. Within a year, Mick and Charlie left to form the Rolling Stones (Jack Bruce would go on to Cream later), but the blues nights at the Marquee were still the rage of London youth anxious for an alternative to the Mersey Sound that was sweeping Britain from the north. Eventually Alexis Korner brought the Stones in from their regular gig at the Crawdaddy Club in suburban Richmond to open for Blues Incorporated. Then the Rolling Stones exploded as well, and never looked back.

Art student Jimmy Page was taking all this in. Rather than play professionally, Jimmy converted the front room of the Page house on Miles Road into a music studio, with a tape recorder, records strewn everywhere, amps, spare electric guitars, a drum kit, and other instruments. Every Sunday Jimmy held court, jamming with Jeff Beck and other young blues scholars of the Richmond and Eel Pie Island crowd. Jimmy's mother, who developed a taste for the music, brewed tea for the lads.

Jimmy liked to have fun too. A friend used to drive him around the Epsom area, and they'd shout insults at people and roar off. Epsom was full of mental hospitals, and the boys were particularly attracted to an institution for young girls with sexual problems, such as compulsive masturbation. One day Jimmy and his friends showed up and tried to pull a couple of girls out of the place, to great merriment but to no avail. Jimmy also would disappear with his guitar on long hitchhiking voyages to Scandinavia, Europe, and points east. On one trip he got as far as India before a recurrence of his fever forced him home.

Soon Jimmy Page abandoned his palette and brushes and started to play again. To get used to working in public, Jimmy would jam with Cyril Davies's interval band at the Marquee, where on one terrifying night these white bluesmen had to support Muddy Waters. A few weeks later, after one of the Marquee blues jams, Page was approached by a young guitarist with a London band called the Roosters. He said that he thought Jimmy sounded a lot like Matthew Murphy, then playing with Memphis Slim. Jimmy was flattered. The guitarist introduced himself. "My name's Eric Clapton."

Cyril Davies died of a blood disease, and Jimmy discontinued the blues nights at the Marquee after a few weeks. By then the Rolling Stones had departed their weekly residency at the Crawdaddy in Richmond, and were replaced by Eric Clapton's new group, an experimental blues band called the Yardbirds. New bands were being invented all over England in the wake of the Beatles and the Stones, and Jimmy was deluged with offers to be lead guitarist in any number of them, but health considerations made him refuse. Instead, he started to work as a studio guitarist, a virtuoso "hired gun" used by producers to fatten the often inadequate sounds of young guitarists in other bands. The session work started after one of the Thursday nights at the Marquee. Recording engineer Glyn Johns, an old friend from Epsom, suggested to Jimmy that he show up for a session the following day. There was a huge demand for new records by English groups, and the sleepy London studio scene had only one electric guitarist, Big Jim Sullivan, considered skilled enough to handle the music the new groups were playing. Jimmy's first session produced the hit song "Diamonds" by Jet Harris and Tony Meehan, who had just left Cliff Richard's band. Then another session, for Carter Lewis and the Southerners, produced "Your Mama's Out of Town," which also hit the English charts, and producers began to consider Jimmy good luck. Not that they had much choice; if you were a producer in that era and needed a studio guitarist, you either sent for Big Jim Sullivan or Little Jimmy Page, as he was known. For a brief time Jimmy joined Carter Lewis's band, but gave it up almost immediately to return to the studios. "I'd been allowed into the whole sort of impenetrable brotherhood," he said, " and it was great fun and games to start with."

In 1965 Shel Talmy, Andrew Oldham, and Mickie Most were the top pop producers in England. They all relied on Jimmy's chameleonlike talent of duplicating any style of guitar—George Harrison, Chuck Berry, Brian Jones. That was how Jimmy Page came to play on the earliest records by the Who, the Kinks, Them, and other top British Invasion bands. When, in January 1965, the Who arrived in the studio to cut their first single, "I Can't Explain," they found that Shel Talmy had Jimmy Page waiting in the hall in case guitarist Peter Townshend was unable to cope. But Townshend proved capable, so Jimmy only added rhythm guitar. On the single's B side, however, Jimmy played lead guitar using one of the innovative effects for which he was famous—the fuzz box. It had been built for him two years earlier. As Jimmy told a reporter, "What happened was Roger Mayer, who later worked for Jimi Hendrix, came up to me when I was still in art school and had started to do a few sessions, and he said, 'I work for the Admiralty in the experimental department and I could make any sort of gadget you want.' So I said why didn't he try to make me this thing that I'd heard years before on this Ventures record, 'The 2000 Pound Bee.' It was a fuzz box, a Gibson fuzz box. We had one in England, but it was a disaster, and I said, 'Why don't you improve on this with the Admiralty's facilities.' Then the Pretty Things got one, and Jeff Beck, and it really swept through."

Of course most of the groups were fiercely proud of their music and were often angry that outside musicians were used on their records. The sessions for Them were really uncomfortable for Jimmy, as the four tough Belfast musicians who backed Van Morrison were replaced, one by one, with London session hacks. "The group went in thinking they were going to record," Jimmy said, "and all of a sudden they find these other people playing on their records. It's a miracle they didn't replace Van Morrison. Talk about daggers!"

The Kinks were less unhappy about Page playing on their tunes; Jimmy's presence on rhythm guitar meant that Ray Davies could move about the studio producing and directing. However, the Kinks were later disturbed when rumors appeared in London that Jimmy was responsible for the trademark fuzz-tone chords of "All Day and All of the Night" and "You Really Got Me." They felt that Page had broken the session player's tacit code of anonymity by talking to the press and giving false impressions.

While he was carving out a well-paid life as a studio hack by day, he would return to Epsom at night (his friends said Jimmy was too miserly to leave his parents' house and get his own place) and revert to his preferred role of blues scholar, auditioning blues discs and learning the guitar solos. Late in January 1965 he played a session that combined his two worlds, the studio and the blues.

Sonny Boy Williamson first arrived in England in 1963 on a tour organized by the American Folk Blues Festival. He returned the following year, recording with vanguard English bands like the Yardbirds and the Animals (who were all terrified of the large, scowling bluesman. Back in Helena, Arkansas, where Sonny Boy lived, the locals were afraid of him too. Sonny Boy was six feet two inches and was said to be quick with a blade). In blues-crazy England, Sonny Boy's career revived. He went to a London tailor and ordered his version of British haberdashery, appearing in concert in two-toned pin-striped suits with a bowler hat at a rakish tilt. He had a bluesman's appetite for whiskey and usually played drunk. On one visit to Birmingham he set fire to his hotel room when he tried to stew a rabbit in a coffee percolator. But if the young British blues scholars who tried to play with him found him menacing, he was also the real thing. He had known the shadowy Robert Johnson and had learned from his stepson, Robert Jr. Lockwood. He was a living link to the shining primitive country blues of the 1930s.

The session that paired Sonny Boy Williamson and Jimmy Page was organized by Giorgio Gomelsky, the Yardbirds' manager. Also on the date were organist Brian Auger, session drummer Mick Waller, and several other blues scholars. Sonny Boy walked into the studio, cracked open a bottle of Scotch, nodded at the awestruck young musicians, rehearsed the tunes once, and recorded them on the spot. Jimmy took solos on "I See a Man Downstairs" and "Little Girl," but mostly Sonny Boy would drown him out with his amplified harmonica. The session was total chaos; Sonny Boy kept the musicians guess-

ing with long pauses and arcane blues structures that he seemed
to be improvising on the spot. Ironically, Sonny Boy returned to Helena right after the session with Jimmy Page. At
home he jammed with a group of white R&B musicians who
called themselves the Hawks (later to be renamed The Band).
Talking to guitarist Robbie Robertson, Sonny Boy derided the
English players he had been working with, saying how miserably the Yardbirds and the others had played. The following May, Sonny Boy Williamson passed away.

The year 1965 was the prime of Swinging London. Beer
was three shillings a pint and the streets were full of Mini
cars and miniskirts. There was something new in the air and
great fortunes to be made from the pop explosion—art, music, and style—that erupted in London that year. By then the
Beatles had become too big to perform in public anymore,
while the Stones had deserted the Marquee and other local
venues for whirlwind tours of provincial theaters and the United
States. The hippest band in London was the loud and trendy
Yardbirds, with their speedy raving R&B jams and hot young
guitarist, Eric Clapton. Ace session player Jimmy Page, partly
because of his friendship with Clapton and partly just to make
the most happening scene in town, often hung out with the
band whenever they worked around London.

The Yardbirds had come out of the Richmond–Kingston
area in the wake of the Rolling Stones. Eric Clapton, rhythm
guitarist Chris Dreja, and singer Keith Relf emerged from west
London art colleges, joined by bassist Paul Samwell-Smith and
drummer Jim McCarty, who'd been in a band together at
Hampton Grammar. At first they played acoustic blues as the
Metropolis Blues Quartet on Friday nights at the Railway
Hotel, Norbiton. But in early 1963 they heard the Rolling
Stones, changed their name to the Yardbirds, and plugged into
the R&B classics the Stones *didn't* play—the rest of the Howlin'
Wolf, Jimmy Reed, and Bo Diddley songbooks. But the
Yardbirds also had a much different approach than the Stones,

who were locked into fairly rigid arrangements. The Yardbirds took off from straight R&B into free-form soloing and
long instrumental sections, mostly improvised from night to
night. When their first album was released, the Yardbirds followed the Stones into the exhausting world of package tours,
playing a different theater every night for two months. Unlike
the Stones, the Yardbirds were unable to translate their wild
art college R&B into a hit single. Late in 1964 Giorgio Gomelsky decided to change tactics and produce a purely pop
single for the Yardbirds by an outside composer with no inkling of their basic R&B act. The song was "For Your Love"
by Manchester songwriter Graham Gouldman (who went on
to form the band 10cc). When "For Your Love" was released
in March 1965, it was an immediate worldwide hit. But blues
scholar Clapton hated the song and the idea of the Yardbirds
doing any kind of music other than the blues. Clapton refused to play on the track after much pleading, and then quit
the band.

Even before Eric Clapton left the Yardbirds, Gomelsky had
asked Jimmy Page to take the job of lead guitar. Page turned
him down immediately. Obviously, Jimmy didn't want a
professional quarrel over the Yardbirds to spoil his friendship
with Eric Clapton. Instead, Jimmy gave the Yardbirds another fine guitarist—Jeff Beck. The Yardbirds had never heard
of him.

For the past year Beck had been developing into one of the
hottest guitar players in London, fronting an obscure dance
band called the Tridents. But he was always too broke even
to afford new guitar strings. Jimmy was so insistent that Jeff
would be the perfect lead guitar for the Yardbirds that they
offered him the job. Jeff Beck joined the Yardbirds in March
1965. Trying to fill Eric Clapton's shoes in a successful band
was daunting, but Gomelsky took Beck to an expensive hair-
dresser for his trademark "puddin' basin" cut and bought him
some flash Carnaby Street stage clothes. Beck took off from
there, inventing new guitar choreography, playing the guitar

behind his head, blowing out his amps with feedback, distortion, and psychedelic effects that would be copied by many other bands. With no strong visual presence like Mick Jagger in the band, the Yardbirds developed their guitarist as the group's trademark and became a laboratory for the guitar showmen who would dominate progressive rock music. To support their next record, "Heart Full of Soul," the Yardbirds decamped for America in June 1965. Before he left England, Jeff showed up on Jimmy Page's doorstep and presented Jimmy with a rare 1958 Telecaster. "It's yours," Jeff said.

Jimmy, meanwhile, was teaching himself the art of record production, working with young engineers like Glyn Johns and Eddie Kramer. Soon Andrew Oldham, the Stones' manager, hired Jimmy as a staff producer for his label, Immediate Records. Page's work for Immediate included unknown groups, singer Chris Farlowe, and the German chanteuse Nico, who later turned up in New York playing her harmonium with the Velvet Underground. Jimmy also produced four tracks for the reigning English blues band, John Mayall's Bluesbreakers, with Eric Clapton on blistering lead guitar. With Clapton and Jeff Beck, Jimmy also recorded a series of informal blues jams on a theme by Elmore James. Clapton and Beck thought they had been playing rehearsals, so when Immediate later released the recordings as a bogus "archive" of British blues, they were incensed and blamed Jimmy for betraying their friendship.

Jimmy also produced his own first single in late 1965. "She Just Satisfies" by Jimmy Page was released on the Fontana label late that year; it had a fuzz-tone, Kinks guitar figure but inane lyrics and Jimmy was clearly no singer. Describing the record to friends as "tongue in cheek," Jimmy had played all the instruments himself, except for veteran session drummer Bobby Graham. The B side was better. "Keep Movin' " was a hard British R&B instrumental with Jimmy overdubbing good blues harmonica and a copy of an Eric Clapton 1965 Bluesbreaker guitar solo. The record didn't make the charts.

By early 1966 Jimmy had played on literally hundreds of London sessions. He was the wise hack of the pop world, a consummate pro, making a fortune while the rest of his generation of English musicians toiled in bands for lots of fame, especially in America, but little money. Outside the insular world of the London recording studios, Jimmy Page was unknown. He took his vacations in Los Angeles and checked out the Byrds and Buffalo Springfield so he could hold his own with returning bandsmen back home. To keep his mind off the drudgery of sessions, he experimented with new techniques.

At one session in 1966 a violinist idly asked Jimmy if he had ever tried to bow the electric guitar. Jimmy borrowed a bow and had a go. Out of the Gibson Black Beauty came a long, sonorous electro-drone on the bass string and unearthly piercing cries on the higher strings. The neck of the guitar isn't curved, so he could "play" only two strings, but when Jimmy irritated the bow across all six strings, wild whoops and great blats of noise emitted from the amplifier. It was an obviously dramatic devise, and Jimmy Page started to play around with it. Coincidentally, a guitarist named Eddie Phillips with an English group called Creation (bass guitar: Ron Wood) was already bowing his electric guitar in London clubs at the time.

Now Jimmy began to burn out from studio work. The last straw was a session Jimmy did for French star Johnny Halliday. To one writer he admitted, "I was becoming one of those sort of people that I hated." But in the spring of 1966, salvation arrived in the form of another invitation to join the Yardbirds. This time, Jimmy Page didn't say no.

By then Jeff Beck had been with the Yardbirds for a desperate year of lows and highs. The band toured America on the proto-psychedelic "Shapes of Things," and Jeff dazzled American teen-agers with his sexual poses and the visceral nerve of his playing. Under the mad tutelage of Giorgio Gomelsky, the Yardbirds would try anything. After a show in Memphis Gomelsky rang up Sam Phillips, the legendary producer who had first recorded Elvis, Jerry Lee Lewis, and other major deities of rock and roll. Gomelsky asked for studio time and later talked Phillips himself down to supervise the session where the Yardbirds cut "Train Kept A-Rollin'," probably the artistic zenith of their career. Later the band cut "Shapes of Things" and "I'm a Man" at Chess Studios in Chicago. Yardbirds legend has Bo Diddley and henchmen showing up at the studio to claim instant royalties after the band left.

But Jeff's attitude was increasingly frustrating to the other musicians. Temperamental, vain, vulnerable to crushing headaches from a childhood accident, Jeff would play inspired, sustained bent-note blues guitar one night, and then play erratically for the next three concerts. He'd met a girl named Mary Hughes in Los Angeles, the Yardbirds' American stronghold, and would occasionally miss concerts in order to stay with her. While the Yardbirds were heavily influencing the new California bands with their loud droning blues trance music, they were rupturing from within. Jeff Beck was bored and losing interest. By then Gomelsky had burned out and sold the Yardbirds to Simon Napier-Bell, a London boulevardier who won the musicians over by telling them he could obtain *advances* against royalties from their record company, something they had never heard of.

By early 1966 Jeff Beck was already trying to convince Jimmy Page to join him in the Yardbirds so they could play dual lead guitar on stage. Beck thought the combination of two howling psychedelic lead guitars would be devastating; he was also desperate to put life into the band. By April the music press was full of rumors that Jimmy Page would be joining the Yardbirds, and Jimmy confirmed it that month at a session he played for singer Ian Whitcomb, saying that he might *replace* Beck, who Jimmy said had burned out in America. Jimmy taught Whitcomb to read the charts for the session ("kind soul," commented the singer). The bass player was a ubiquitous session arranger who called himself John Paul Jones.

By this time Paul Samwell-Smith was musical director of the Yardbirds, and he produced the group's next single, "Over

Under Sideways Down," whose guitar part was reportedly sung to Jeff Beck by Simon Napier-Bell. Samwell-Smith was also burned out. He was disgusted at the Yardbirds' slack attitude and just wanted to produce records. In May 1966 tension within the band was obvious. Jimmy Page drove up to Oxford one night with Jeff Beck to see a Yardbirds show at the May Ball held every year by the university's undergraduates, who had hired both the Yardbirds and the Hollies to play three sets apiece. As soon as the two guitarists made their way backstage and saw the hunchbacked Keith Relf reeling around drunkenly, they knew it was going to be a long night. The Yardbirds' first set went well but got little response, which annoyed Relf and got him drinking even harder. Backstage, Relf and Hollies singer Allan Clarke started to smash refectory trays with judo blows. Relf broke all the fingers of one hand, which swelled up like sausages, and this sent him back to the bar to deaden the pain. During the Yardbirds' second set Relf was shit-faced. While the band played their hits, Relf farted into the mike, told the formally attired students to fuck themselves, then started groveling on the floor. When he got up again he fell back into the drums and had to be dragged off. Out in the audience Page was doubled over with laughter. For the third set they strapped Relf to the mike stand and played all their numbers as instrumentals.

Backstage after the show, Paul Samwell-Smith quit the Yardbirds in disgust. He invited Chris Dreja and Jim McCarty to leave with him, but they refused. Instead, Jimmy volunteered to replace Samwell-Smith on bass until they found somebody else. Chris Dreja says, "Page had been doing sessions for years. He wanted to get out on the road, and I think he saw it as a good opportunity to join a band that was out in the thick of it. And he jumped at the chance. He was prepared to possibly play *drums* if necessary." (In an aside, Dreja nervously added, "I'll get the evil eye for saying that.")

Jimmy made his debut as the Yardbirds' bassist at the Marquee in London in June 1966. At first Simon Napier-Bell tried

to dissuade the group from taking on a shrewd professional like Jimmy. To Jeff Beck, he said, *"You're* the genius guitarist in the group. To bring in someone as good as you is crazy."
But Beck and the others insisted, and Jimmy was asked to stay with the band. "He was happy to stay," according to Dreja, "and although it wasn't his normal instrument, he was happy to remain on bass. I think he just liked being in the band . . . He was very sweet and wanted to please. He'd do anything for you until his ego got in the way."

Jimmy's first American tour with the Yardbirds began in August 1966. They played the Whiskey in L.A. and the Carousel Ballroom in San Francisco, as well as state fairs all over the Midwest and the South. Jimmy, in high spirits, tucked his slender frame in an antique officer's jacket and hid his long black hair under an American Civil War cap. He took along his performing ax of the day, the 1958 Telecaster, now painted in Day-Glo psychedelic whorls and backed with Perspex to reflect rainbow beams back from spotlights. Musically the Yardbirds were at their apogee. Jimmy's urge to rock was even more exaggerated when he played bass, and "Train Kept A-Rollin' " and "I'm a Man" burned away under Jeff's blurry washes of drone and feedback. They played a memorable outdoor show on Catalina island before flying to San Francisco to play the Carousel Ballroom, one of the breeding grounds of the San Francisco bands. But Jeff Beck got a sore throat and refused to play; the group decided to switch Chris Dreja to bass and go on with Jimmy on lead. In the past one of Beck's collapses meant a crisis for the band; Beck was undeniably the star of the Yardbirds and their fans wouldn't accept a show without the pouting guitarist. But now Jimmy Page seized the moment and tore the place apart. Pairing the acidic Telecaster with a pair of Fender amps, Jimmy reproduced the familiar Clapton and Beck solos from the Yardbirds records, and then dazzled on his own. He astonished the Carousel audience by bowing the guitar, conjuring bizarre, oceanic swoops of sound that meshed with the hall's psychedelic light show. By the end of the evening the Yard-birds were relieved. Everyone had the feeling that Jeff might not stick around much longer, but the Yardbirds *could* go on with Jimmy Page in his place.

But Jeff did come back to the band, and they finished their summer tour and went home still in one piece. Chris Dreja took over on bass; Jeff and Jimmy were playing lead, with Keith Relf bitterly complaining that their amps were too loud. Back in England Jimmy and Jeff spent hours rehearsing at Jimmy's new digs, a converted Victorian boat house on the upper reaches of the Thames. The two guitarists taught themselves a few Freddie King solos note for note—"I'm Going Down" sounded best—and practiced playing in unison or in har-mony until they got it sounding right. Dual lead electric gui-tars in a rock band were very flash and new, and the two musicians were confident they'd come across something commercially explosive. And while they lasted, the two gui-tars were *magic*, producing shuddering, sirenlike wails that filled the air with queer countertones and overtones. Sadly, little of the Yardbirds' dual-lead music was recorded. The next Yardbirds single, "Happenings Ten Years Time Ago," was recorded while the group was waiting for Beck, who was late for the session. The only dual-lead track that captured the wild flight of the Yardbirds was called "Stroll On." It was recorded in late summer 1966 for the band's appearance in *Blow-Up*, Michelangelo Antonioni's cryptodocumentary of the Swing-ing London era. Antonioni had scripted a scene calling for a rock band in a club and tried to cast the Who, which he had witnessed violently destroying their instruments as part of their act. But the Who wouldn't do the film and Napier-Bell got the Yardbirds involved. They recorded some original music for the sound track, but at the audition they had played "Train Kept A-Rollin'," and that was all Antonioni wanted to hear—those two harmonic lead guitars. But some sort of contractual glitch surfaced concerning the old rockabilly song, so Keith Relf rewrote the words slightly and the song was reborn as

"Stroll On." The Yardbirds were filmed, Jimmy playing bass, at Elstree Studios outside of London, on a set that was a painstakingly re-created version of the Ricky Tick in Windsor. Still obsessed with his image of the Who, Antonioni told Jeff Beck to smash up his guitar. Beck refused, since he was playing a precious instrument; anyway that wasn't his act, it was Peter Townshend's. (Actually, when playing America, the easily frustrated Beck often knocked over his malfunctioning amps. Once in New Mexico he stopped a show by throwing his amp out an open window next to the stage.) But Antonioni insisted, and Beck was supplied with a cheap prop guitar. Grinning like a droog, he smashed it as the camera caught Jimmy Page smirking in his long hair and muttonchops.

In September the dual-lead Yardbirds came to life in a package tour of Britain with the Stones, Ike and Tina Turner, and the Jaywalkers, with singer Terry Reid. On good nights the Yardbirds were blazing, but gradually competition between the two guitar prima donnas flared into the open. When the stereo effects and guitar harmonies didn't work, the other musicians blamed Beck. Jimmy Page, wise hack and consummate pro, was good every night and quickly started to outshine Jeff on the tour.

Jeff Beck's days in the band were obviously numbered, and he was already working with Mickie Most, the veteran singles producer who was then very hot with Donovan and Herman's Hermits. Since Beck couldn't sing and didn't fit in well with groups, Most cast him as a solo instrumentalist and arranged a session even before Beck had departed the Yardbirds. That session almost turned into Led Zeppelin, two years early.

The idea was to record a variation of Ravel's "Bolero" for rock guitar. Jimmy Page was arranging and playing electric twelve-string rhythm guitar, Nicky Hopkins was on piano, and the proposed rhythm section was drummer Keith Moon and bassist John Entwistle, both of whom were tired of the ever-battling Who. At the last moment, Entwistle bowed out; his place was taken by Most's young session arranger, John Paul Jones. "Beck's Bolero" was recorded at IBC Studios in Langham Place, into which the loony Moon sneaked, wearing shades and a great Cossack hat, because he wasn't supposed to play any sessions outside the Who.

"Beck's Bolero" was so appealing that there was serious talk about forming a band. Keith Moon and John Paul Jones were ready, Page and Beck were keen, but they needed a singer. Steve Winwood (then about to form Traffic) and Steve Marriott of the Small Faces were approached, but the plan was killed when Jimmy, who had queried Marriott's manager, was asked in turn how he'd feel playing guitar with ten broken fingers. The Led Zeppelin prototype crashed right there.

In October the Yardbirds took off for a five-week tour of the United States as part of Dick Clark's Caravan of Stars. The tour was a disaster. After three days of bus travel and playing two shows a night, Jeff Beck cracked. He kicked over his stack of amps, smashed his guitar, walked offstage, and caught the next plane to Los Angeles. The Yardbirds continued as a four-piece. When they reached Los Angeles, Beck was apologetic, but at a band meeting the three original Yardbirds refused to play with Jeff anymore and fired him. Jeff got up to leave and asked Jimmy if he was coming. Jimmy looked at him and said, "No. I'm going to stay behind." With Jeff's departure, the Yardbirds became Jimmy's. Opinions vary as to who was ultimately responsible. "This is all very touchy," he told one writer. "There was a lot of cloak and dagger stuff going on and I didn't want to be a part of it at all . . . He and I were very close. This strange professional jealousy came between us, and I don't understand why."

While the Yardbirds slogged through the remainder of the Dick Clark tour, they learned that Napier-Bell was selling his share of the Yardbirds to Mickie Most and his partner, Peter Grant. Most was chiefly interested in Jeff Beck while Grant, a veteran of the British music wars, took over the Yardbirds.

Before he left, Napier-Bell told Peter Grant to watch out for Jimmy Page, who asked too many questions about where the band's money was going. As Grant remembers, "He told me, 'It's a good band, but you need to find a guitarist. He's a real troublemaker, that Jimmy Page.' When I met Jimmy, I told him this. 'Troublemaker!' he said, 'You're dead right. We did *Blow-Up*, five weeks in America and a Rolling Stones tour of Britain and we got just £118 each.' I took them on."

Soon after buying their contract, Grant took the Yardbirds to Australia and Singapore. Unlike other managers, Grant went along and suffered the same hardships as the musicians. Jimmy loved this, and the fact that Grant's gangster manners and 250 pounds of east London bulk intimidated anyone who tried to screw the band. After years of mismanagement, this was the first tour where the Yardbirds made any money. After Australia, Jimmy flew on to India, where he wanted to hear Carnatic music. He arrived, alone, in Bombay on the Arabian Sea at three in the morning with a duffel bag over his shoulder, and spent days in the streets, listening to itinerant musicians.

Mickie Most was the hottest manager/producer in 1967 England, and might have seemed the ideal producer for the Yardbirds. Three of his acts—Herman's Hermits, Lulu, and Donovan—were among the biggest in the world. But Jimmy Page was concerned. During trips to California he had heard how groups like Paul Butterfield and the San Francisco bands were stretching into improvisational styles. The rigid, three-minute single format—Mickie Most's specialty—was already dead. Jimmy wanted to take the Yardbirds into the psychedelic unknown, not make jingles for teen-agers.

Peter Grant was the perfect foil for Jimmy's discontent. Born in 1935, he had lived a Dickensian life of hardship: broken home, wartime evacuation, no education. By the age of thirteen he was a stagehand at the Croyden Empire theater. He grew up as a runner on Fleet Street, rushing wet film around.

A hard-eyed, hulking man, he'd been a nightclub bouncer, a movie extra in *The Guns of Navarone*, Robert Morley's double in films, and wrestled professionally as Prince Mario Alassio. Growing up in the streets had given him a tenacious gut instinct for cash and how it flowed. By the end of the fifties he was a tough U.K. tour manager for American rockers like Little Richard, Gene Vincent, and the Everly Brothers. A famous English music legend has him beating up a promoter who tried to stiff Little Richard after a show, and then beating up the six bobbies who had arrived to calm him down. By the mid-sixties, Grant had learned the ropes of touring in the States as tour manager for the Animals, one of Mickie Most's acts. After undergoing several close scrapes with the Animals, he let it be known that he carried a gun. Intimidating and indomitable, he was the opposite of the reticent, epicene Jimmy Page, who just wanted to play his guitar for stoned-out American kids, travel the world, make millions of pounds, and be left in peace to read Aleister Crowley and practice magic spells, or whatever he did. From the moment Page and Grant met, the end of the Yardbirds was preordained.

Meanwhile, contracts had to be fulfilled, and Mickie Most booked the Yardbirds into the studio. Jimmy was eager to record as head of the Yardbirds, inspired by the revolutionary new bands springing up. Eric Clapton, Jack Bruce, and drummer Ginger Baker had formed Cream to play gritty, speeded up electric versions of Robert Johnson and Skip James. Cream was *the* hot band in England. Steve Winwood had formed Traffic and was recording a rock raga called "Paper Sun," and newer bands like the Move, Soft Machine, Pink Floyd, and Free (with a teen-age singer named Paul Rodgers) were extending the boundaries of what groups could do in the studio. Rumors of a new Beatles masterpiece called *Sgt. Pepper's Lonely Hearts Club Band* were flying. So Jimmy was horrified when the Yardbirds were given the Mickie Most treatment. Jimmy remembered, "On half the tracks we didn't hear the playbacks. Some of them were first takes. We'd spend time on the singles, but Micky Most thought that albums were nothing . . . just something to stick out after a hit single." When Jimmy asked to hear the playback, Most would growl back over the intercom, "Don't worry about it." The other Yardbirds weren't even invited to play. Jimmy was joined by Most's usual arranger, John Paul Jones, on bass, and other session musicians were brought in. The result was a sorry batch of songs, mostly demos from unknown composers. Among the standouts were "Little Games," which had a nice bowed cello section by John Paul Jones; "White Summer," Jimmy's Carnatic madrigal that was his solo showpiece in concert; and "Tinker, Tailor, Soldier, Sailor" and "Glimpses," both of which featured Jimmy's strange bowing technique for the first time on records. "Glimpses" is also an example of the mixed-media presentations the Yardbirds were performing in concert, bedrock psychedelia with ominous chanting, sitar and bowed guitar fragments, and distorted radio voices. The Yardbirds also recorded at CBS Studios in New York. Two of these tracks, "Think About It" and "Goodnight Sweet Josephine," were released as the Yardbirds' last single early in 1968. There's an incendiary Jimmy Page guitar solo on "Think About It," goosed with a metal slide and backward echo, that would resurface later as the key second solo that brought Led Zeppelin's version of "Dazed and Confused" to its molten climax.

At home in England, Eric Clapton's Cream and the Jimi Hendrix Experience were the reigning bands, and the Yardbirds were ignored. But "Little Games" was a hit in America, where the Yardbirds virtually moved in 1967. In March *Blow-Up* was released and the Yardbird's blistering segment made them underground stars. While Keith nourished himself with daily LSD voyages, Jimmy took care of business and gave interviews to teen mags like *Hit Parader*, which headlined "Yardbird Jimmy Page says, 'Open Your Mind.' " After expounding on Carnaby Street fashions, Clapton and Beck, Indian music and his guitars, Jimmy lays out his hippie-era philosophy: "I'm not actually concerned with clothes. In actual fact, I'm pleased to see people walking around in outrageous things. They're throwing off the chains of a society that was. It's probably making England completely decadent, but so what? Actually it's a forecast of the end of society. But I don't care because I'll be dead before it ends. If we've come this far in five years, it should *really* be something in another five. I'd like the new society to be a peaceful one, but it won't be, because violence seems to be the answer to every problem. Every fringe society must be experiencing this. We walk around with long hair and someone shouts something, so you give him an answer back which is a little sharp which they don't quite expect, so they come to fists. What sort of mentality is that?" Jimmy finished the interview with some veiled remarks against the war in Vietnam, and expressed his deep love of Hollywood, especially Sunset Strip.

Most of the Yardbirds were by then burned out and addled by drugs, but Peter Grant kept them on the road all year. In April they toured Scandinavia, followed by shows in Japan and France, which featured psychedelic backing tapes of bombs and trains and old newsreels of Hitler, augmented by a troupe of dancers called Pan's People. For Relf and McCarty, the gigs had become a joke. But Jimmy was still fresh and enjoying every minute of his stardom, playing the costumed pre-Raphaelite dandy, in long hair, love beads, crushed velvet bell-bottoms, frilled lace shirts, silk caftans, buckskin jackets, cowboy boots, and paisley robes. They played on flatbed trucks at open-air amusement parks in the South, as well as hip dance halls like the Boston Tea Party and the Kinetic Circus in Chicago, where Jimmy reportedly accepted the invitation of the Plaster Casters, that city's primal groupie clique, which made casts of the erect penises of the rock stars who passed through town. With Peter Grant along to scare the shit out of everybody, the Yardbirds were at last making money. Somehow Grant had hooked the band onto the Mafia club circuit. One typical incident took place at an amusement park in Warwick, Rhode Island, as the Yardbirds' bus pulled up an hour late. The two Italian promoters jumped on the bus, took out their guns, and started telling the musicians they were going to die. But Grant rose up and started butting them back toward the door with his mountainous belly, yelling, *"You're gonna do wot?"* And things cooled down and the show went on.

On one of their free nights in New York, the Yardbirds trooped down to the Café a Go Go to hear Janis Ian, who had a big hit with "Society's Child." But they were floored by the opening act, a folksinger named Jake Holmes who performed with two other acoustic guitarists. One of Holmes's songs, "Dazed and Confused," had a sinister descending bass scale and jittery, paranoid lyrics that described a bad acid trip with unsparing accuracy. As played by Holmes and his guitarists, the song had a percusssive, ritualistic solo, almost flamenco in nuance, which dissolved into an acid guitar drone. "Dazed and Confused," the band agreed, was a brilliant number—dramatic, frightening, and very stealable. The next morning they bought the album it was on, *The Underground Sound of Jake Holmes*, and set about adapting it for their act, Keith Relf rewriting the lyrics and Jimmy patching in his furious guitar lick from "Think About It." Calling their version "I'm Confused," they played it that December when they opened for the Young Rascals at the old Madison Square Garden in New York.

Early in 1968 Peter Grant booked what was to be the last Yardbirds tour of the United States. There was already a serious rift in the group between the slack hippie faction (Relf and McCarty) and the serious professionals (Page and Grant). Chris Dreja was somewhere in the middle. Relf was always making fun of Jimmy's show-must-go-on attitude; at one band meeting he bitterly told Jimmy that for him, all the magic left the Yardbirds when Eric Clapton quit the band.

In late January 1968 the Yardbirds returned to America for a tour of colleges and psychedelic ballrooms that provided the

main audience for the new "progressive rock" that had re-
placed rock and roll. Almost every big city had one or more
FM stereo radio stations that broadcast rock twenty-four hours
a day, in sharp contrast to the catholic pop music policies of
the BBC at home. Sustained by pills, shots, and dope, the
Yardbirds prepared to hit the road. Managing the tour was
Richard Cole, a recently hired English employee of Peter
Grant's. Twenty-two years old, six feet two, a gold earring
dangling from one ear, Cole became a central character in
Led Zeppelin's rise to the top. In time his antics with Led
Zeppelin created his own legend for Richard Cole, the ulti-
mate road manager, the compleat rock soldier.

Cole was born in east London in 1945. He started his career as a scaffolder, but in a pub one day in 1965 someone
offered him a job as a roadie for an English band called the
Unit Four plus Two. By 1966 he was making twenty pounds
a week road-managing the Who until his driver's license was
revoked for speeding. Then he worked for the Searchers and
lived in the south of France. At night he slept in a van owned
by an English group called the Paramounts, who later changed
their name to Procol Harum. A timid little piano player named
Reg Dwight was hanging around that scene. Later he changed
his name to Elton John. Cole's next job was driving a van for
a band called Ronnie Jones and the Night Timers, with John
Paul Jones on bass and John McLaughlin on lead guitar. In
late 1966 he took a job with the New Vaudeville Band, who
hit with "Winchester Cathedral." That band fulfilled Cole's
fervent desire to see America. As he puts it, "It was anyone's
dream, if you're an English road manager, to come to America. They used to leave their English roadies behind and pick
up a crew over there. They *used* to. I fucking reorganized that
very sharply. I said, 'Fuck that. Let's take our own equipment
over there, wot we're used to working on.'" The New Vaudeville Band was managed by Peter Grant. When Cole went to
Oxford Street to ask about the job, Grant offered him twenty-
five pounds a week. Cole said, "Naw, fuck that. Thirty a week,

take it or leave it." Grant looked at the tall, muscular Richard Cole, sized him up as a better-looking, less dangerous version of himself, and said he would take it. Cole worked for Grant—and Led Zeppelin—for the next thirteen years.

Richard Cole stayed with the New Vaudeville Band until the end of the year. (One night in Birmingham a young local drummer, whose kit had been repossessed, asked Cole if he could set up and play the band's drums. Taking pity on the sixteen-year-old John Henry Bonham, Cole said yes.) Cole then moved to America and went to work with the Vanilla Fudge as a sound engineer for a hundred dollars a week, touring on the strength of the Fudge's big hit, a light/heavy version of the Supremes' "You Keep Me Hangin' On." When he heard the Yardbirds were coming back to America, he wrote to Peter Grant and asked for the job of tour manager, and got it.

For a month Richard Cole dragged the recalcitrant, stoned-out Yardbirds all over America. Cole was as hard as Grant, and actually took physical chances to protect the musicians under his care, intimidating dishonest clubowners and beating on aggressive autograph hounds. He knew every groupie in every town, and could actually say to a homesick drummer as they were arriving in some wretched midwestern town that he knew a girl there who loved English drummers. Mother hen, field pimp, hit man, Richard Cole was dearly loved by every band he worked for. Cole was the ultimate sergeant—big, nasty, a natural leader, an Anglo-Irish pirate who would have been at home with the notorious White Companies, looting France during the Hundred Years War.

The Yardbirds arrived in New York in April 1968 for a date at the Anderson Theater, a dingy rock palace two blocks from the Fillmore East. It was a bad, dismal night and the band was jet-lagged from their flight from Los Angeles, the Yardbirds' adopted home. So they were angry when a staff producer from Epic, their American record company, announced that he was going to record the show. Nevertheless, the Yardbirds went on and opened with their theme, "Train Kept A-

Rollin'.'" "I'm Confused" sounded like the sound track of a horror film, featuring dramatic hushes (this was in the depths of the Doors' "rock theater" period), Jimmy's dramatic bow showpiece, and the dazzle guitar solo at the climax. For "Shapes of Things," Keith Relf introduced "Jimmy 'Magic Fingers' Page, Grand Sorcerer of the Magic Guitar." After Jimmy's Indo-Celtic showpiece, "White Summer" (played on an Indian-tuned Danelectro guitar), the show ended with "I'm a Man" and a full blast Yardbirds rave-up, Jimmy playing a wild, flashing solo on his knees.

A few days later the group went to Epic to hear the play-back. "It was a total embarrassment," Jimmy recalled. "It was recorded on jet lag, and by a guy who had never recorded a rock band in his life. . . . He had one mike on the drums, which was unthinkable, and he miked the wrong cabinet for the guitar so that the fuzz tone, which gave us all the sustain, wasn't picked up." Even worse, the producer had tacked on bullfight cheers and sound effects of clinking glasses to make the concert sound "live." The Yardbirds forbade Epic to release the record.

While the Yardbirds were in New York, Richard Cole hung out with Keith Moon and John Entwistle at Salvation, the hot disco of the day. One night Moon and Entwistle were bitching about the Who, about how they hated Roger Daltrey and Pete Townshend and wanted to break up the Who and form a band with Jimmy Page and Steve Winwood. And Entwistle said, according to Cole, "Yeah. We'll call it Lead Zeppelin. Because it'll fucking go over like a lead balloon." Moon roared out his maniacal bray, and Richard Cole told Jimmy about the idea the minute he got back to the hotel.

Back in England in the late spring the Yardbirds disintegrated. Keith and Jim didn't like the music anymore, preferring the softer styles of Fairport Convention and the Incredible String Band. For them, the Yardbirds were through. "I tried desperately to keep them together," Jimmy maintained later. "The gigs were there, but Keith would not take them very

seriously, getting drunk and singing in the wrong places. It
was a real shame. The group were almost ashamed of the very
name, though I don't know why. They were a great band. I
was never ashamed of being in the Yardbirds." The band's
last show was at Luton Technical College in July. The next
day Peter Grant called Jimmy and told him that Keith and
Jim McCarty had quit. Grant also reminded Jimmy that they
retained the legal rights to the Yardbirds' name and that there
was a tour of Scandinavia planned for the fall if Jimmy wanted
to go on. Jimmy said he was keen.

Years later, Chris Dreja reflected on Jimmy's role in the
Yardbirds: "He worked very hard at fitting in and contribut-
ing music. He had a very professional attitude; he was very
prompt, and we [by the time he joined] were almost degenerate, undisciplined rabble. We were getting tired, and Jimmy
was fresh and enthusiastic . . . he tried to put as much in as
he could . . . but he was also using it as a platform for himself, getting into bowing the guitar and other experiments.

"I think Jimmy had really preconceived the demise of the
band. He knew he wanted to continue, with another band
. . . I think that both Peter Grant and Jimmy realized the
potential of the coming years, and we'd just done five years
of it, at a time when rock bands and venues were an unknown quantity. But they realized the potential and they were
obviously right."

And, with the endless painful wisdom of hindsight, Jim
McCarty added, "The worst thing was, just after we split up,
the whole thing exploded, didn't it?"

TWO

ZEPPELIN RISING

We could have called ourselves the Vegetables or the Potatoes. . . . What does Led Zeppelin mean? It doesn't mean a thing.

—JIMMY PAGE

Jimmy retreated to his boat house in Pangbourne and weighed his options. With Peter Grant retaining the name, Jimmy could go on playing Yardbirds-style hard rock indefinitely, all over the world. A Scandinavian tour was already set up for the fall; Japan, Australia, and America were available after that. But, lulled by the bucolic river life, Jimmy's tastes ran to softer, folkish music like Pentangle, the Incredible String Band, and Joni Mitchell. There must, he thought, be a middle ground between light and heavy music. By summer 1968 there was little indication of whether the second wave of English bands would have the same unqualified success as the first. But late in July the response to the Jeff Beck Group's gigs at the Fillmore East showed both Jimmy and Peter Grant that they had to carry on.

After Beck had left the Yardbirds, he didn't play a note for five months. But in March 1967, inspired by one of Jimi Hendrix's aural firestorms, he put together the first Jeff Beck Group, with Ron Wood on bass, Aynsley Dunbar on drums, and a Scots singer named Rod Stewart. His first album, *Truth*, came out in July 1968. Mixing Willie Dixon R&B classics ("You Shook Me," "I Ain't Superstitious") with updated Yardbirds ("Shapes of Things") and softer songs like "Greensleeves," "Beck's Bolero," and folksinger Tim Rose's "Morning Dew," *Truth* had a bluesy, rough-edged feel. Jeff made his guitar bark like a dog and whine like a tomcat in rut. This was also the debut of Rod Stewart's gritty, emotional vocal style and mike-swinging stage act. When Peter Grant and Mickie Most brought this band to Bill Graham's Fillmore East, they found a lot of anticipation on the street due to Beck's exalted status with the Yardbirds. Opening for the Grateful Dead, with Rod Stewart so frightened that he hid behind the amps for the first three songs, the Jeff Beck Group shook the audience with its dramatic, white man's blues.

At home by the Thames, Jimmy almost never touched his electric guitar, preferring to strum and pick acoustically. But he and Grant knew that they had to follow their gut instinct for where the real money was, "heavy music" in America. The biggest selling band there was Iron Butterfly, whose album *In-A-Gadda-Da-Vida* consisted of repetitious, droning blues scales and had survived on the charts for years. The other big band of the day was Vanilla Fudge, who played it somewhat lighter, alternating "white blues" with softer, less bombastic passages.

There were other factors for Page and Grant to consider, if

a new "supergroup" was going to be successfully manufac-
tured. By August 1968, Cream was breaking up after three
successful albums. At first it looked like Jeff Beck was going
to fill the gap. The new progressive rock FM stations that
Jimmy so loved would be desperate for a new British blues
act. But Peter Grant knew the real truth. The Beck group was
already unstable. Rod Stewart and Ron Wood were already
giggling like schoolgirls, and Beck was odd man out. No matter how thrilling they were on stage, if the personalities didn't
mesh, the band couldn't last.

Jimmy insisted that his new band be self-owned and finan-
cially and artistically independent. He had seen the Yardbirds
fall apart, and the only real cause had been poor management. Jimmy Page would never let himself be manipulated
again. Early in September he and Peter Grant formed a new
company called (ironically) Superhype Music Inc., which
liberated them from further obligations to record for Mickie
Most. But within a month the Yardbirds had to fulfill contracts for a short tour of Scandinavia, and Jimmy had to find
a band. Chris Dreja was still on bass at that point. And if
Jimmy had been able to choose, they probably would have
been joined by pop crooner Terry Reid and drummer B. J.
Wilson, then with Procol Harum. Wilson had been the
drummer on a 1968 session that Jimmy had played for Joe
Cocker, "With a Little Help from My Friends," and he expressed interest in the much-rumored new group that Jimmy
was forming. Jimmy was uncertain. In his ideal group the
drummer was the key, a lead instrument almost co-equal with
Jimmy's guitar. Unfortunately for Terry Reid, he had just
signed with Mickie Most as a solo act, which put him out of
reach of the New Yardbirds.

Another musician who asked Jimmy about his plans was
John Paul Jones, the session bassist and arranger who had already played with Jimmy on dozens of recording sessions since
1965. Even before the demise of the Yardbirds, Jimmy recalled, "I was working at the sessions for Donovan's 'Hurdy

Gurdy Man,' and John Paul Jones was looking after the musical arrangements. During a break he asked me if I could use a bass player in the new group I was forming. Now John Paul Jones is unquestionably an incredible arranger and musician—he didn't need me for a job. It was just that he felt the need to express himself, and he thought we might be able to do it together. . . . He had a proper music training and he had quite brilliant ideas. I jumped at the chance of getting him."

His real name was John Baldwin, and he was born January 3, 1946, at Sidcup, Kent. His parents were "in the business" with a variety-style double act. By the time he was two, he was already on the road. His father had played piano at the silent movies, and John himself was playing piano by the age of six. Later John and his father had a piano/bass duo, working at hunt balls, bar mitzvahs, and cocktail parties. In the summer they had a residency at the Isle of Wight Yacht Club. John had gotten his first bass at the age of thirteen, bought reluctantly by his dad and only because he had joined a band and couldn't get his piano in the van. His father had said, according to John, " 'Don't bother with it. Take up the tenor saxophone. In two years the bass guitar will never be heard of again.' I said, 'No Dad, I really want one; there's work for me.' He said, 'Ah, there's work?' And I got a bass right away."

He was living at his boarding school, Christ College, when he formed his first band. He was heavily influenced, he says, by jazz bassists like Charles Mingus and Scott LaFaro, who played with Bill Evans. One day he heard Phil Upchurch's bass solo on "You Can't Sit Down" on the radio and the proverbial light went on in his head. The bass *could* be a lead/solo instrument in rock, just as Mingus had proved it could be in jazz.

By the time he was sixteen, John Baldwin had a band that was playing at American military bases all over the south of England. Huge black sergeants used to make them play "Night Train" all night long. The following year, 1962, he left school and got the first job he auditioned for, with Jet Harris and Tony Meehan, who had just left the Shadows and had a number one single, "Diamonds" (on which Jimmy had played guitar). Just seventeen, John was hired on bass. The rhythm guitar was John McLaughlin, already the best jazz guitarist in England. This job lasted eighteen months, and gradually John Baldwin began to turn up at recording sessions to play bass. In 1964, at the age of eighteen, he changed his name to John Paul Jones and put out his first record, an instrumental called "Baja." The B side was an original composition called, presciently, "A Foggy Day in Vietnam."

By 1965 John Paul Jones was one of the top session bassists in London, working regularly with singers like Tom Jones and Dusty Springfield, and session players like Jimmy Page. "It was always Big Jim and Little Jim," he says, "Big Jim Sullivan and Little Jim [Page] and myself and the drummer. Apart from group sessions, where he'd play solos, he always ended up on rhythm guitar because he couldn't read too well. I used to see him just sitting there with an acoustic guitar, just sort of raking out chords." After two years John Paul moved up to arranger and musical director. It happened at a Mickie Most session for Donovan's "Sunshine Superman," where John Paul decided the arranger was incompetent and demonstrated a better rhythm section to Most. Hired on the spot as a staff arranger, one of his first assignments was Herman's Hermits. Mickie Most would later claim that the Hermits records John Paul arranged outsold the Beatles in 1965–66, selling twelve million singles in America alone. Working with Donovan, Lulu, and other acts, he spent his days strapped in his Fender bass, often directing large studio orchestras. By 1967 he was twenty-one years old. He had married his wife, Mo, the previous year and had a daughter and another on the way. His most prestigious session came that year, when Andrew Oldham hired him to produce the string charts for "She's a Rainbow" on the Rolling Stones' *Their Satanic Majesties Request.* He also worked with Jeff Beck and Terry Reid, whose first album for Most had many of the same chord changes as Led Zeppelin's first, a testament to Jones's presence. But by 1968 he was burned out. He remembers: "I had started running and arranging about forty or fifty things a month. I ended up just putting a blank piece of score paper in front of me and just sitting there and staring at it. Then I joined Led Zeppelin, I suppose, after my missus said to me, 'Will you stop moping around the house; why don't you join a band or something?' And I said, 'There's no bands I want to join, what are you talking about?' And she said, 'Well, look, I think it was in *Disc*, Jimmy Page is forming a group . . . why don't you give him a ring?' So I rang him and said, 'Jim, how're you doing? Have you got a group yet?' He said, 'I haven't got anybody yet.' And I said, 'Well, if you want a bass player, give me a ring.' And he said, 'All right. I'm going to see this singer Terry Reid told me about, and he might know a drummer as well. I'll call you when I've seen what they're like.' "

If this account seems somewhat fey and tongue in cheek, consider that the dry-humored Jones told another interviewer he got the job as bassist in Led Zeppelin after he answered an ad in *Melody Maker*.

It was obvious to Jimmy and Peter Grant that there weren't any good singers in London who were available. Since the new band was patterned on the Jeff Beck Group, they needed a singer with the romantic persona of a Rod Stewart, someone with the nerve to get on a stage and emote vocally along with an electric guitar. But all the good singers—Steve Marriott, Steve Winwood, Joe Cocker, Chris Farlowe—were busy. Terry Reid, only eighteen, had been snatched by Mickie Most at the last moment. One day Jimmy and Peter ran into Reid on Oxford Street. Reid told them about an unknown singer with a band called Hobbstweedle up in Birmingham, a great tall blond geezer who looked like a fairy prince with this caterwauling voice, who was heavy into blues and the West Coast bands. They called him "The Wild Man of Blues from the

Black Country." His name was Robert Plant, and Terry Reid recommended him highly, having gigged with Robert's previous group, the Band of Joy. Peter's office telegraphed Robert at home and Jimmy got on the phone with him. They made plans for Jimmy and Peter to see Robert at a Hobbstweedle gig that weekend. When Robert asked about a drummer, Jimmy said he was still looking. Robert said he knew someone Jimmy should hear.

Robert Anthony Plant was born August 20, 1948, at West Bromwich, Staffordshire. His father was an engineer and the Plants lived in Kidderminster, a rural Worcestershire suburb of Birmingham. Enrolled at King Edward VI Grammar in stolid, four-square Stourbridge, the heart of the "Black Country" of the English west Midlands, Robert was well read and a good student until he discovered girls and Elvis at age thirteen. He spent hours in front of a mirror, trying to copy every Presley move. By this point Elvis was in the army and past his peak as a fifties rock and roll star, but his earlier rockabilly songs really *got* to Robert. By the time he was fifteen, his disapproving father would drive Robert to the Seven Stars Blues Club in Stourbridge every week, where Robert jammed with the Delta Blues Band, murdering Muddy Waters, bleating out "Got My Mojo Working" and other bucket-of-blood blues tunes with all the beery, extroverted soul of the Midlands working class. They had an eight-string guitarist named Terry Foster who could sound like Big Joe Williams. Another of Robert's bands, Sounds of Blue, included Chris Wood, who would later play in Traffic.

But if blues musicians were taboo in their own Mississippi Delta communities, they were abominated in middle-class Kidderminster, especially when young Robert first went Mod—the French crew hairdo, the parka, the tight jacket and Chelsea boots, the chrome side panels for the scooter—after seeing the Who and Small Faces as they passed through Birmingham. Robert was the only member of Led Zeppelin (and one of the few English pop musicians of his generation) to be musically discouraged at home. His parents were adamant that he study accounting, and when Robert left school at sixteen he was apprenticed at two pounds a week to a doddering chartered accountant who was to train Robert for a life of balance sheets and ledgers. But all Robert did was make tea for the old man and dream about Robert Johnson, who could make his darkling, nasal voice sound so much like his guitar. "It almost seemed to me as if the guitar strings were really his vocal chords," Robert later recalled. At night he jammed with various forgotten Birmingham blues combos—the New Memphis Bluesbreakers, Black Snake Moan (after Blind Lemon Jefferson), and the Banned. He participated in every conceivable English youth subculture of the sixties, beginning as a beatnik blues geek blowing a kazoo and thrashing a washboard with thimbles, then fighting Rockers at Margate with the Mods, then going over to the Rockers for a while, before returning to beat-dom and eventually apotheosizing as a premature hippie. His blond mane was now so long that he could only go home at night. Finally he left home at sixteen for the life of a blues magician. Later he would reflect on the decision: "I decided that if I didn't get anywhere by the time I was twenty, I would pack it in. Of course it didn't really matter what happened because I wouldn't have packed it in anyway. The whole scene was amazement, enlightenment, a total trip-out. You just cannot reproduce those moments. . . . You can't give up something you really believe in for financial reasons. If you die by the roadside then you die by the roadside—so be it. But at least you know you've tried. Ten minutes in the music scene was the equal of one hundred years outside of it."

In 1965 Sonny Boy Williamson played in Birmingham and Robert went backstage and stole one of his harps, which put him in physical contact with one of his idols. Years later he was quoted: "I always got a shiver every time I saw Sonny Boy Williamson—the way he would strut out on stage. . . .

He was everything I wanted to be at the age of 70." He also tried to mimic the gravel-coarse, nasal blues delivery of Bukka White.

Later that year Robert joined another blues band, The Crawling King Snakes, named for the John Lee Hooker boogie tune. They played twenty-minute sets at clubs and dance halls bursting with young Mods who'd come to see main acts like Solomon Burke and Wilson Pickett, or Birmingham area bands like the Spencer Davis Group or the Shakedown Sounds with singer Jess Rhoden.

For a while, the Snakes were joined by a big long-haired drummer whom everyone called Bonzo. He was a sweet, generally quiet guy with the same goofy affability as Bonzo, the old British cartoon dog. His idol was Keith Moon of the Who, and he used to line the inside of his bass drum with aluminum foil to make the thing rattle off like cannon fire. Bonzo and Robert became fast friends. Years later Robert would tell a Zeppelin employee about how he used to hang around Bonzo's house (having no real home of his own), so horny he'd start playing with himself until Bonzo would go, "Hsssst! Hey! Stop that! Me mum's comin'.''

Robert's next band was called the Tennessee Teens, a three-piece, Tamla-style soul band who asked Robert to join. The group changed its name to Listen and their style to basic Young Rascals. They even cut a single, Robert Plant's first record, a cover of the Rascals' "You Better Run." Backed by horns and a female chorus, Robert was produced to sound like a younger, even more overwrought Tom Jones. The single was released by CBS in 1966 and disappeared. The B side was called "Everybody's Gonna Say," co-written by Plant. CBS released two other singles under Robert's name later that year and early in 1967: "Our Song"/"Laughin', Cryin', Laughin' " and "Long Time Coming"/"I've Got a Secret." Neither single was successful but the latter (on which Bonzo played) got Robert his picture (light beard, mustache, velvet caftan, garlands of love beads) in *New Musical Express*. Robert was described as eighteen, Birmingham-born, with A levels in English, history, and math and the ability to play violin, piano, organ, and guitar. "Now he works all over the country with his backing group, The Band of Joy. Already the disk has hit the Birmingham Top Twenty, which is at least Planting the seeds of his talent."

By this time Robert had found a new home in the extended, communal Anglo-Indian family of his girl friend Maureen, whom he had met at a Georgie Fame concert in 1966. They lived in a crowded house in Walsall that was full of hard-working first generation immigrants from India. It was a soulful scene of hot curries and great people, the first real home the earnest urban bluesman Robert Plant had found since his bitter departure from his father's house.

There were actually three versions of the Band of Joy. Robert was fired from the first in early 1967 when the group's manager told him he couldn't sing. Defiantly, Robert formed a different Band of Joy, whose act was to paint their faces and perform in hippie regalia. This was the beginning of the influence of the San Francisco Sound, and Robert plunged right in. "I got hold of a copy of a Buffalo Springfield album," he said. "It was great because it was the kind of music you could leap around to, or you could sit down and just dig it. Then I got the first Moby Grape album, which was a knockout. . . . I had loved good blues, but all of a sudden I couldn't listen to old blues anymore. . . . Now I was sobbing to Arthur Lee and Love doing 'Forever Changes.' " The second Band of Joy disintegrated, and the third rose on the strength of its new drummer, John "Bonzo" Bonham. Riding the San Francisco Sound, singing Jefferson Airplane songs, this band broke out of Birmingham and played London clubs like Middle Earth and the Speakeasy. After that they backed American singer Tim Rose on an English tour. Singer Terry Reid was the other act. Robert and Bonzo loved playing together, but by the spring of 1968 the Band of Joy had run its course. Bonzo joined Tim Rose's new band and Robert was left at loose ends.

It took some time for Robert to find another band. Many musicians in the Wolverhampton area considered Plant more of a dancer than a singer and thought that he was in bands to dance around and look good as much as to sing. He was almost invited to join the Wolverhampton band Slade, whose guitarist, Noddy Holder, had been a roadie for the Band of Joy. But the other members of Slade hated Robert's flamboyant posing, and he wasn't hired.

For a while he let Maureen support him, and then joined a road paving crew to earn a few quid. He made six shillings tuppance per hour, laying hot asphalt. The other workers called him "the pop singer." For a time he had a duo with Alexis Korner, the London bluesman, and they played a few gigs around Birmingham and cut a record that was released years later as a Korner album track. Then Robert failed an audition with Denny Cordell, Joe Cocker's manager. Somewhat dispirited, Robert joined a band called Hobbstweedle, named after the J. R. R. Tolkien trilogy *The Lord of the Rings*, which every good hippie had read by then. That was when he got the first telegram from Peter Grant.

The following weekend Jimmy, Peter Grant, and Chris Dreja turned up at the Hobbstweedle gig at a dismal teachers college in Birmingham. They were let in the back door by a "big, rug-headed kern" whom they assumed was the bouncer. But when they saw him onstage in his caftan and beads, doing "Somebody to Love" in this bluesy, sirenesque soprano, they gave each other *the look.* "It unnerved me just to listen," Jimmy said later. "It still does, like a primeval wail." There were twenty-five kids at the dance, and they were all drinking. After finishing his set of Moby Grape and Buffalo Springfield songs, Robert approached Jimmy to see what the star of the Yardbirds thought of the show. But Jimmy and the others were low-key and vague. Jimmy only said, "I'll call you within a week." But on the way back to London, Jimmy was intrigued. That voice . . . it *had* it, that distinctive, highly charged sexual quality that Jimmy needed. It was as good a white man's blues voice as Rod Stewart's, but it was even wilder, even a little crazy-sounding. Jimmy wasn't sure. He couldn't *believe* that Robert was still scuffling, undiscovered, in Birmingham. "When I auditioned him and heard him sing, I immediately thought there must be something wrong with him personality-wise, or that he had to be impossible to work with, because I just could not understand why, after he told me he'd been singing for a few years already, he hadn't become a big name yet." So Jimmy called Robert back and invited him down to Pangbourne for a few days to suss him out. Robert called Alexis Korner and asked for advice. Korner said, by all means, *go*.

In the boathouse on the Thames, Robert Plant and Jimmy Page played records and made friends. Fortunately, California bands excluded (Jimmy had appeared with all of them in the Yardbirds era and was sick of them), the two shared many musical tastes. Early on, when Jimmy had walked down to the village for a newspaper, Robert picked through Page's pile of records and pulled some out to play. When Jimmy returned he told Robert they were the *exact* records he would have played to him. Much lifting of eyebrows at this instance of synchronicity. Jimmy played Robert some soft things, like Joan Baez doing "Babe I'm Gonna Leave You" and Robin Williamson's Incredible String Band, updated English folk airs that poured down like honey. He played rock and roll tunes, like Chuck Berry doing "No Money Down." He played Little Walter's harmonica blues, and explained to Robert his idea for a new kind of "heavy music" with slower and lighter touches, music with dynamics, light and shade, *chiaroscuro*. They talked about a band where the singer and guitar might play in unison. Jimmy played Robert "You Shook Me" from an old EP by Muddy Waters, with Earl Hooker playing the melody on electric guitar behind Muddy's voice. Jeff Beck and Rod Stewart had done the same thing with the same song on Beck's new album, but that didn't matter. It was the sound Jimmy wanted.

After a few days of this, Robert was almost beside himself. It was all so—*heady*. Here was this attractive, mysterious, soft-spoken rock star offering vistas of stardom in America, brocaded with vague intimations of immense riches. It was all so *new*. For the first time, Robert had found somebody who might know what to do with his boundless reservoir of adrenaline.

So excited was Robert that, when he left Pangbourne, he hitchhiked up to Oxford to find Bonzo, playing somewhere that night with Tim Rose, to recruit him for the New Yardbirds.

John Henry Bonham was born on May 31, 1948, at Redditch, Worcestershire. The son of a carpenter, he grew up near Robert in Kidderminster, hammering things. His first drum was a bath salts can with wires on the bottom and a coffee tin that his dad rigged with a loose wire for a snare effect, plus his mother's cooking pots. When he was ten, his mother bought him a snare drum. Five years later his father got him a used, slightly rusted drum kit. When Bonzo was sixteen he left school and went to work with his father, carrying hods around building sites. Bonzo actually liked to work: It built him up and left him free to play at night. He started off with Terry Webb and the Spiders, wearing purple jackets with velveteen lapels. The singer wore gold lamé. There was another band, the Nicky James Movement, that had its gear repossessed after a gig. When he was seventeen he went on to another group called A Way of Life and married his sweetheart, an English rose he'd met at a dance at Kidderminster. Pat Bonham wasn't keen to be married to a musician so poor that they had to live in a fifteen-foot trailer and her husband had to give up smoking cigarettes in order to pay the rent. Bonzo had sworn to Pat that he'd give up drumming if she married him. But soon Bonzo looked up Robert Plant, who lived nearby, and joined his band. Bonzo of course couldn't afford a car, and at first it was debatable whether Robert and the Crawling King Snakes could actually afford the gas money to pick him up and get him home. But Bonzo already had a great reputation as a drummer around Birmingham; he played the strongest, loudest drums in the Midlands and would occasionally break his bass drum head when he really got excited. Some bands wouldn't hire Bonzo, since local clubs often wouldn't even book bands that Bonzo played with. They said he played too loud. But Bonzo gradually developed a lighter touch as well; he stopped breaking drum heads when he learned to play louder without hitting as hard—when he learned how to swing. He was one of the first drummers to line his bass drum with aluminum foil, and was already playing drum solos with his hands when he started out with Robert. His only acknowledged influences were early soul records, the raucous Keith Moon, and the "astonishing" Ginger Baker, who with Cream in 1966 became the first rock drummer to step out as a featured instrument, co-equal with the mighty lead guitar. Baker's sometimes mesmerizing (and sometimes excruciating) drum solo, "Toad," became a paradigm for Bonzo. Like most drummers, he had an aggressive streak. He liked to drink and give a little aggro now and then. He didn't go looking for fights, but he didn't run either.

Eventually Bonzo left the Snakes and went back to A Way of Life, closer to Kidderminster. Later he and Robert played together in the Band of Joy until that collapsed in 1968, and Bonzo accepted the offer to tour with Tim Rose, which is where Robert found him in Oxford one night that summer in 1968.

It had been three months since Bonzo had last heard from Robert, and the drummer listened to his friend's breathless spiel about Jimmy and Pangbourne and the new band, which ended up with, "Mate, you've *got* to join the New Yardbirds." But Bonzo was unimpressed. He was making forty pounds a week with Tim Rose, more than he'd ever earned in his life, and had even gotten noticed by the music press when Tim Rose had last played in London. He told Robert, "Well, I'm all right here, aren't I?" Robert pleaded that they could make a lot of money with the New Yardbirds, but Bonzo still wasn't sure. To him, the Yardbirds was a name from the past with no future.

Shortly after, Jimmy saw Bonzo for the first time, playing the Country Club in north London with Tim Rose. At the time Jimmy was still considering making the new band sound something like Pentangle, the acoustic band that featured guitarist Bert Jansch. But when he heard Bonzo's merciless attack, he knew what his new band would sound like. There followed an intensive Superhype campaign to snare John Bonham. (Grant said he knew Page was serious about Bonham because it was the first time Page hadn't called Grant collect.) The problem was that Bonzo was too poor to afford a phone. Robert sent eight telegrams to Bonzo's pub, the Three Men in a Boat, in Walsall. These were followed by forty telegrams from Peter Grant. Still, Bonzo wouldn't join. The success of the Tim Rose gigs had brought in *other offers.* Joe Cocker wanted him, and Chris Farlowe offered him a job. It was a hard decision. Farlowe was well established and had a new album produced by Mick Jagger. Everybody in London was sure that Cocker, the spastic blues belter from Sheffield, was going to be very big. But as Bonzo later recalled, "it wasn't a question of who had the best prospects, but also which music was going to be right. When I first got offered the job, I thought the Yardbirds were finished, because in England they had been forgotten. Still I thought, 'Well, I've got nothing anyway so anything is really better than nothing.' I knew that Jimmy was a good guitarist and that Robert was a good singer, so even if we didn't have any success, at least it would be a pleasure to play in a good group. . . . So I decided I liked their music better than Cocker's or Farlowe's." Finally Bonzo wired Peter Grant, accepting the drummer's chair with the New Yardbirds. Jimmy got back to John Paul Jones, who agreed to come to the first rehearsal and, if it worked out, to invest in the band. Jimmy himself plowed in almost every penny left over from his sessions and Yardbird days. John Paul was the last to join the band, which was due to leave for Scandinavia, as the New Yardbirds, the following week. Chris Dreja retired from music when Jones joined the band.

All four musicians have since used the same word to describe their first rehearsal: *magic.* As Jones later recounted, "The first time, we all met in this little room to see if we could stand each other." Bonzo was in awe of the brainy, wizardish Page and didn't say much. "It was wall to wall amplifiers, terrible, all old. Robert had heard I was a session man, and he was wondering what was going to turn up—some old bloke with a pipe? So Jimmy said, 'Well, we're all here, what are we going to play?' And I said, 'I don't know. What do you know?' And Jimmy said, 'Do you know "Train Kept A-Rollin'?" ' I told him no. And he said, 'It's easy, just G to A.' He counted it out, *and the room just exploded.* And we said, 'Right, we're on, this is it, *this is going to work*!!!" In another interview, seven years later, Robert was equally effusive about that first meeting. "I've never been so turned on in my life," he said. "Although we were all steeped in blues and R&B, we found out in the first hour and a half that we had our own identity." They played old Yardbirds war-horses like "Smokestack Lightning," old Band of Joy numbers like Garnet Mimms's "As Long As I Have You," and all sorts of blues and R&B classics. Jimmy tried to teach the band "Dazed and Confused," but John Paul kept getting the chords wrong. The unspoken assumption was that Jimmy was the soloist, he had all the talent, and what he needed was a good backing band with a singer. But now Page realized he had more than that. He remembered the initial shock: "Four of us got together in this room and started playing. Then we *knew.* We started laughing at each other. Maybe it was from relief or from the knowledge that we could groove together."

With the rehearsal over, Robert and Bonzo, the two Brummies, were almost numb with joy, slightly tempered by other feelings when, as they were leaving, rich pop star Jimmy Page asked the literally penniless musicians to help pay for the food and beer. They didn't know Jimmy's reputation as a miser. Soon they would be calling him Led Wallet.

On September 14 the New Yardbirds left for Copenhagen. The act consisted of "Train Kept A-Rollin'," which evolved into a verseless version of "Communication Breakdown;" Jimmy's version of "Dazed and Confused" with new lyrics; Jimmy's showpiece "White Summer;" a blues called "I Can't Quit You Baby," and innumerable spontaneous variations on themes by other musicians—"Fresh Garbage" from Spirit, "We're Gonna Groove" from Ben E. King, "Shake" from Sam Cooke and Otis Redding, "It's Your Thing" from the Isley Brothers, and the entire *oeuvre* of Elvis. The Scandinavian shows were the laboratory in which the band brewed its alchemy and invented—or reinvented—a sound, judging the success or failure of each new direction by whether the Danish kids responded or not. The best thing was the pairing of Robert's Klaxon-loud wailing and Jimmy's guitar in full cry, in unison. "It happened the first time on stage in Denmark," Robert noted. "I wasn't trying to scat sing, but the voice was imitating the guitar. There was no spoken instructions about it . . . but we broke into it on 'You Shook Me' and we all broke into smiles." And Jimmy later remembered a telling incident during the first gig in Copenhagen, when Robert's amp broke down. But the group kept playing and, according to Page, "you could still hear his voice at the back of the auditorium over the entire group."

Even in Scandinavia the band knew that they weren't the New Yardbirds anymore. A name had to be chosen: Initially they came up with Mad Dogs (which Joe Cocker would later use) and Whoopee Cushion. Then Jimmy recalled the Entwistle/Moon brainstorm of the lead zeppelin. "We were sitting there kicking around group names," Jimmy said. "Eventually it came down to the fact that the name was not really as important as whether or not the music was going to be accepted. I was quite keen about Led Zeppelin . . . it seemed to fit the bill. It had something to do with the expression about a bad joke going over like a lead balloon. And there's a little of the Iron Butterfly light-and-heavy connotation." When the band got back to London, the *a* was taken out of *lead* so the thick Americans wouldn't mispronounce it *leed*.

The group's first album, *Led Zeppelin*, was recorded in October 1968 at Olympic Studios in Barnes, south London. Jimmy was producing with engineer Glyn Johns. The nine tracks on the album were basically Led Zeppelin's Scandinavian act, minus "Train," "We're Gonna Groove," and John Paul Jones's long organ introduction to "Your Time Is Gonna Come," improvised in the style of Garth Hudson's "Chest Fever." The album was recorded in only thirty hours of studio time, spread throughout two weeks that month. (By 1975, after this one album had already grossed over $7 million, Peter Grant would claim it cost only £1,750 to produce, *including* the artwork depicting the catastrophic death of the ocean-going zeppelin *Hindenburg*.

Led Zeppelin was intended to duplicate the band's early live shows so the new band would have something to sell while it spent the following year touring America. The album had to have a minimum of overdubs that would be difficult to reproduce onstage, so the tracks were recorded almost "live" in the studio. Typically, adhering to Jimmy's light/heavy scheme, the songs started as acoustic white blues *études* that mutated into Bonzo's stomping thud coupled with Page's hard-raunch guitar. "Good Times Bad Times" built slowly until the whole band stopped for an instant and—like a burst of pent-up electrical energy freed from a capacitor—Jimmy rips into one of his thousand note flurries. Again, Joan Baez's folkish lament "Babe I'm Gonna Leave You" begins with Jimmy strumming an acoustic Gibson J-200 guitar, and then alternates with grinding hunks of sludge. Robert sounds like he's been listening to Van Morrison. But the album really broke open with "You Shook Me," Willie Dixon's old blues, but taken even slower, heavier, and more literally than Jeff Beck's previous version. Here Robert's voice and Jimmy's guitar coined a trademark unison wail that would be copied by garage bands for the next fifteen years. The first side ends with the epic headphone-classic "Dazed and Confused" (credited to Jimmy Page with no mention of Jake Holmes), whose lyric had again been rewritten. Originally about a bad trip, "Dazed and Confused" now elucidated some of Jimmy's devilish views on the female sex: "Lots of people talking, few of them know/The soul of a woman was created below." Dreamy, morbid, glowing with whooshing flocks of baby vultures produced by bowing the E string of the guitar, "Dazed and Confused" was the album's *tour de force,* and when Jimmy digs out the "Think About It" riff during the second solo and Robert lets loose a fanfare of stygian shrieks, it sounds like a Wagnerian rock *götterdämmerung.* A generation of fans would grow up wondering what Robert was yabbering, submerged under the wah-wah, before Zep drops the bomb one final time.

This mood is mercifully lifted with the lighter second side. John Paul's ecclesiastic organ intro to "Your Time Is Gonna Come" leads into Jimmy's new acoustic guitar prelude, "Black Mountain Side," a modal version in mock-sitar tuning of an old English folk riff that had been played in clubs by a folk-singer named Annie Briggs and recorded by Bert Jansch. A tabla player, Viram Jasani, was brought in to provide a raga-like rhythm track. "Communication Breakdown" followed, which replaced "Train Kept A-Rollin'." The moment when Robert's moan decays into a shouted "Suck!" and Jimmy fires a deadly burst is a Zeppelin classic. Another Willie Dixon-copyrighted blues, "I Can't Quit You Baby," was another showcase for Jimmy's blues textures and clichés, mostly borrowed from B. B. King and Jimi Hendrix's "Voodoo Chile." The record's climax is "How Many More Times," which the Band of Joy used to do. Taking lyrics and riffs from Albert King's "The Hunter" and a medley of other verbal blues clichés, this is primal, brain-beating, overwrought Zeppelin at its most shameless, full of Jimmy's bowed whoops and slides (the guitar solo is from "Shapes of Things") and a blues rant by Robert, who announces that he's nervous because he's got a child on the way, which was indeed the case. The song reaches its denouement with a strummed "Bolero" figure from Jimmy, which could be a tribute, an inside joke, or a spiteful jab, depending upon whether or not one was Jeff Beck.

But the songs and the guitar licks on *Led Zeppelin* were only part of the story. Somehow Jimmy was able to capture the elemental, elusive excitement of a rock band in heat. He had strong ideas about how rock music ought to sound, reflected in his eccentric methods. Most producers just stuck a microphone in front of an amplifier. But Jimmy would also put a mike twenty feet in back of the amp, and then record the balance between the two. "Distance is depth," he would murmur in the studio. Microphone placement was an arcane science; by close-miking and distance-miking, Jimmy was one of the first producers to record a band's *ambient* sound, the distance of a note's time-lag from one end of the room to the other. Jimmy thought that this is where a previously hidden ingredient lay, that this was the reason that the early rock and roll records sounded as if they were recorded at a party. "The whole idea, the way I see recording," Jimmy said later, "is to try and capture the sound of the room live and the emotion of the whole moment and try to convey that across. . . . You've got to capture as much of the room sound as possible. That's the very essence of it."

The excitement of these first Zeppelin sessions was electrifying. Listening to the playbacks, the musicians and crew just shook their heads. Glyn Johns remembered, "It was tremendously exciting to make that album. They'd rehearsed themselves very healthily before they got near the studio. I'd never heard arrangements of that ilk before, nor had I ever heard a band play in that way before. It was just unbelievable, and when you're in a studio with something as creative as that, you can't help but feed off of it."

Most ecstatic of all was Robert, who at last sounded close to what he knew was his potential. He remembered that mo-

ment years later: "That first album was the first time that
headphones meant anything to me. What I heard coming back
to me over the cans while I was singing was better than any
chick in all the land. It had so much weight, so much power—
it was *devastating*. It was all very *raunchy*."

But when the sessions were complete (only "Babe I'm Gonna
Leave You" required significant overdubbing), Peter Grant tried
to book Led Zeppelin into a quick tour of English clubs and
universities and was met with total indifference. Hardly anyone wanted a group called the New Yardbirds, and nobody
wanted an unknown band called Led Zeppelin. But Grant was
told by Jimmy to take whatever was offered at any fee under
any billing. So the band made its world debut as Led Zeppelin at Surrey University for £150. Three nights later they
played the Marquee in London as "Jimmy Page with the New
Yardbirds." Playing above the human pain threshold in the
old jazz club, they played twelve bars of "Train Kept A-Rollin' " as an invocation before roaring into "Communication
Breakdown," Bonzo cruising, Robert singing vocalisms—the
music was too fast for words, Jimmy burping out controlled
spouts of wah-wah. Then they went right into "I Can't Quit
You Baby," Robert screaming his brains out, trying to get noticed while Jimmy played huge chordal slabs and then did his
Hendrix fire-power impression, all show-offy technique and
undeniable blues feeling. This dissolved into one of Led Zep's
peculiar early medleys, encompassing Howlin' Wolf's "Killing Floor" with "Fought My Way Out of Darkness" and the
lewd lemon lines ("You can squeeze my lemon/till the juice
runs down my leg") from Robert Johnson's "Travelling Riverside Blues." In the middle of this Jimmy broke into Elvis's
"That's All Right." Then Robert, frantic, singing anything that
came into his head just trying to keep up with Jimmy, went
into a jam on, incredibly, Milt Jackson's "Bags' Groove." The
set was climaxed by eleven minutes of "Dazed and Confused." It was a blistering show, but the audience was only
mildly interested. The management complained about the

volume. The following night the New Yardbirds played their last date at Liverpool University. From then on they were billed as Led Zeppelin.

The initial reaction to the band from Britain's acerbic, often loutish music press was good. Later it would deteriorate into open hostilities. One paper described Led Zeppelin "as the most exciting sound to be heard since the early days of Hendrix or the Cream." The first Marquee date was reviewed positively, especially what was called "Days of Confusion," but most critics chided the "heavy music group" for playing too loud.

On November 9 Robert married his Maureen, now eight months pregnant. That night Led Zeppelin played its London debut at the Roundhouse in Chalk Farm. Robert's old car broke down on the way to the gig, and he almost didn't make it. Shortly after, Maureen bore Robert Plant a daughter, named Carmen Jane.

While the four musicians had been launching their Led Zeppelin, Peter Grant had been preparing for his assault on New York to procure a record deal. Jimmy Page so far had only half of what he wanted. Jimmy wanted *complete control*—of production, cover art, publishing, scheduling, concerts, promotion. Jimmy never wanted to be owned again. So Peter Grant left England in November 1968 with audition tapes, a rough mix, and cover art for *Led Zeppelin*. His mission was to secure a world distribution deal from an American recording company that granted total artistic and commercial control to the musicians.

He got it from Ahmet Ertegun and Jerry Wexler of Atlantic Records, the label that had pioneered pop rhythm and blues twenty years earlier. At the time Atlantic was comfortably on the charts with Cream, Buffalo Springfield, and Aretha Franklin. But Wexler also had his eye on the future, as forecast by the sales performance of two other Atlantic acts, Iron Butterfly and Vanilla Fudge. These two groups—so-called "heavy" bands that spewed lugubrious blues and rock—were selling like crazy. Rarely in the Top Twenty, they neverthe-less stayed on the charts for *weeks*. Iron Butterfly's *In-A-Gadda-Da-Vida* stayed on the charts for several years and became the first album to be awarded platinum status. Wexler and Atlantic chairman Ahmet Ertegun could also see that the au-dience for rock music had changed radically in the past two years. In the wake of Eric Clapton and Cream, Led Zeppelin would appeal to this new audience, boys and young men be-tween fifteen and twenty-four, an audience who like their rock to be loud, Anglo-Saxon, violent, 4/4, *martial*. The girls weren't really at this party. It wasn't a dance.

Wexler had already spoken to Peter Grant by telephone and told him that Atlantic wanted Led Zeppelin. He had gotten a glowing recommendation for the new group from singer Dusty Springfield, who had worked with both Page and Jones in London. "But you don't know my price," Peter replied.

In New York Peter and his American lawyer, Steve Weiss, negotiated an awesome deal for the day, which reportedly gave Led Zeppelin a $200,000 advance and the highest royalty rate ever negotiated for a group of musicians (said later to be five times that of the Beatles) in return for worldwide distribution by Atlantic Records and its licensees. The contract gave com-plete artistic control to the band, and an added perquisite—demanded by Jimmy—that Led Zeppelin would be the first rock band on the hallowed Atlantic label. All the other white rock acts appeared on Atlantic's déclassé subsidiary, Atco Records.

Atlantic had given away a small chunk of the farm to Led Zeppelin. Peter Grant went back to the Plaza Hotel and called Jimmy to come to New York to sign the deal.

Then, perhaps with joy in their hearts, Grant and Weiss called on Clive Davis, then president of Columbia Records, whose Epic subsidiary had the rights for the Yardbirds (and Jeff Beck) in America. Jimmy of course felt that Epic was an inept and exploitative label, while Clive Davis had con-sidered the Yardbirds one of his pet projects and was confident that Jimmy Page's new band—the word on the street was they were *hot*—would be on Epic. It was the first time Peter and Clive Davis had met, and they talked friendly music gossip until Davis finally said, "Well, aren't we going to talk about Jimmy Page?" And Grant said, "Oh no, we've already signed the Zeppelin to Atlantic."

Silence. Then the meeting deteriorated into a shouting match. Davis tried to harangue Grant: The Yardbirds had been with EMI in England, with Epic owning North American rights. The Epic contract also covered the individual Yardbirds, and they assumed EMI's contract did too. But part of Jimmy's deal when he joined the band was that he retained his own recording rights. Grant explained that Jimmy had never been signed to EMI as an individual, and that CBS therefore had no claim. The meeting ended with the CBS executives in a rage.

Jimmy Page landed in New York a few days later, carrying the master tapes for *Led Zeppelin*. After meeting the Atlantic people and signing contracts, Jimmy and Peter joined the Jeff Beck tour in progress. Jimmy didn't play; he just followed the tour through New York and Boston, staying at the same hotels, lurking quietly in the dressing rooms, closely observing this new, young, mostly male audience at the Fillmore East and the Boston Tea Party. Sergeant-Major Richard Cole mustered the troops and saw to it that they were well boozed and laid. At the Image Club in Miami Jimmy did get up to jam with Beck and Rod Stewart. Then in New York, after one of Beck's Fillmore East triumphs, Jimmy played Led Zeppelin's demo of "You Shook Me" for Jeff, which of course was one of Beck's showstoppers.

According to Beck, Jimmy said, "Listen to this, listen to Bonzo, this guy called John Bonham that I've got." When Beck heard the version, his heart sank. "I looked at him and said, 'Jim, what?' and the tears were coming out with anger." With *Truth* still in the stores, Beck assumed that Jimmy was out to upstage him again, just for the thrill. Why couldn't he have come up with something on his own?

*   *   *

When word of Led Zeppelin's monumental deal with Atlantic hit the streets, the land was rife with accusations of "hype." The musicians and fans of the late sixties were highly ambivalent about the unprecedented commercial success of rock music; young record company employees were known as "corporate freaks" and were ideologically suspect as agents of bourgeois capitalism. Any new band that hadn't been through 1967 was suspected of the sin of corporate hype—being foisted upon the rich and gullible public by some big conglomerate without authentic anarcho-hippie credentials. When rumors of huge advances and royalties began to spread, Led Zeppelin was smeared as a hype band. To counter these charges, Jimmy dropped by the *Melody Maker* office unannounced one day, ostensibly to correct the paper's spelling of the group's name. (They had spelled it Lead Zeppelin.) He was quoted on the topic of hype: "If somebody wants to hype a group they only suffer, because people know what's going on now. People understand the economics of bands, especially in the States where it is the fashion to ask who is getting what out of what." That same month in New York Columbia Records took out ads in the alternative and underground press (which was in turn heavily dependent on record advertising) which proclaimed "The Man Can't Bust Our Music!"

Back in London in December Jimmy took his band through more low-paying trial runs. They played the Marquee, then Bath Pavilion for £75, and Exeter City Hall for £125, finishing at Fishmongers Hall, Wood Green, in London. With no album and the Yardbirds dead, Led Zeppelin couldn't get arrested in England. Just before Christmas Jimmy and Peter decided to take the band to America and start to tour even before the album was out. "We couldn't get work here in Britain," Grant recalled. "It seemed to be a laugh to people that we were getting the group together and working the way we were."

And Jimmy was also bitter about what he perceived as his rejection by the music business in England. "It was a joke

. . . we really had a bad time. They just wouldn't accept anything new. . . . We were given a chance in America."

Led Zeppelin left London on Christmas Day, 1968, bound for the subtropical splendor of Los Angeles. The Zeppelin had risen. A new era had begun.

THREE

THE YEAR
OF THE SHARK

Zeppelin, flieg!　　*Zeppelin fly!*
Hilf uns im Krieg　　*Help us in war*
Flieg nach England　　*Fly to England*
England wird abgebrant　　*England will be burned up*
Zeppelin, flieg!　　*Zeppelin fly!*
—GERMAN CHILDREN'S RHYME, *1915*

Peter Grant was going for America's throat. With no album out yet, Led Zeppelin was taking a calculated risk in coming to America. But Peter Grant based his strategy on years of experience and his instinctive savvy for the unslaked cravings of American youth for English rock. Pushing Jimmy's name, Peter and his agent, Frank Barsalona of Premier Talent, booked Led Zeppelin into the key regional venues for breaking a new act—Bill Graham's Fillmores West and East, the Whiskey in Los Angeles, the Kinetic Circus in Chicago, the Boston Tea Party, and others. Then Atlantic sent out 500 white-label promo copies of *Led Zeppelin* to FM stereo rock stations and record stores, which generated a 50,000 unit advance order (excellent business for a first LP by a new band) and genuine listener interest in the newest band to emerge from the lamented Yardbirds. Once in the States, Peter Grant, doing his own promotion, would call ahead to the FM station in the next town the band would play in, reminding the program director that Led Zeppelin was coming and asking what cuts from the new album his listeners were responding to. The Yardbirds had been getting $2,500 a night, but Led Zeppelin was happy to take gigs at $1,500, and as low as $200. The idea was simple: Go out and play.

The result of Grant's strategy would be phenomenal success. Led Zeppelin would spend the next year and a half on the road (including six separate tours of America), earning their fortune and trying to shake a devoutly deserved reputation for bawdy mayhem and excess. The real cause of this reputation, road manager *extraordinaire* Richard Cole, first met the four members of Led Zeppelin in October at Peter's office on Oxford Street. He had just left the New Vaudville Band in Canada and was about to pick up Terry Reid in the States, who was opening shows for Eric Clapton's new supergroup, Blind Faith. Richard, buccaneering veteran of myriad rock voyages, immediately took to the new band, especially the eager, inexperienced young drummer Bonzo, who reminded Cole of the night he let Bonzo set up and play New Vaudville's drum kit in Birmingham, two years before. The shrewd Cole also foresaw big things ahead for Jimmy. "He knew he was going to be a big leader in rock. You could tell. When the Yardbirds finished—somehow, although he'd only been in the group for a year—he ended up owning the name. Don't ask me how, but he owned the name, and it was a gold mine and he *knew* it. He also knew what he wanted to do with a group and he just needed the people to complement him. I'm sure he was born with a fucking gold nugget up his arse—and he's probably still got that fucking original gold nugget, with two coats of paint on it. He's the meanest in the world, that's why they call him Led Wallet."

On December 26, 1968, Richard Cole met Jimmy, Robert, Bonzo, and Peter Grant's flight from London at the Los Angeles airport. John Paul Jones, who with his wife had spent Christmas with singer Madeline Bell in New York, arrived separately. Los Angeles was a fun house for English rock bands. Robert Plant and Bonzo, who had hardly even been out of England, were incredulous. Robert kept remarking about how he'd never seen a policeman with a gun before. Even before they played a note, Led Zeppelin became the darlings of the main Hollywood groupie clique, Girls Together Outrageously, the GTOs. Unlike most English stars, Led Zeppelin actually liked to go to sleazy rock clubs and just *hang out*. Jimmy was an old hand at this, but Robert and Bonzo— country bumpkins from the Midlands—were amazed to find themselves propositioned by beautiful young GTOs with kohl-rimmed eyes and big heaving bosoms hanging out of their brazen, frontless frocks. Under Richard Cole's relentless philosophy of sex and booze, Led Zeppelin found themselves keeping company with the starlets of the groupie scene and such novelties as the Dog Act, which would bring a Great Dane to the band's hotel for special shows that Richard arranged.

Right after Christmas the band flew to Denver to make its American debut, accompanied by its two-man crew, Richard Cole and roadie Kenny Pickett, whom the band called Pissquick. It was the first time Cole had *heard* Led Zeppelin. "Fucking monsters," he thought. But they weren't even listed on the bill. Two days later they were in Boston to play the Tea Party, which Grant considered a key show in the key American taste-making college town. Here the group had its first inkling of Zeppelin hysteria when, after they had already expanded their hour-long show by half an hour, they were called back for seven encores by the cheering crowd. With their brand-new L.A. hippie regalia drenched in sweat, they had to play unrehearsed jams on Elvis Presley, old Yardbirds war-horses, and Chuck Berry classics. At one point, during a reprise of "How Many More Times," Jimmy nudged John Paul to look down in front, where the entire first row of boys were banging their heads against the edge of the stage.

Led Zeppelin next touched down in New York and met the press. Atlantic's publicist took them on the obligatory visit to *Billboard* magazine, where one of the staff kidded the group about their hair, unusually long even for that era. Jimmy was also interviewed by *Hit Parader*; he described Led Zeppelin as an improvisatory blues group, defended himself from charges that he was stealing ideas from Hendrix and Clapton, and held forth on his bowing technique and his new acquisition, a pedal steel guitar, which he had used on the forthcoming album. Asked what advice he would give to aspiring guitarists, he was succinct: Use lighter strings.

The Yardbirds' old stronghold had been the West Coast, and Peter Grant had booked a heavy concentration of gigs there, usually opening for Vanilla Fudge. (On other dates they opened for the rabble-rousing Detroit band, the MC5.) On the last day of the year the group played in Portland, Oregon, and then found itself unable to fly to Los Angeles because an arctic blizzard had closed the airport. But all were adamant that they make the date at the Whiskey, the main rock show-case in Los Angeles. The show *had* to go on. So Richard Cole rented a station wagon and started to drive the group to Se-attle through the worst snowstorm in local memory in order to catch a plane at Seattle's still-open airport. Pissquick was an hour behind, driving the truck carrying the band's equip-ment. The road was deserted except for abandoned vehicles and the visibility was completely whited-out, but Cole reso-lutely crept ahead, prompted by Peter Grant's ominous mut-tering about making the plane on time. When Led Zeppelin arrived at the Squalamie Pass, they found the road blocked by a state police car; the pass was closed by heavy drifting snow. The police pulled Richard Cole over and told him to stay off the road. But Richard waited until the police car had driven off and been enveloped in the opaque whiteness, and then got the car back on the road, bypassing the roadblock by driving under an overpass marked "closed." They drove on through the stormy pass, past closed gas stations and idle snowplows. They assumed that Pissquick had been stopped by the roadblock and that they would arrive without their instruments or equipment. Morale was at a nadir, especially among Robert and Bonzo, who were terrified in the back of the wagon, wishing they were back on the safe, familiar road to Wolverhampton. "Bonzo and I were really babies then," Robert said later. "We were twenty years old and scared to death, never having been in a big group or anything."

Halfway through the pass, Richard Cole pulled over and announced he had to piss. He put on the brake and jumped out, unbuttoning and wondering aloud which of his organs would freeze first. Suddenly the car began to move backward. The band and Peter Grant found themselves sliding toward a precipice, ten yards from oblivion, as Cole continued to pee unaware of the tragedy occurring behind him. But Robert and Bonzo started to shriek in terror, and Cole ran back, managing to brake and steer the car to a stop. Robert and Bonzo were cowering with fear, which seemed to perversely amuse the battle-hardened likes of Page, Jones, Cole, and Grant. An hour later the car approached a deserted suspension bridge. Robert and Bonzo looked closely: The huge gales were actually making the bridge *sway*. Oblivious, Cole plunged them toward their doom and Robert and Bonzo screamed for him to stop. Cole thought they were putting him on, but they were actually *freaking out*. So the motherly Cole pulled over and gave Robert and Bonzo a ration of whiskey to calm them down. An hour later they had both drifted into a stupor and Cole drove on through the tempest.

Four hours later Led Zeppelin reached Seattle. But their plane's engines had frozen, so they gave up and headed for the airport bar to sulk. Half an hour later Pissquick drove up with the gear, having evaded the same roadblock via the same closed overpass. Led Zeppelin got to L.A. the next day in one piece. "Fools that we were," Cole says, "we only knew that we had a job to do and that was it." But the passage through the storm had been too much for the frail Page; he came down with flu and high fever and spent New Year's Day in bed. Cole and John Paul Jones were the only ones old enough to celebrate with a drink. The two twenty-year-olds, Robert and Bonzo, were thrown out of the bar.

The Whiskey engagement was a wild success, and Hollywood embraced Led Zeppelin as it had the Yardbirds four years earlier. On January 9, 1969, Jimmy's twenty-fifth birthday, the band began three days at the Fillmore West in San Francisco, supporting Country Joe and the Fish. Taj Mahal opened the show. In spite of the headbangers in Boston and the enthusiasm in L.A., it was this Fillmore West weekend that showed the musicians they were going to be very big. Here they ran out of Elvis medleys and were forced to play unrehearsed Garnet Mimms tunes and improvise current hits like Spirit's "Fresh Garbage." Through all this, Jimmy suffered with flu and a fever, reminiscent of his glandular fever in the Crusaders days.

As Led Zeppelin headed for the hinterlands, Atlantic geared up its hype machine. Thousands of posters were distributed showing a bushy-headed Jimmy reaching out, palm extended (copied from the Doors' first poster), while the three hairy "sidemen" glowered behind him. *Led Zeppelin* was released in America the last week of January while the band played the Image Club in Miami. But on progressive rock stations like WBCN in Boston and KSAN in San Francisco, the album had already been an underground hit for several weeks, with disc jockeys mostly leaning on "Communication Breakdown," "Babe . . . ," and "Dazed and Confused." (In New York singer Jake Holmes heard Jimmy's version of his song and wondered what to do. Jimmy had lifted intact the title, bass line, and *gestalt* from Holmes's song, but the words were completely different. Years later Holmes recollected, "I said, what the hell, let him have it.")

But Led Zeppelin's pleasure at radio airplay and strong sales was offset by a cool reception from the press. *Rolling Stone*, which Jimmy then considered the best American music paper, was very sour in its review, which started, "The popular formula in this, the aftermath era of such successful British bluesmen as Cream and John Mayall, seems to be: add, to an excellent guitarist who, since leaving the Yardbirds and/or Mayall has become a minor musical deity, a competent rhythm section and a pretty soul belter who can do a good spade imitation. The latest of the British groups so conceived offers little that its twin, the Jeff Beck Group, didn't say as well or better three months ago, and the excesses of the Beck Group's *Truth* album . . . are fully (most notably its self-indulgence and restrictedness) in evidence on Led Zeppelin's debut album." After slagging the record track by track the reviewer concluded: ". . . if they're to fill the void created by the demise of Cream, they will have to find a producer and some material worthy of their collective attention." (Published in March 1969, this negative review drew hundreds of protest letters to the paper.)

After three weeks of honing their show at provincial clubs and colleges, Led Zeppelin finished its first American tour opening for Iron Butterfly at the Fillmore East in New York on January 31. Before the show Peter Grant told Jimmy that Led Zeppelin's job was to blow the clumsy Butterfly off its own stage. So Jimmy took the stage in his red velvet suit and played for two hours before the expected half dozen encores, with Bonzo leaping high in the air above his drums during the last climax. By the time they finished their show with "Train Kept A-Rollin'," Iron Butterfly refused to go on, realizing that Led Zeppelin—fellow musicians, hip brethren, and label-mates—had left them nothing.

The band returned to England in February, flushed with success. *Led Zeppelin* was Number 90 on the American charts and heading up. Not every show had been perfect; in Detroit "Killing Floor"—soon to evolve into "The Lemon Song"—fell apart with each musician playing a different melody, leaving the audience confused. In other cities the reaction teetered on the brink of mania. Most important, the band was beginning to jell. Jimmy was playing his controlled, furious guitar lines better than ever and exuded more weird charisma than anybody. John Paul Jones, content to go unnoticed, had suffered equipment problems but remained the ultimate pop professional. Bonzo had gotten a lot of attention as, obviously, the most powerful new drummer in rock since Keith Moon. Night after night he was steady-on, playing louder and heavier than anyone had ever heard, but playing with precision and definition. Most English drummers had been small men like Ringo Starr, Charlie Watts, Keith Moon, or Kenny Jones of the Small Faces. But Bonzo was a big man with correspondingly greater physical strength. He was also playing with the biggest bass drum available, twenty-eight inches in diameter, which was lined with aluminum foil for extra reverberation. Bonzo's style was brutal rather than artistic, but his time was impeccable and his developing long drum solo, patterned on Ginger Baker's "Toad," was often the biggest ovation-getter in the act, especially when Bonzo threw away his sticks and played with his hands. In Portland Bonzo had even complained that he couldn't hear himself; he wanted to add another bass drum. John Paul Jones said that he didn't see why Bonzo wanted a double bass kit, since he was already doing more with one foot than most drummers did with two hands and two feet.

Of the four members of Led Zeppelin, it was Robert Plant who was most savagely criticized, both within the band and without. Throughout America the pop critics insulted his aria-like blues wails and his prissy, hyper-masculine posing. Cole remembers that "I used to hide the press write-ups from him because they were so critical. I wouldn't let him see them." Indeed, Robert's stage presence was rather *outré*, and sometimes even the band thought he had gone too far. Someone came up with a nickname for Robert: "Percy." Cole says it started as an inside joke concerning a famous English gardener, Percy Thrower; but it stuck among the band. From then on Robert *was* Percy. But even Jimmy wasn't absolutely positive about Robert. Cole recalls, "It was a very touch-and-go thing whether Robert would even be in the group after the first tour, because he didn't quite seem to make it up to Pagey's expectation. At the time there was a possibility he wouldn't do another tour. That was the truth."

Significantly, Robert had gone unnamed on the song publishing credits for *Led Zeppelin*. Later it was explained that he was still under a songwriting contract to CBS at the time. But Robert's status within the band was relatively low during the earliest days. Once, Richard and Jimmy were sitting by the hotel pool in Los Angeles and Cole asked Robert (who was earning less money than Cole) to go for sandwiches, an unheard of breach of tour protocol. Robert got the food, but never forgave him.

Yet Robert stayed in the band. It was decided by Jimmy and Peter that Robert would get better with more experience. Meanwhile, everyone was *buzzing*. Jimmy was quoted: "I can't really comment on why we broke so big in the States. I can only think that we were aware of dynamics at a time when everyone was into a drawn-out West Coast style of playing. We knew we were making an impression after the incredible response at the Boston Tea Party and the Kinetic Circus in Chicago, but it was the Fillmore West when we knew we'd really broken through. It was just . . . *bang!*"

But in England no one cared. As Cole says, "They came back like victors. They were the hottest new act in the States.

They had *conquered America*. And all of a sudden they were back on the little English circuit playing to four hundred people. But that was the circuit then. You didn't go on tour in England, you just went to work, doing your venues." Jimmy was really down on the situation at home; he bitched to *Melody Maker* that his ultra-long hair was getting him in trouble in London's West End, where skinheads in suspenders and boots called him rude names. In America, he said, they had a decent phone system and radio stations that played only rock *all the time*. In England *Led Zeppelin* had been belatedly released in March 1969 and was being ignored by the BBC Radio One, the only station of any significance in the country. "I hate the whole scene," Jimmy pouted. "A new group can sit around for 10 months and have no notice taken at all."

For two months Led Zeppelin introduced itself to Britain, playing at pubs like the Toby Jug in Tolworth and almost every club around London. They returned to Denmark and Sweden to play before making their first (and last) appearance on English television. Substituting for the Flying Burrito Brothers on a late evening show, they played "Communication Breakdown." Meanwhile, the press was starting to take notice. The underground magazine *Oz* noted: "Very occasionally, an LP record is released that defies immediate categorization, because it's so obviously a turning point in rock music that only time proves capable of shifting it into perspective. This Led Zeppelin album is like that."

But England was a disappointment. Led Zeppelin had tasted its power in America, which now beckoned to them with money, girls, and fame. So on April 20 they flew back to Los Angeles for another tour, again shepherded by Richard Cole. Back on the first tour, at the Carousel Ballroom in San Francisco, Cole had made an unusual request of Peter Grant. "I said, 'Look, let me stay with this band and not do all the others. Let me stay with one fucking band instead of jumpin' about, let me have a bit of the glory.' Because I *knew* they were gonna make the money. I *knew* they were gonna be monsters. And they were."

The tour opened with four nights at the Fillmore West. Twenty-nine shows in thirty-one days, co-headlining with Vanilla Fudge, which meant that whichever band was strongest in that market went on last. By then Led Zeppelin's act was growing out of proportion. Their original hour-long show had expanded to an hour and a half onstage. When they added their utility Ben E. King and Garnet Mimms numbers, they played for two hours. The encores demanded in America expanded the show to two and a half hours, and the new riffs and songs Led Zeppelin were writing on the road added an hour to that. Even Vanilla Fudge, who the band was friends with, was leery about going on after Zeppelin had wrung a crowd for three and a half hours of nonstop crunch.

In Los Angeles Cole installed the group in bungalows at the Château Marmont Hotel, where Led Zeppelin's orgies wouldn't disturb the other guests. Everyone in the band but Jimmy was married, which only heightened the forbidden pleasures that Hollywood night life offered the band. At one point Bonzo dressed up as a waiter, laid Jimmy on a room service cart, and wheeled him into a suite full of tumescent girls, whom Jimmy fancied on the youngish side. "I don't think you will ever find an English musician who would ever put down those girls who were called groupies," Cole says. "Cos those girls were not *sluts* or *slags* or whatever. They fucking saved my arse as far as patience goes, cos you're talking about twenty-year-old guys away from home. The girls took care of them and were like a second home. You could trust them. They wouldn't steal from you. Most of them are dead now."

By early May *Led Zeppelin* had entered the American Top Ten, and the band was raging. The long shows usually began with "Communication Breakdown," and segued into "I Can't Quit You Baby" with Robert's yawping howls and Jimmy's delicate blues fugues. Often the shows would bog down in the bombastic sludge of "Killing Floor"/"Lemon Song" and "Babe I'm Gonna Leave You" before ending with the usual oldies medley. At one show at Winterland, this started with

Garnet Mimms's "As Long As I Have You" and ran through an improbable melange of the lullaby "Hush Little Baby," "Bags' Groove," "Shake" a la Otis Redding, and "Fresh Garbage."

Two days later Led Zeppelin's sojourn in Seattle proved to be the end of their reputation as normal humans. Seattle was where The Shark Episode took place.

The show itself was another success. Playing at an open-air festival, Robert and Bonzo were thrilled to be on the same bill with Chuck Berry (whom the jaded Jimmy knew from Yardbirds tours as a moody recluse). Their awe was increased when they beheld the brown-eyed handsome man emerge from his dusty Cadillac, which he'd driven from St. Louis, unpack his guitar, and play a set with a strange pickup band, and then deposit his cash fee in his briefcase and drive off. Led Zeppelin took the stage after the Doors had finished their set, made anticlimactic by Jim Morrison's disconnected rambling, and then revived the faded audience with their punchy, explosive rhythms. It was no contest, and Led Zeppelin gave no quarter.

Back at the hotel the band started drinking. Richard Cole says that what happened later was his fault. "The sharks thing happened at the Edgewater Inn in Seattle. How it came about is that in 1968 I was with Terry Reid, supporting the Moody Blues in Seattle, and their road manager told me the band should stay at the Edgewater Inn, because there's a tackle shop in the lobby and you can fish right out the window of the hotel. I said, 'Go on, fuck off ya cunt.' He said, 'Come on Richard, I'm not kidding, it's true.' So the next time I was in Seattle was with Led Zeppelin and Vanilla Fudge, and we started to catch sharks out the window. By this time the tours were more and more risqué, and you could do what you liked with the girls who showed up at the hotel. For me, that second fucking Led Zeppelin tour was the fucking best time of my life. *That* was the one. We were hot and on our way up, but no one was watching too closely. So you could fucking *play*. And these birds were coming up to my suite wanting to fuck, and me and Bonzo were quite serious about catching these fish." What happened next isn't really clear. One girl, a pretty young groupie with red hair, was disrobed and tied to the bed. According to the legend of the Shark Episode, Led Zeppelin then proceeded to stuff pieces of shark into her vagina and rectum.

Richard Cole says it didn't happen that way. "It wasn't Bonzo, it was *me*. Robert and Bonzo didn't know *anything*, they were kids. It wasn't shark parts anyway: It was the nose that got put in. Yeah, the shark was *alive*! It wasn't dead! We caught a big lot of sharks, at least two dozen, stuck coat hangers through the gills and left 'em in the closet. . . . But the *true* shark story was that it wasn't even a shark. It was a red snapper and the chick happened to be a fucking redheaded broad with a ginger pussy. And that is the truth. Bonzo was in the room, but I did it. Mark Stein [of Vanilla Fudge] filmed the whole thing. And she *loved* it. It was like, 'You'd like a bit of fucking, eh? Let's see how *your* red snapper likes *this* red snapper!' That was it. It was the *nose* of the fish, and that girl must have come 20 times. I'm not saying the chick wasn't drunk, I'm not saying that *any* of us weren't drunk. But it was nothing malicious or harmful, no way! No one was *ever* hurt. She might have been *hit* by a shark a few times for disobeying orders, but she didn't get hurt."

In this incredible year-long spurt of debauchery, the musicians and management of Led Zeppelin, according to Cole, often kiddingly reminded each other that silent film star Fatty Arbuckle's career had been ruined when he was alleged to have accidentally killed a girl he was rogering with a champagne bottle. This was often talked about, because Led Zeppelin quickly discovered that *lots* of girls wanted to be rogered with champagne bottles. Cole blames it all on alcoholism. "I'll tell you how much we used to drink. I think we bankrupted Steve Paul's Scene in New York because we *never* paid our bar bills. All the so-called Led Zeppelin depravity took place the first two years in an alcoholic fog. After that we got older and grew out of it. It became a realistic business."

Meanwhile, the tour madness only increased. In British Columbia they discovered that their two dates were five hundred miles and one day apart. The distance had to be driven overnight. From there they flew to Hawaii and a couple of days of rest before plunging back into battle with shows in Detroit. After flying all night the group staggered into their Detroit motel at seven in the morning and stumbled onto a gruesome murder scene. The corpse was being taken out as the band walked in, and steam was rising from a pool of blackened blood on the carpet. A man had been shot to death just a few moments before. Robert grabbed his bags and his room key and headed for some sleep. "I only knew I'd spew if I looked at it for another second," he said.

In Detroit Led Zeppelin's entourage was joined by its first writer/photographer team, covering the band for *Life* magazine. Back in Los Angeles the band had been upset by its decidedly mixed reviews in the local press. A Hollywood press agent was hired to correct that situation, and *Life* was convinced to assign a team to the tour. Writer Ellen Sander and her photographer had originally proposed covering the Who, also touring America that summer (they were one of the few English bands to play at Woodstock), but that had fallen through and Sander and *Life* had settled on Zeppelin instead. It was Sander's first job for *Life* and a plum for Zeppelin, since new bands weren't often afforded such mainstream press coverage. It was decided that Sander would join the band in Detroit. There Cole organized an informal betting pool based on which of them would have her first.

As Sander traveled with the band, she recorded her impressions for her article. Robert was "wooly, handsome in an obscenely rugged way." Jimmy was "ethereal, effeminate, pale and frail." Bonzo "played ferocious drums, often shirtless and sweating like some gorilla on a rampage." John Paul Jones held the whole thing together and stayed in the shadows." "No matter how miserably the group failed to keep their

The Yardbirds in action at the Shrine in Los Angeles, April 1968. From left: Chris Dreja, Keith Relf, Jim McCarty, and Jimmy Page, dressed in velvet and lace and playing his psychedelic Telecaster.

The Yardbirds Christmas card, 1967. Peter Grant is dressed as Santa Claus at Jimmy's right.

DARTREY ROAD

Robert Plant, circa 1966, sporting caftan and love beads when he was the vocalist for a Midlands group called the Band of Joy. The beard didn't last the year.

John Baldwin, alias John Paul Jones

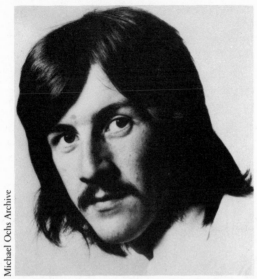

John Henry Bonham as a lean and hungry young drummer

Robert Plant just after he had joined Led Zeppelin

Led Zeppelin's first publicity group photograph. The floral shirts were the height of fashion in 1968.

Robert in action, 1970

Bonzo, in 1970. His huge drumsticks ("trees" in drummer jargon) were the largest available.

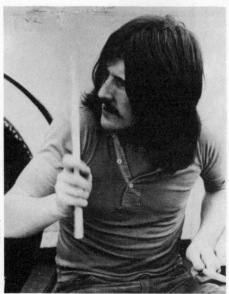

Led Zeppelin in late 1971, around the time "Stairway to Heaven" was released. Note Jimmy's beard.

Jimmy Page and Lori Maddox, Los Angeles, 1972

Jimmy raises the bow during "Dazed and Confused," 1972.

A photo call after a Led Zeppelin press conference in Miami before the 1973 American tour

On May 5, 1973, Led Zeppelin played for this crowd of 56,800 in Tampa, Florida. At the time, it was the largest crowd and the biggest gross ($309,000) for a single artist performance. Some of Led Zeppelin's single-act attendance records still stand.

behavior up to a basic human level," Sander noted, "they played well almost every night of the tour. If they were only one of the many British rock groups touring at the time, they were also one of the finest. The stamina they found each night at curtain-time was amazing, in the face of every conceivable foul-up with equipment, timing, transportation and organization at every date. They had that fire and musicianship going for them and a big burst of incentive; this time around, on their second tour, from the very beginning, they were almost stars."

Sander couldn't help noticing the frantic air of sexual tension and competition between the members of the group. Jimmy didn't like to approach girls himself, preferring to have Cole solicit for him. But Cole was too dangerous and Sander was not a groupie, so Jimmy had his publicity agent tell Sander to call him instead. And Sander did end up spending the most time with Page, since Robert was too wild and preoccupied with sex, Bonzo and Cole were too drunk, and Jones was never around. One night Cole burst into her motel room to tell her that the group was leaving for a gig, and noticed that both beds were unmade. "Pagey's been with you then," he exclaimed, and rushed out to tell the rest. But it wasn't true.

When Robert Plant awoke from his afternoon nap in Detroit, he stank so badly he was dispatched to buy some shampoo and deodorant for himself. As he stepped out of the motel onto the street, a motorist stopped at a light, cursed his long hair, and spat in his face. Robert was upset. "I'm white," he said later. "I can imagine how a spade feels here."

That night the show was at the Grande Ballroom, an old warehouse that was one of the original rock palaces. The house was packed and restless; armed police were arresting customers for lighting joints. The house loudspeakers failed during the first set, which sounded terrible. Backstage, the dingy dressing room was crowded with groupies angling for a shot at the band. According to Sander, "A pair of grotesquely painted, greasy-cheeked, overweight sexbombs in their late twenties pushed their way through the young things to Robert Plant. One placed her hand on his thigh and brassily declared, 'You're spending the night with *me*.' Robert grimaced and exploded. 'Hey wot, you bloody tart, old Robert's a married man!' The others tittered as he squirmed away, pausing to shoot them a leering wink." Huddling together for protection, the band discussed the situation. The two elder groupies were dubbed "the ugly sisters," but it was decided they did possess a certain slatternly allure. A plot was hatched to get them back to the motel, gang bang them, and then stuff them full of cream-filled doughnuts. Pleasant memories of The Shark Episode still danced in their fevered brains. In fact, once Led Zeppelin acquired a taste for abusing groupies, it just got worse. With smug self-justification, Jimmy explained it to Sander: "Girls come around and pose like starlets, teasing and acting haughty. If you humiliate them a bit they tend to come on all right after that. Everyone knows what they come for. . . . I haven't got time to deal with it."

Just then John Paul Jones walked in the door, looked in the room full of girls and dope dealers, and walked out again, sulking miserably outside while fans pestered him. Jimmy Page, "with that febrile, forlorn look that brought out perversity in fifteen-year-olds" (according to Sander), sat inside and chatted with whoever spoke to him, neither offering or accepting any sexual invitations.

The following morning the group met outside the hotel, waiting for Richard to show up with the station wagon. Robert was annoyed. Not only had the cream doughnut event fallen through when they couldn't find a store after the gig, but Robert had been with one of the ugly sisters and she wouldn't come all night. "Can you believe that?" he asked. "I was embarrassed."

The next gig was in Athens, Ohio. Between his own hectic sexual escapades (he usually ended up with the girls he solicited for others), Richard got the band to the airport, handled the reservations and tickets, got them drunk on the flight so they wouldn't complain, rented a car at the next airport, and got them to their next motel and gig. No time for supper, just visits to the motel bar before and after the show. Then up in the morning, and the musicians would collapse into a sleepy stupor, heads lolling with the turns, as he drove them through springtime Ohio farmland back to the airport and the next gig in Minneapolis. When Robert got on the plane he galloped down the aisle like a demented ape, shouting, "Toilets! *Toilets for old Robert!*" The other passengers gaped as the big hippie with the blond mane clawed at the door of the lavatory.

The plane was delayed, and the band was late getting onstage at the staid Guthrie Memorial Theater, where the audience chuckled in genteel chagrin at Robert's screaming orgasm sequence during the new song "Whole Lotta Love." Afterward the band was obliged to attend a party for the country club set at the promoter's suburban manse, where the exhausted Englishmen got quietly drunk and were gaped at by the locals for several excruciating hours. The next morning Richard convened a meeting. There were four days before the next show in Chicago; everyone wanted out of Minneapolis. Jimmy decided the band should go to New York to work on the new album, rehearse, and do interviews.

Work had started on *Led Zeppelin II* the previous January, with riffs left over from the original act and new riffs developed during the constant playing, rehearsal, and improvisation of the tour. *Led Zeppelin II* was the product of an English band's insane life on the road, written in snatches in motel rooms, dressing rooms, and studios all over North America. Since English musicians were allowed only six months a year in America, they were under constant pressure to make every day pay. But actually working in the studio became a problem when word spread among the groupies that Jimmy Page and his hunky band were in town. There was a thirty-ish groupie queen who was particularly annoying to Jimmy. She'd show up at the studio where Jimmy was trying to mix "Bring

It On Home," claiming to be the ex-wife of a famous producer, dressing the part—dyed blond hair, black leather miniskirt, tall boots, a cowboy hat. The most intelligent of the groupies had the foresight to check the studio schedules so they could arrive early to get the best seats: It was this group the blonde tried to intimidate, loudly announcing that Jimmy was so *marvelous* in bed last night. Finally a distracted Page could take no more. He went out in the hall and found the most pathetic of all the aspirant groupies. Cuddling her protectively, he led this wretch back into the studio and demanded the older woman give up her seat for her. Staring straight ahead, her pancaked face crumbling, the blonde got up and left. That night the group saw her cruising Steve Paul's Scene like a barracuda, sniffing fresh blood.

The next stop, Chicago, was old Yardbirds turf. The massive Kinetic Circus was packed; also on the bill were Vanilla Fudge, and in the dressing room the gory details of The Shark Episode were rehashed again with great mirth. Led Zeppelin tore it down that night, and the hall echoed to repeated ovations. "Dazed and Confused" was now stretching into twenty minutes, with Jimmy's bow exhibition drawing much awe for its ritualistic connotations of diabolism. Snooping at the back door, Peter Grant caught the hall's manager surreptitiously selling tickets to an already sold-out show and confiscated the cash. Something else felt wrong. Neither Grant nor Cole believed the tally of heads and cash. In the office Cole took apart the waste bin and came up with ticket stubs of the wrong color. Again, Grant demanded and received whatever illicit cash was due the band. Grant's tenacious instinct for the scent of cash would eventually mean that his clients Led Zeppelin would earn (and keep) more money than any rock musicians before them.

After two nights in Chicago and another in Maryland, the band needed rest. Jimmy's flu returned, but he went on anyway. "That's how you know you're a pro," he chirped to Ellen Sander on the plane to New York the next day, where

Atlantic Records was giving them a gold-record party at the Plaza Hotel. There the group was informed that *Led Zeppelin II* would have to be finished quickly to catch the fall market. Somewhat listlessly, the band went back in the studio right after the party. During this time, the musicians' morale sank into despondency. Bonzo, desperately homesick, was silent and morose. Jimmy became a martinet in the studio, a compulsive workaholic. John Paul Jones kept cool and said little. And Robert Plant, who was rapidly becoming the star of Led Zeppelin much to the sheer dismay of Jimmy Page, spoke constantly of buying a christening gown for his daughter Carmen Jane. One morning, after a night-long drunken fracas that had brought the hotel manager to his door, Robert sighed aloud, to no one in particular, "God, I miss my wife."

Prodded by Cole, soothed with lurid visions of future riches by Grant, Led Zeppelin pressed on. The first tour had lost money, but the second would finish in the black. They were getting between $5,000 and $15,000 a night. For their five weeks' work, the four musicians and Grant would split about $150,000 after booking agents, lawyers, accountants, roadies, and publicity agents had been paid. But they didn't care about this loose change; this tour was only a set-up for the third, where they might gross almost half a million dollars for fewer shows and better traveling conditions. The band's attitude was crystallized by Jonesy: "In this business, it's not so much making it as fast as you can but making it fast while you can. The average life of a successful group is about three years. You have to get past that initial ordeal. The touring makes you into a different person. I realize that when I get home. It takes me weeks to recover after living like an animal for so long."

Next show: the Boston Tea Party, where earlier the kids had been banging their heads on the stage. This time, with all the Atlantic people up from New York to see the show, the Zeppelin soared and were called back for the usual multiple encores. After five encores the group was backstage, swigging

Watney's Red Barrel ale, about to drop but still high on adrenaline. Outside, the crowd was *bonkers*. Robert urged, "Let's give 'em another." Jimmy Page shook his head, laughing. "We don't *know* any others," he gasped. But as Robert walked out again, the crowd began to roar and the others followed him into an unrehearsed, sloppy medley of Beatles and Stones songs. Backstage after the show, the band was limp. Robert was enraged because a fan stole his favorite shirt. Jonesy lovingly wiped his bass down with a towel before carefully depositing it in its plush-lined case. They were besieged by groupies as usual. (Earlier, a bridegroom had followed his bride to the band's motel, where she had tried to find Led Zeppelin, and had beaten her up on the street outside the restaurant where the band ate, unaware of the whole incident.) This time, too tired to cope, they asked a deejay from the Boston FM station to find them some nice girls.

The second tour of the States ended with two shows at the Fillmore East on May 30 and 31. On the last night Ellen Sander from *Life* showed up backstage to thank the band for letting her travel with them and to say good-bye. She walked into Led Zeppelin's dressing room, she remembers, unprepared for what would happen next. "Two members of the group attacked me, shrieking and grabbing at my clothes, totally over the edge. . . . Bonzo came at me first, and then there were a couple more. After that I didn't see much. All of a sudden there were all these hands on me, and all these big guys. My clothes were half torn off; they were in a frenzy. I was absolutely terrified that I was going to be raped and really angry. . . . And then I saw Peter Grant—who was bigger than all of them—and I thought, 'Him too? Oh no, I'm gonna be *killed*!' But what he did was pull Bonham off me. Peter Grant just picked him up and pulled him off me, so all they did was tear my clothes. They didn't hurt me, except for my feelings."

Led Zeppelin never did get their pictures in *Life*; Ellen Sander refused to write the story. And when she later published her bitter account of Led Zeppelin's second American tour, she concluded, "If you walk inside the cages of the zoo you get to see the animals close up, stroke the captive pelts, and mingle with the energy behind the mystique. You also get to smell the shit firsthand."

The American entertainment press wasn't much kinder. Of that final show at the Fillmore, *Variety* opined, "This quartet's obsession with power, volume and melodramatic theatrics leaves little room for the subtlety other Britishers employ. There is plenty of room for dynamics and understatement in the Zeppelin's brand of ultra-hard rock. But the combo has forsaken the musical sense for the sheer power that entices their predominantly juvenile audience."

Already Led Zeppelin was in trouble because it was the younger kids, the little brothers and sisters of the great sixties generation, who loved Zeppelin the most. For this Led Zeppelin would never be forgiven by the rock establishment.

In June they went home. By then the English media had publicized their American notoriety and welcomed them with anticipation. On the thirteenth they started another English tour, and three days later played "Communication Breakdown" on the BBC, the first of three English broadcasts they did that month. The following week they played Robert Johnson's "Travelling Riverside Blues" on Radio One's *Top Gear* program. Even while touring, Atlantic's schedule for *Led Zeppelin II* kept them in the studio, where "Ramble On" and "Living Loving Maid (She's Just a Woman)" were done. Also recorded, at Morgan Studios, was their sometime set-opener "We're Gonna Groove." On June 27 they broadcast a live, hour-long show from the Playhouse Theater over Radio One, the first time England had a chance to hear their whole show. "Communication Breakdown" led the set with Jimmy's flashing wah-wah solo, with snatches of "Season of the Witch" and the Isley Brothers' "It's Your Thing" in the improvised middle section. Then the segue to "I Can't Quit You Baby,"

with Robert screeching over the lumbering blues cadence:
"Oooooooooooooooaaaaaaaauuuuuuuuuugggghhhhhh! I can't
quit you baaaabe/But ah'm gonna hafta putcha down for a
while." White blues at its most highly posed. "Dazed and
Confused" sounded gothic even over the radio, as the bowing
section emitted painful, demonic blasts of stygian murk before the crazy fast section began to hurtle like an Exocet missile. Unseen, over the radio, Led Zeppelin still had this
uncanny ability to project strong feelings of movement and
magical display. Jimmy's showpiece, "White Summer"/"Black
Mountain Side," calmed things before "You Shook Me"
and "How Many More Times" ended the show. Two
major concerts followed. At the Bath Festival of Blues and
Progressive Music, Zepp added 12,000 victims to its sacrificial list. The next day, June 29, they headlined the first night
of the Pop Proms series at the Royal Albert Hall, where the
staff turned the houselights off at 11 P.M. after one encore.
Led Zeppelin went back onstage anyway and played "Long
Tall Sally" before showering the fans with confetti and flower
petals from the foot of the stage. Finally Led Zeppelin was
triumphant at home. Even the music press applauded Bonzo's "uncluttered approach" while sneering at the band's "hippie
ideals."

Led Zeppelin's third American tour began July 5 at the Atlanta Pop Festival and would last all summer. Gradually fan
hysteria began to pile on the band. At the once semi-respect-
able Newport Jazz Festival, where they played with Jeff Beck,
James Brown, B. B. King, and Jethro Tull, hundreds of kids
rushed the stage to get close to the band, marking the end of
the bucolic Newport scene. The same reaction occurred at
the Baltimore and Philadelphia Jazz Festivals the following
week. On July 13 they played the Singer Bowl, an open-air
stadium in Flushing Meadows on Long Island, on the bill
with Jeff Beck, Ten Years After, and Vanilla Fudge. During
Beck's set Jimmy walked out to jam, followed by a very drunken
Bonzo, who sat down at a drum kit and began to play a

"stripper" beat, removing his clothes at the same time. Finally Bonzo got down to his bikini shorts; as he dropped these a squad of police started toward the stage to prevent a Bonzo moon. But Peter Grant, watching from the wings, reached Bonzo first and picked him up, complete with drum stool and sticks still flying, and carried him offstage to the dressing room, where he told Bonzo he was fired if his clothes weren't on by the time the police broke the door down.

While in New York they also played with B. B. King at a beer company's music festival in Central Park, where police estimated that 25,000 fans turned up at a space that held only 10,000. After four encores the crowd was swept up in Led Zeppelin's raucous frenzy, and the metal framework of the stage and light towers was creaking from the strain. Just before the band left for dates on the West Coast, Atlantic Records told them they had an unbelievable 400,000 advance orders for the new album.

Led Zeppelin arrived back in Los Angeles, its spiritual home, as conquering heroes and naughty devils intent on further lechery and copulation. By then the rumors had gotten out of control. The Shark Episode had been embellished to include the sadistic beating of scores of girls with dead octopusses. The Ellen Sander attack had become full-fledged rape and murder. Richard Cole again moved the band into the Château Marmont and the fun began.

Led Zeppelin regarded Los Angeles as their Sodom and Gomorrah, an improbable subtropical fantasyland that offered its most nubile daughters and every conceivable vice to them on a platter. When young Brummies like Robert and Bonzo beheld these gorgeous California girls with psychedelic outfits and fuck-me eyes, *blatantly coming on to them*, their young minds snapped. Egged on by Cole, the outrageous was pursued to its most mindless limits. For some reason food and sex were inextricably linked in the band's mind. Perhaps it was a reaction to growing up in the puritanical, postwar Britain of shortages and rationing. One of the stars of the food scene was the girl Richard called the Dog Act. One day he tried to get her Great Dane to penetrate her and perform cunnilingus. But the dog wasn't interested. He even fried some bacon in the kitchenette of his bungalow and stuffed it up her. Still the dog wouldn't go for it. "So I'm fuckin' her," Cole says, "and I said to Bonzo, 'C'mon, you can fuck her and all.' Now Bonzo truly loved his wife and usually didn't get involved with girls, but this time he said yes. So Bonzo's in there fuckin' her, and I swear he says to me, 'How'm I doing?' I said you're doing fine. Then Grant walks in with this giant industrial-size can of baked beans and dumped it all over Bonzo and the girl. Then he opened a bottle of champagne and sprayed them." Jimmy had himself photographed covered with beef entrails and offal, which GTO Miss Cinderella pretended to eat. The pictures were suppressed.

Richard Cole attributes such madness to the melancholy of homesickness on the road. So insecure were Robert and Bonzo that they insisted on sleeping with the light on for the first five tours. Sometimes their fear was comical. Sharing bungalow B, Robert and Bonzo refused to sleep in their room if the other wasn't there. Cole remembers that one night Robert came in and Bonzo was missing, so Robert climbed into bed with roadie Clive Coulson, who was bunking in the living room. Later Bonzo came in with a girl and he couldn't find Robert; so Bonzo sent the girl home, and also tried to get in Coulson's bed, waking Robert and the unamused roadie, who needed his sleep.

The queens of the L.A. groupie scene were of course the GTOs, the groupie clique loosely affiliated with Frank Zappa's Mothers of Invention. And the most beautiful of the GTOs was an eighteen-year-old seamstress named Miss Pamela, who sewed beautiful shirts for boys in bands and who caught Jimmy's gimlet eye one night on that tour, in a trashy Hollywood nightclub called Thee Experience.

"He pursued me," Miss Pamela recalls. "I just didn't want to know from Led Zeppelin then, because I knew about their reputation and anyway I was into the Byrds, but it was actually the Burrito Brothers by then—local country and western. Also I preferred hanging out with the girls, the GTOs, because we were so locally famous and we had such a great time—Miss Mercy, Miss Lucy, Cinderella, Sparky, the two Michelles. And, you know, we'd *heard* about Led Zeppelin, how crazy they were. They'd been back East first. We heard all the rumors and everything because communication among the groupies—I *hate* that term—was on an up-to-the-minute level. We knew some of the girls back East—Devon and Emaretta. We heard how *wild* Led Zeppelin were, that they fucked *everybody*, a different girl every night. They already had that reputation a month into their first tour! *Absolutely!* And I always prided myself that I would always have whoever it was for the whole tour, at least locally, ha ha! I was too romantic for one night stands."

The big rock club that summer of 1969 was Thee Experience. Led Zeppelin was one of the only bands actually to go as a group and hang out; they loved to be seen and fawned over. Their local notoriety actually began when Richard Cole and some groupie pushed two tables together and went at it right in the club to the sweaty cheers of the assembled patrons. (The girl was immense on the street for weeks afterward.) A few nights later Jimmy sent Richard over to Miss Pamela's table. "Jimmy likes you," Richard said. Miss Pamela said she thought that was nice. Later Richard came over with a note from Jimmy, including his room number at the hotel, but Pamela ignored it. The next night Jimmy sent Cole over again; this time Miss Pamela was lured to Led Zeppelin's table, where the usual riot was going on, except for Jimmy, sitting quietly in a corner. "Jimmy was too 'sensitive' to ask out girls," Pamela says. "He was really like a rosebud, so demure, almost feminine, so pink and so soft. I really was sucked into that—who wasn't? It was so beautiful, the image he was portraying then." Later Richard told her that Jimmy wanted her to come along to Led Zepp's show in San Diego the following night. It was a nice invitation. Miss Pamela became Jimmy's American girl friend and road-wife for the next year and a half.

She remembers her time with Jimmy with genuine fondness. "He was so romantic, so devoted, so goo-goo eyed and all that stuff. I was swept off my feet, and at the concerts I was *somebody*. I remember that in those days, if you were a musician, silver and turquoise were the thing. And with all their new money Led Zeppelin went out and bought the biggest, most grotesque and gaudy pieces they could find—huge silver necklaces with gigantic rocks of turquoise—and they'd drape these things all over me before they went onstage. They trusted me with their jewelry! You don't know what this meant to a nineteen-year-old girl in 1969!

"And Jimmy was amazing; he didn't take any drugs and only drank wine occasionally. Mostly he was vain; he'd be in the bathroom working on his hair twice as long as I was, primping and all that. I had a curling machine he would put on his hair to get these perfect little curls that hung just like *that*."

Miss Pamela traveled with the band that summer, to New York, Dallas, San Francisco. "Jimmy would take me shopping at the most expensive stores, and did I flaunt it. He was also collecting art, and bought a lot of M. C. Escher prints in California just before Escher died. We'd go to shows at the Whiskey and he just adored sitting around, being fussed over. Jimmy was so romantic and really into the woman he was with. He bestowed you with all his favors. He never looked at someone else and made you feel like a princess."

Around this time a documentary film was being shot in Los Angeles on the groupie phenomenon. In one sequence, shot in Miss Pamela's parlor, an unidentified girl describes Jimmy Page's skill with whips. When the film, *Groupie*, was released the following year, Led Zeppelin's tattered reputation sank even lower. Now it was "Jimmy Page—scourge of the groupies."

"Well, he would *never* touch me that way," Pamela says.

"He was always very gallant in the sack. In fact, he was *fabulous!* But he *was* very into whips. I saw them in his suitcases and I'm sure on the road he used them on someone else. I know Cinderella, he used to whip her. He was seeing her simultaneously, just as I started going out with him. He used to tie her up and whip her and . . . *she loved it!* She was *proud* of it!" Miss Pamela laughed at the memory. She also says that Jimmy was definitely not involved in most of the orgies at the Château Marmont and the Continental Hyatt House, where the band moved after the Manson killings had scared everyone in Southern California that summer. Once, one of the roadies knocked on their door to inform Jimmy that they were gang banging Cynthia Plaster Caster upstairs in a tub of baked beans. Jimmy went up to watch.

Mostly, Pamela says, Jimmy was obsessed with the eccentric English mage Aleister Crowley, and was trying to build a collection of Crowley artifacts. Once, when Jimmy had returned to England, Pamela found an annotated Crowley manuscript in Gilbert's Bookstore on Hollywood Boulevard, and bought it for Jimmy. Since Pamela was herself obsessed with the tarot deck, she was sympathetic. "He was *really* into that stuff," she says. "I believe that Jimmy was very into black magic and probably did a lot of rituals, candles, bat's blood, the whole thing. I believe he did that stuff.

"And, of course," she says, "the rumor that I've heard forever is that they all made this pact with the Devil, Satan, the Black Powers, whatever, so that Zeppelin would be such a huge success. And the only one who didn't do it was John Paul Jones. He wouldn't do it. Who knows where the rumor came from? But that was the rumor."

As the summer tour ground on, *Led Zeppelin II* had to be mixed down and completed as well, and Jimmy's schedule got to be insane. For one mixing session in New York, Peter Grant and a journalist drove out to the airport to pick up Jimmy, who was flying in from a Zeppelin date in Salt Lake

City to mix at A&R Studio. After the session Jimmy would fly immediately back to L.A. so he could rejoin the tour in Phoenix the day after that. Peter and Jimmy were usually together on the road, and Peter was upset when they got to the airport and found that Jimmy's flight had come in early and he had already left for the studio. Peter was fretting as they tore back into the city, expecting harsh words from the flinty guitarist, who hated to fly in the first place, and especially hated to fly alone.

By August the *Led Zeppelin II* songs had been written and recorded all over England and North America, reflecting the intense, raw mental state of a touring English band. Whereas *Led Zeppelin* had been mostly Jimmy's ideas, the new album showcased the new group identity that had surfaced on the road. Jimmy's sound was different too, since he had switched to a Les Paul guitar from the Telecaster. The album's engineer was Eddie Kramer, an English rock ace who had worked with both Jimi Hendrix and Traffic. He remembers the pressure to finish *Led Zeppelin II* on time: "We mixed it at A&R Studios in two days on a 12-channel Altec console with two pan pods, the most primitive console you could imagine. The tapes were from everywhere; 'Whole Lotta Love' had been recorded in Los Angeles, some were from London, Robert had done voice-overs on the run in Vancouver in a studio with no headphones, and some, like 'What Is and What Should Never Be,' I had recorded myself in New York in obscure studios like Groove Sound and Juggy Sound, any place we could scrounge studio time. We overdubbed a lot, and recorded solos in hallways. We scrambled all over New York trying to find studio time. It was a wild scene, and the band was *very* boisterous. I left the depraved side of it to them."

Finally, one day in late August, the album was done. Jimmy settled into a studio chair to hear the playback, dressed in his usual Regency look—the rose-colored velvet jacket, scarlet crushed velvet bell-bottoms, buckled boots of wine-dark patent leather. Other people (like Jerry Wexler) were saying the album was a masterpiece, but Page was by then sick of hearing it anymore, and had even begun to lose confidence in some of the tracks.

"Whole Lotta Love" opened the album with a nervous chortle from Robert and one of the most memorable guitar stutters in rock. The track then began to roar like a nuclear-powered Panzer division coming down the autobahn at 120, before Robert's sirenesque vocal, begging for the most carnal style of love, falls into the track's famous "middle section." This was an abstract (but carefully rehearsed) gyre of sound—clamoring trains, women in orgasm, a napalm atttack on the Mekong Delta, a steel mill just as the plant shut down. It had a strange, descending riff that Page sculpted with a metal slide treated with backward echo. There were frightening whooping sounds from Page's theramin, an electronic oscillator invented in France in the 1930s. By passing a hand over the antenna that stuck out of the little black box, one could change pitch and produce bizarre, interplanetary noises. Jimmy had first seen it used by the California band Spirit earlier in the year. The lyrics were plain: "Way down inside I wanna give you every inch of my love . . . I wanna be your back door man." But it was Robert's voice, not what he was saying, that was stark and craven. His boiling, wordless gallop into the night was like some mad, Indo-Celtic mantra that wouldn't go away.

"What Is and What Should Never Be" was next, and introduced a standard Zeppelin flight path: the soft, whispered, melodic opening verse and then—blast off! Bombs away! An acoustic ballad of limpid romance suddenly boils over into a martial chant of fire power and domination. The Plant vocal persona is emerging, somewhere between fawning and strutting. The lyrics to this great rock song—insipid verses of seduction and forbidden love, "It's to a castle I will take you"—supposedly, according to Richard Cole, chronicle the beginning of a long and secret liaison between Robert and a close woman friend. "When he first started with the group, he brought her down one day to see us," Cole says, "and we all fucking *laughed*. We said, 'You're fucking *mad*' . . . That was the big thing when the group started. He was playing with both of them. That's in one of the songs as well. It's on the second album."

"The Lemon Song" was cut live in the studio just as it came off onstage (but with guitar overdubbed on the bridge), a base rendition of Howlin' Wolf's "Killing Floor" with rearranged words and Robert's cliché white blues recitative. The first side ended with "Thank You," said to be the first fruits of Robert Plant's new lyric book. A maudlin love song, written for his wife, patterned on the Young Rascals' blue-eyed soul, it was the first song that Robert and Jimmy actually wrote together. It ends with an organ solo by John Paul Jones, an ominous, doomy theme that brought the first side set to a mysterious close. The raunchy, bump-and-grind "Heartbreaker" started the second side, a pastiche of Robert's banal West Coast lyrics plus a regulation blues guitar solo that finished with a rave-up and segued immediately into the brilliant "Living Loving Maid," a portrait of the aging New York groupie who had plagued Jimmy all summer. "With a purple umber-ella and a fifty cent hat/Missus Cool rides around in her aged Cadillac." Later Jimmy would be quoted: "It's about a degenerate old woman trying desperately to be young."

The next track, "Ramble On," began with massed acoustic guitars, a reminder that California in 1969 was captivated by the new sound of Crosby, Stills, and Nash. An evocative drone was achieved with matched harmonic feedback. For the first time though, Robert's vocal power stands alone, taking the place of Jimmy's lead guitar. The song took its theme from J.R.R. Tolkien's *The Hobbit* and *The Lord of the Rings* saga. The "Mordor" mentioned in the song is the site of the spiritual quest undertaken by Tolkien's hobbits. Bonzo's drum solo, "Moby Dick," sounded much like it did when the band took five minutes (or twenty) for a beer and a smoke while Bonzo bashed away onstage. The last track, "Bring It On Home," was most eccentric. Beginning as a tasteless send-up of the old blues by Sonny Boy Williamson, with slurred nigger singing, a crude parody of an old black man, it ended with an unexpected Led Zeppelin blast-off—loud, raw, skillful, electric white blues that ends with Jimmy's creditable, even faithful, acoustic blues playing.

That was the running order. Atlantic already had half a million advance orders for the album. By October of that year Jimmy Page would learn whether his last-minute misgivings had been justified.

The third American tour ended in Dallas on August thirty-one, where the band received a tour-high $13,000 for their show. Shortly after, Led Zeppelin flew back to England to recuperate, where customs agents hassled them over their platinum albums. Jimmy went to Spain for a few weeks before Led Zeppelin's first shows in France. The employees of Atlantic's French licensee, Barclay Records, knew that the Zeppelin was very important because Atlantic chairman Ahmet Ertegun accompanied the group, a favor only accorded to superstars like Crosby, Stills, and Nash. In Paris Led Zeppelin also appeared on the live television variety show *Tous en Scene.*

By October Led Zeppelin was ready to return to the States for a fourth time that year. But first there was a concert in London with an ironic twist. During World War One, fifty-four years earlier, England had been victimized by terrible zeppelin bombing raids flown by the German Navy. Giant hydrogen-filled war zeppelins took off from their German bases at night, flew over the North Sea, and dropped bombs over London in history's first prolonged aerial bombardment. Although Kaiser Wilhelm specifically directed that his zeppelins not bomb royal palaces or London's poorer districts, his pilots were navigating by dead reckoning and ground lights, and couldn't be sure where their bombs fell. Gruesome death and carnage followed the moonlit shadows of the zeppelins. The zeppelin raids were considered a terrible atrocity by the English, who were almost powerless to stop the zeppelins until the RAF pilots learned how to attack the slow, lumbering balloons and turn them into searing fireballs of hydrogen.

On October 13, 1915, the German naval zeppelin *LZ 15* bombed the city of London; one of the bombs exploded in the Lyceum Theater, Aldwych. Fifty-four years later, almost to the day, Led Zeppelin's show in the Lyceum on October 12 had a similar, if slightly less violent, effect. The band got what was said to be the largest fee paid to an English group for a single performance. The screaming, delirious audience finally proved that Led Zeppelin was a lot more than just the hype it had been accused of being.

Five days later Led Zeppelin opened its fourth American tour with two shows at New York's Carnegie Hall, the first rock band to play the prestigious theater since the Rolling Stones five years earlier. Robert's girlish chiffon blouse and snakeskin boots and Jimmy's antique, Edwardian clothes were a sensation. After the bent-note arabesques of Jimmy's solo on "White Summer," someone walked up and put a cold bottle of good champagne on the stage. (After the shows the theater charged the band for cleaning gum off the seats.) Then it was back on the road—Chicago, Cleveland, Boston (where the band got a $45,000 fee for a single show), Buffalo, Toronto, Providence, Syracuse, Kansas City, *ad nauseam*. On October 22 *Led Zeppelin II* was released. Life was never the same for the band after that. At that time the first album was still at Number 18 on the charts, having sold almost 800,000 copies in forty weeks. The Beatles had just released *Abbey Road* and the Stones had put out *Let It Bleed*. In spite of *Led Zeppelin II*'s heavy competition, it entered the charts at Number 199 and jumped the following week to Number 25. For a month it sat at Number 2. But by late December it had even displaced *Abbey Road* as the number one album in America. Led Zeppelin was ecstatic. Bigger than the Beatles!

There was a big row with Atlantic over the lack of a single. "Whole Lotta Love" was widely popular. In America the FM stations blared it constantly, and even in France it was played twice a day by the normally turgid "long wave" stations, as if it were a French hit that couldn't be ignored. But at five and a half minutes the song was too long for the American AM Top Forty stations, and Led Zeppelin was refusing to chop out the middle section to fit "Whole Lotta Love" into the three-minute radio format that Jimmy and Peter considered passé. Led Zeppelin had made a conscious decision to bypass the media—radio and the press—and go directly to its audience by playing live without diluting its sound. When the band refused to release the song as a single, some American stations simply edited out the middle section and spliced "Whole Lotta Love" into a single format. Audience reaction was so strong that Atlantic released its own edited version as a single, over the strenuous objections of Peter Grant and Jimmy. "I just don't like releasing album tracks as singles," Page pouted. "The two fields are not related scenes in my mind." In five weeks "Whole Lotta Love" (with "Living Loving Maid" on the B side) sold a million copies. In England the band flatly refused to have the single out, and it was never released. Grant was quoted as saying that he refused to grovel to state-controlled radio.

But in America, late in 1969 and through 1970, "Whole Lotta Love" was an emergency telegram to a new generation. In its frenzy of sex, chaos, and destruction, it seemed to conjure all the chilling anxieties of the dying decade. The lyrics reduced the struggles of the sixties generation to its most base element, its unbridled craving for *love*. Ironically, the song (and Led Zeppelin) didn't much appeal to the kids of the sixties, who had grown up with the Beatles, the Stones, Bob Dylan. Tired, jaded, disillusioned, they were turning toward softer sounds, country rock. But their younger siblings, the high school kids, were *determined* to have more fun. Led Zeppelin was really their band. For the next decade Led Zeppelin would be the unchallenged monarchs of high school parking lots all over America. In forsaking England Led Zeppelin became an American band for all practical purposes, and America would embrace them in strange ways. In Vietnam that year "Whole Lotta Love" was an actual battle cry. American soldiers and marines bolted eight-track stereos onto their tanks and armored personnel carriers and rode into battle playing the song at top volume. The irony was murderous.

Pleased by their (only half-expected) success, the musicians were also baffled by the harsh criticism of the album by the press. *Rolling Stone* ridiculed the album, accused the band of robbing authentic bluesmen of royalties (aside from covering Howlin' Wolf and Sonny Boy Williamson without credit, some writers claimed that "Whole Lotta Love" was closely related to Willie Dixon's "You Need Love"), and implied that heavy white blues like theirs was best listened to in a stupor induced by mescaline, Romilar (a narcotic cough syrup), Vietnamese marijuana, and Novocain to deaden the pain. But Led Zeppelin *needed* acceptance by its peers, its own generation; when it wasn't forthcoming, when their audience proved to consist solely of their younger siblings, the musicians had to hide their mild disappointment all the way to the bank. One of the high points of the tour was Las Vegas, where Zeppelin saw their hero Elvis perform in a giant Vegas nightclub.

The fall tour wore on. In Philadelphia they were playing the Spectrum basketball stadium. Jethro Tull was supposed to open, but Led Zeppelin was bored and wanted to get back to Steve Paul's Scene in New York so they could get drunk and chase girls. So Richard Cole went to the promoter and demanded to go on first because Jimmy was sick. The promoter flatly refused. Cole said, "Look, there's a problem. Look at Jimmy, look how fucking ill he looks. He's taking pills for his liver and either we go on first or fuck it, we're leaving now."

"*You can't do that!*" the promoter screamed.

"Well," Cole said, "I can't risk the fucking guy's *health* for the sake of you. The money doesn't mean anything to us. His welfare is more important to me." The promoter was given no choice. Led Zeppelin went on first, played an hour, and rode their limousines back to New York and the Scene.

Their last American concert in 1969 took place on November 8 at Winterland in San Francisco, with Roland Kirk and Isaac Hayes opening the show. The Rolling Stones 1969 tour was also in full swing; the Stones would play the next night in Oakland. Richard Cole saw both shows. "And that's when I realized how *big* Led Zeppelin were gonna be," Cole says. "Because the people were fucking dead at the Stones show, but the Led Zeppelin crowd was completely crazed. They were younger, they had a lot of energy, and they still wanted to rock."

By then led Zeppelin had spent nine months on the road. Although the first tour had lost money, the others had done well. Led Zeppelin made about a million dollars in its first year. Its airfares alone came to £25,000. After six months in America they all had to get out for tax reasons, so Jimmy, Robert, and Richard flew to Puerto Rico for a few days of fun—mostly whoring, according to Richard. They were in the bar of their hotel one evening and a hooker sidled up and put her hand in Richard's crotch. *"Grande,"* she purred. Then she reached for Robert and her eyes widened. *"Mucho grande,"* she exclaimed.

Led Zeppelin spent the remainder of 1969 resting and giving interviews. To *Hit Parader*, Jimmy complained about the constipated BBC. "With the music we're playing, the people in the street know what it's all about, but the adults don't know at all. If the music had enough exposure, so many more people would understand it." (The same issue featured Eric Clapton complaining about the incredible violence he saw between American rock fans and police while on tour with his ill-fated supergroup, Blind Faith.) To another writer, Jimmy said, "We were a completely untried group of people who got together to produce an album which only had one ingredient we were sure of—genuine enthusiasm. We were unabashed rock and roll, and the secret of our success lies in that fact, and the ability to interpret the excitement of those early rock sounds to the idiom of today." Jimmy missed a gold record presentation on December 11 when his car was involved in an accident on the M4 on the way into London. He then bought a new Rolls.

In America "Whole Lotta Love" and *Led Zeppelin II* had changed the sound of rock. The old terms—"white blues," "heavy music"—didn't fit Zeppelin. A new term was coined: "heavy metal." It had first been used by the writer William S. Burroughs, then by the group Steppenwolf in their hit "Born To Be Wild." But Jimmy took umbrage: "It's a bastard term to us. I can't relate that to us because the thing that comes to mind when people say heavy metal is riff-bashing, and I don't think we ever just did riff-bashing at any point. It was always inner dynamics, light and shade, drama and versatility that we were going for." To another journalist, Jimmy put the group's political stance in perspective: "I feel that some so-called progressive groups have gone too far with their person-alized intellectualism of beat music. Our music is essentially emotional like the old rock stars of the past. . . . We are not going to make any political or moral statements. Our music is simply us."

Back in England Robert had bought a dilapidated property called Jennings Farm at Blakeshall, Wolverly, near Kidder-minster. It was an ancient place, where local legend had it that Charles I had stopped for tea after losing the Battle of Worcester. Robert moved in with Maureen, his baby daugh-ter, and some of his old friends. They bought a tractor and started raising chickens and goats. To a local reporter he mused: "It seems funny that a few months ago I was an ungratified singer, and now they're calling me the next sex symbol. It can't be bad. . . . Maybe if the audience can see a cock through a pair of trousers, that must make you a sex symbol."

Bonzo had also bought a house nearby, an old farm in West Hagley. He spent thousands of dollars on cars. By the end of the year he had eight, including his first Rolls. John Paul Jones also moved his family into a house at Chorleywood, Hertfordshire.

Led Zeppelin had triumphed, helped by their professionalism and compatibility. Great bands like Cream couldn't stand each other and broke up. The Beatles dissolved in rancor that year. Brian Jones was replaced by the Rolling Stones and died in his swimming pool. Somehow Led Zeppelin had by-passed the self-indulgent egocentricity of the other pop stars. They had the self-awareness and long-term goals that enabled them to push through. By refusing to appear on television and rejecting sure-fire hit singles, they were succeeding against otherwise impossible odds. They were almost handicapping themselves. It was a strange glue that held them together, since the four musicians were very different from each other. While Page and Jones were professional, cynical London hacks, Robert and Bonzo were naïve provincials who had played music more for love than for money. Page and Jones tended to be detached and withdrawn, but Robert and Bonzo were open and accessible. Page and Jones were patient, dry-humored, and in control. Plant and Bonham were violent, funny, and manipulated by the other two and Peter Grant.

But none of that really mattered then. What mattered was that Led Zeppelin had found its audience. And Led Zeppelin kept the grown-ups out.

FOUR

VALHALLA
I AM COMING

Do what thou wilt. So mete it be.

—ALEISTER CROWLEY
The Book of the Law

By 1970 Jimmy Page had already been preoccupied with the life and work of Aleister Crowley for several years. He had a growing collection of Crowley books, manuscripts, and memorabilia, and that year he collected one of the most Crowleyan artifacts of all—Boleskine House on the shore of Loch Ness in Scotland.

Since Crowley's strange career imprints so heavily on Led Zeppelin's, it is worth considering. He was born to a well-off middle-class English family in 1875 and developed into a tall, charismatic young man who published his own poems at Oxford and was recognized as one of the most talented rock climbers and mountaineers of his day. His nature was both perverse and dramatic. Crowley assumed titles of nobility, lived under aliases ("The Chevalier MacGregor" was one), cultivated strange accents and prostitutes. Thirsty for secret and esoteric knowledge, he joined the Order of the Golden Dawn, but was denied higher rank by William Butler Yeats himself, who wrote to Lady Gregory, "We did not think that a mystical society was intended to be a reformatory." Crowley then went to Mexico where he spent a year trying to make his image vanish in a mirror. Traditional magicians had built an arcane system of spells, ritual, and drama around magic. But Crowley felt that real magic was hidden in man's will and could be summoned by an unconscious process. In magic was the survival of the pre-Christian era, a natural world of spirits and powers that had been suppressed by the Church. Conventional morality was worthless; Crowley's credo, with which he began his letters, became "Do what thou wilt shall be the whole of the Law." Accordingly, he lived a life of imponderable adventure, excess, and decadence. He participated in great Himalayan mountain expeditions (some of them disastrous), wrote prolifically and craved recognition as a writer (although his books were considered pornographic or demented), fought duels with rival necromancers by summoning platoons of demons. Regarded by most as a mountebank and by his cult as a true magus, he lived openly with several women at a time and was legendary for his unabashed use of euphorics—hashish, opium, cocaine, and heroin. He was deported from Sicily after one of his entourage died at his rustic "abbey," Thelema. Crowley also achieved notoriety with what he called "sex magick," or sexual intercourse continued indefinitely, without orgasm, to produce long, drawn-out states of ecstacy and intoxication. London society was shocked when some of its most respectable married matrons were discovered to visit Crowley's satanic temple in the Fulham Road where "The Great Beast 666" and "The Wickedest Man in the World" (as

he occasionally called himself) initiated them into the rites
of sexual magick.

Crowley ended his days moving from one country to the
next, just ahead of creditors and the police. Suffering from
asthma and bronchial infections, addicted to heroin, he died
in Brighton in 1947, and was almost forgotten until the English rock musicians, who alone had the money and incli-
nation to live as Crowley did, started reading about him years
after his death.

Jimmy bought Boleskine House in 1970. It was an eighteenth-century U-shaped house with a grim history. Overlooking the foreboding Loch, home of supposedly extinct
reptilian "monsters," it had previously been the site of a church
that had burned with its parishioners inside. A man had been
beheaded there, according to local lore, and his head could
occasionally be heard rolling around the halls at night. When
Crowley moved in after the turn of the century, he styled
himself the "Laird of Boleskine," adopted the kilt, and began
trying to summon demons like Thoth and the Egyptian magical deity Horus. He practiced the dangerous magic of Abra-
Melin the Mage to contact his guardian angel. Subsequently,
the house and terraces at Boleskine became awash with
"shadowy shapes"; the lodgekeeper went berserk and tried to
murder his family and, according to Crowley, the room became so dark while he was trying to copy magical symbols
that he had to work by artificial light even though the sun
was blazing outside.

Jimmy bought the house from the Canadian who owned
it. Since Crowley had lived there, it had been the site of a
notorious swindle involving many of the local farmers and a
fictitious pork sausage works. Everybody on the Loch thought
the place was haunted and bad news. Jimmy Page, looking
for a country seat, thought it was perfect.

Led Zeppelin began 1970 with a short experimental tour
of England. In the past year the band had repeatedly encoun-
tered curfew problems when its long set had to follow an

opening act. This time Peter Grant sent the band out alone to see if Zepp's two-hour blitzkrieg of dynamic blues and pelvic thrust would be enough. As usual, the audiences were wrung out like sponges. John Paul Jones was now playing Hammond organ as well as bass; this extra layer of drone sent Jimmy spiraling into even more febrile displays of blues loop. After shows in Birmingham and Bristol, the band gave a stopsout show at the Royal Albert Hall in London on January 9, Jimmy's birthday. Backstage, someone had brought along a stunning French model named Charlotte Martin, who was coveted by every major rock star in London. Richard Cole remembered that she had first surfaced on the arm of Eric Clapton, who walked into the Speakeasy with her one night and stopped all conversation until Roger Daltrey piped up, "Fucking hell, Eric, where'd you get *that* bird!" That night was the beginning of a long and stormy relationship between Jimmy and Charlotte, who would later bear Jimmy's only child, Scarlet Page.

The tour ended in Leeds later that month, and Jimmy and Charlotte settled in Pangbourne, enjoying an Edwardian lifestyle along the river amid Jimmy's growing collections of antiques and pre-Raphaelite furniture. Jimmy's indecently long hair and tartan fashions now provoked hostility even in the streets of his village, and he began to be increasingly reclusive. His between-tour idyll was shattered when the police banged at his door on a rainy night in early February, demanding to know if Jimmy knew a Mr. Robert Plant, who had been injured in an auto accident. Jimmy's heart almost stopped. Had he lost his singer? Was the baby in the car? When Jimmy called Kidderminster Hospital, he found that Robert's Jaguar had gone off the road after a Spirit concert near Birmingham. Still estranged from his family, Robert had given Jimmy's name as next of kin. Robert's arm was badly bruised, and he had a cut over his eye, but he said he'd work in a wheelchair if he had to. A show in Scotland was canceled while Robert recuperated. Car crashes would prove a terrible nemesis for Led Zeppelin in the future. Meanwhile, Peter Grant had given Jimmy a Bentley for his birthday. To celebrate, Jimmy learned to drive.

Later that month Robert was well enough to join the band on Led Zeppelin's first European tour, which began inauspiciously in Copenhagen. While the band was rehearsing in a studio, they were rudely interrupted by a woman named Eva von Zeppelin, who claimed descent from the Count von Zeppelin who had designed the first German airships. The woman was hysterical. She threatened terrible lawsuits if the band played as Led Zeppelin. To the Danish press she blurted, "They may be world-famous, but a couple of shrieking monkeys are not going to use a privileged family name without permission." The band was due to appear on Danish television, and she tried unsuccessfully to stop the show. Finally she was calmed down by Peter and Jimmy, but as she was leaving the studio she saw the first album cover with the zeppelin going down in flames, and she blew up again. Intimidated by the legal threats, Led Zeppelin played their Scandinavian dates billed as "The Nobs," Cockney slang for what hung between Led Zeppelin's legs.

This tour also broke in some new material, especially a blues extravaganza called "Since I've Been Loving You," the prettiest of all Zeppelin's bluesy compositions. In their free time, Cole took them to the sex clubs. All went peacefully until the Danish record licensee held a press reception in an art gallery, despite what he had heard about Led Zeppelin's violence. Jimmy was offended by the insipid modern art, and goaded Bonzo into "rearranging" a couple of pictures whose paint was still wet. When the manager objected, Peter Grant bought the pictures to keep things calm. But soon a fight broke out between Bonzo, Cole, and two reporters, who were bodily thrown out.

Back in England in early March Peter Grant announced plans for Led Zeppelin's fifth tour of the United States, to begin later in the month. London's prestigious *Financial Times* ran a story on the band, noting that they would earn $800,000 playing twenty-one concerts over one month. The paper described Robert as "a painfully thin pre-Raphaelite heroine, with delicate features and wild curls, which cover his face when he tosses his head. Plant screams into the hand mike . . . low pessimistic snatches from American blues singers of the 30s, and culminates with a belligerent cry from the silent depths of the hall: Squeeze my lemon till the juice runs down my leg." The musicians thought this was funny, but for Robert it was more important. The *Financial Times*'s approval of Led Zeppelin as an earner of significant foreign exchange gave Robert new credibility with his father and marked the beginning of Robert's armistice with his family.

The fifth American tour was a hellish ordeal for the band. They were returning to America during one of the worst periods of civil disturbance in its history. The nation was divided by the Vietnam War along generational lines. College-age Americans—Zeppelin's target audience—were restless and alienated. Mass demonstrations against the war occasionally became violent when crowds were attacked by riot police. The mood of the authorities, especially local governments and the police, was jittery; the murder of protesting students at Kent State University in Ohio occurred right after the tour. In this climate of unrest and fear, rock concerts like Led Zeppelin's grope-feasts were considered a public danger and a needless excuse to get an already excitable youth population *really* riled up. Led Zeppelin's ultra-long hair, shaggy beards, and unabashed hippie ideals were particularly hated by the cops, who arrived at many shows in helmets and riot gear, ready for trouble. More often than not, they got it.

The tour began in Vancouver. On the way to Canada Jimmy's favorite Les Paul guitar was stolen off a truck at the airport. Page later advertised for it in *Rolling Stone*, just a photo with no name and a reward offer. But it never turned up. During the Vancouver show Richard Cole spotted a man in the crowd holding a shotgun microphone aloft as the band played. He pointed out the microphone to Grant. Led Zeppelin had already been a victim of record bootlegging, which captured unpolished performances and robbed musicians of royalties on their music. The Beatles, the Rolling Stones, Bob Dylan, and Jimi Hendrix had been heavily bootlegged, and the first unauthorized Zeppelin recordings had already started to appear. Grant was already notorious in English record shops for confiscating any Zeppelin bootlegs he might find. Earlier that year *Melody Maker* published a front-page story that drew attention to a double-live LZ boot which was being distributed by a man named Jeffrey Collins, who ran a record store in Chancery Lane. Grant and Cole visited the shop around six in the evening the same week. Grant put a CLOSED sign on the door while Cole threatened the terrified bootlegger with his life until he handed over his entire stock of pirated Zeppelins. "The group was tired of being robbed of their work," Cole says, "so we sent a couple of roadies out to drag the guy backstage. I said, 'C'mere ya cunt,' and smashed his mike and his tape recorder for him." But it turned out to be an agent of the Canadian government testing decibel levels, and a big row ensued. Backstage, an annoyed Bonzo destroyed the dressing room, which cost Grant another $1,500.

Led Zeppelin's gangsterish reputation preceded them to their next date, which Cole remembers well: "We were stuck in Winnepeg, and we had a reputation for being hard, very hard. Tough to deal with. Peter Grant wanted the group to get what it was owed, and I was supposed to enforce that this was done. We were supposed to play an open-air concert, but it had begun to rain and there was some kind of riot going on. So the promoter comes in and hands us our money. I said, 'That's nice, we ain't even fuckin' played. I like *this!*' And he said, 'And you won't play either.' And I said, 'What do you mean we won't fucking play. We broke our fuckin' backs to get here. We had to charter a fuckin' plane for the equipment.' He said that our agents in New York had told him that Zeppelin wouldn't play in the rain and would break someone's leg if they weren't paid anyway. But I said, 'Man, we didn't come all this way to upset people. These people are musicians, and *they will play*, even if we have to tear our equipment apart and rebuild it into a sound system.' And that's what we did." Roadie Clive Coulson objected; there was a problem with the amps. "Shut your fuckin' mouth and do what you're told," snapped Richard.

The next day was off, and Led Zeppelin was rotting in its hotel. One of Cole's specialties was finding things to keep the band amused. So Grant said to Cole. "What are we gonna do?" And Cole replied, "I dunno. Let's look in the Yellow Pages. Maybe we could go on a boat trip or something." Grant said, "Not that, you cunt. Can't we get some strippers or dancers?"

So Richard rounded up four strippers for a private perform-ance in the hotel. They brought their own record player. Grant called room service and ordered sixty screwdrivers. *"I told you fucking sixty! Six zero! Ten times six! That's what we want!"* When everybody was very drunk, the girls were shown in by Richard, who then sneaked into their changing room and dressed himself in their street clothes. When Cole then ap-peared to strip, much hilarity ensued. The others were laugh-ing so hard that they were vomiting. "Then I fucked one of the girls on a table in her own clothes," Cole remembers. "There's nothing that immoral in it. It's just that most people wouldn't *dream* of doing it. That's the whole story of Led Zeppelin right there."

Problems continued on the road, especially violence be-tween fans and security forces. At Pittsburgh and several other dates, Led Zeppelin was forced to stop playing and quit the stage until a brutal melee stopped in front of the stage. This was especially frustrating for the band, since the tour had been organized with precision to come off like an efficient military campaign. This was the first time that the band had appeared alone in America, without a supporting group, the total focus of the audience's attention. Cole explains: "Peter Grant was a brilliant manager, believe me. He realized that if the act was *that* big and *that* good and could hold an audience's attention for a couple of hours, there was no fucking point putting a support group on, wasting peoples' time waiting for the main attraction. If you go to a concert, you don't want to see the Shmuck Sisters singing for 30 minutes. You'll sit in the bar, right? It stopped all that fucking aggravation, the arguments between groups about equipment and all that shit. It was like, we go in, that was it, our stuff was there and we were ready to work. There was no fuckin' around; it was tested, it worked, and as soon as it was switched on a minute before the curtain went up, it was on the button. That was it!"

The South gave the band the most trouble. Led Zeppelin would stop to eat in some roadside diner and find themselves in a scene from *Easy Rider*. A half dozen flamboyant, shaggy, bearded English hippies would be glared at and cursed out by the native rednecks. They were spat on and laughed at. Waitresses refused to serve them. Death threats were telephoned to concert halls. People were forever pulling out their guns and pointing them at Led Zeppelin. A typical incident: On April 6 Led Zeppelin visited Memphis where they were made honorary citizens, an honor previously reserved for the likes of Elvis and Carl Perkins. That night the crowd went berserk when Jimmy pulled the trigger on "Communication Breakdown." It was total Zeppelin blast-off, and soon ten thousand southern kids were shaking like pagans. The promoter lost his nerve when he beheld this frenzy and told Peter Grant to pull the group off. Grant said, "Go and fuck yourself, *I'm* not pulling 'em offstage." So the promoter pulled out his gun, stuck it in Grant's ample ribs and said, "If you don't cut the show, I'm gonna shoot ya." Grant stared him down and laughed in his face. "You can't shoot me, ya cunt," Grant said. *"They've just given us the fucking keys to the city!"*

Soon afterward, Zeppelin was playing in Raleigh, North Carolina. After setting up the gear, one of the Zeppelin roadies, Henry Smith, was sitting in the toilet backstage when he heard two Raleigh cops discussing a plan to "bust those motherfuckers Led Zeppelin tonight." Henry told Cole, who called Steve Weiss in New York. An hour later several dozen private security goons from the Burns and Pinkerton agencies arrived at the hall, hired by Weiss as a buffer between the band and police. When the band got to Georgia, eight bodyguards were deployed after death threats were received against the group. Two armed agents rode in each Zeppelin limo. In Texas some dumb cracker shouted that their hair was too long, and the musicians told him to fuck off. As Bonzo recalled: "We were leaving after the show and the same guy shows up at the door. He pulls out this pistol and says to us, 'You guys gonna do any shouting now?' We cleared out of there *tout de suite.*" Later on, at the airport, Jimmy and Robert were being ridiculed and hassled by two drunken sailors for their very long hair. Ever protective of his act, Peter Grant went up to the sailors and lifted them both off their feet, one in each hand, by their collars and roared, *"What's your fucking problem, Popeye?"*

There were other hassles as well. Jimmy and Robert were both sick. And despite his exuberant, cock-o'-the-walk sexuality onstage, Robert was sometimes transfixed with bouts of fear and nerves. Peter Grant would have to soothe him and tell him he wasn't a failure, that he was a *big star*. And there was no denying this fact. The young fans were *rabid*. They swirled and stomped in front of the stage, wriggling like slippery eels, and when one line rushed the stage literally over the backs of those in front, it was like a human wave breaking upon a beach. Often Robert had an epiphany of singing to an ocean of tidal humanity as he poured out his songs. The kids even let poor performances go by. Once, at the Philadelphia Spectrum, the sound failed entirely, and Jimmy and Robert walked off and left Bonzo to play "Moby Dick" for an hour or so. The kids didn't care. They *loved* it. When Robert and Jimmy went back on, there was another mad dash for the stage. Kids wanted just to *see* the interaction between the tightjeaned blond singer with the rolled mustache and pointed beard and the raven-haired magical guitarist with the wild-eyed licks. When Jimmy and Robert touched heads or leaned their bodies on each other, the audience whooped as if it could sense a flow of pure sexuality. Led Zeppelin was creating its own private universe for its fans. The music was only one part of it. Something else was going on.

The tour ended on a bum note in Arizona when Robert's voice turned into a frog's croak following a show in Phoenix, after twenty-nine shows (several having been added after the band's arrival). Led Zeppelin was supposed to play its last date in Las Vegas, but Robert's voice had collapsed and there could be no show. Gratefully, the band flew home. The wives had joined them for the last part of the tour, and the musicians had been miserable. "The atmosphere was just different," Cole says. "Fucking business is business. That was the last time the wives got to go along."

The musicians had been disgusted and frightened by the police brutality they had experienced and witnessed on that tour and were relieved to be home. Jones was quoted by one of the English music papers: "Yes, the violence does frighten me, mainly because the U.S. is the biggest power in the world. It just seems to be in a terrible mess at the moment. . . . The glaring fact is that there is just so much money involved. The government seems to be so corrupt." And Jimmy complained about their ill treatment in restaurants that wouldn't serve them and at hotels where they were told to keep out of the pool so they wouldn't infect the other guests. Robert carped about James Taylor and his weepy, introspective soft rock that was being touted in America as the great new trend. But Robert knew better. A couple of hundred thousand American kids had just shown Robert that *he* was the great new trend.

In England the band had a few weeks off before they had to record their third album, which Atlantic wanted to release that autumn, with *Led Zeppelin II*—fans called it the "Brown Bomber" because of its sepia jacket—still high on the charts. Some songs the band had already worked out; "The Immigrant Song" reflected Robert's fascination with Celtic Britain and the tides of English history, especially the four-hundred-year period from the eighth to eleventh centuries when the English fought for their island with generations of Viking invaders from Denmark and Sweden. "The Immigrant Song," with its images of barbarous Norse seamen and pillaged abbeys, was the first of Led Zeppelin's many hammers-of-the-gods threnodies, and the band was considering opening the shows with it on the next tour. Late in April, meanwhile, Jimmy made a rare television appearance by himself, playing "White Summer" and "Black Mountain Side" on the BBC Two program hosted by Julie Felix.

Led Zeppelin was now burned out from fifteen months of continuous work, most of it on the road in America. Bonzo and Jones went home to their families, but Jimmy and Robert had to write an album. Originally, since their personal tastes were running to Crosby, Stills, and Nash and Joni Mitchell, and since they wrote well together on the road, they considered getting a house in northern California and writing there. But they wanted to be close to their own families, so Robert suggested they retreat to Wales to a remote rural cottage in the mountainous wilds of Snowdonia called Bron-Yr-Aur (pronounced "Brom-rahr"), which Robert had visited as a child. The fashion in those days was for young hippies to retreat from the evils of city life and get back to the land, living communally on old farms, returning to "the basics." Jimmy had never been to Wales and thought the quiet, mysterious Welsh countryside would be good for him after the gruesome rigors of touring.

Robert took along Maureen and the baby, and Jimmy brought his Charlotte. Three of the roadies (Clive Coulson, Henry Smith, and Sandy MacGregor) went along to look after things. Bron-Yr-Aur (the name meant "Golden Breast" in Welsh) lay in a black mountain vale far off the road near the river Dovey. With guitar cases clattering in back, the entourage had to drive across the fields in jeeps to reach the house, which had no electricity. The trip was originally planned not so much to write songs, but to rest. It was springtime and Wales was in flower. They spent long hours walking the countryside, carrying tape recorders and working on melodies. They drove around in their jeep and visited a nearby estate and mansion that was being restored by a gang of young volunteers. One of the kids seemed to recognize them and handed Jimmy a guitar, but Page protested demurely that he had no idea how to play. Another time their solitude was broken by a group of kids on motorbikes. Robert was enraged by the trespassers and was about to mobilize the roadies to do mayhem, but the kids turned out to be farmers' sons with shooting and fishing rights on the property. One of them gaped and managed to blurt out "Are you *really* Robert Plant?"

Evenings were spent before the fire, drinking cider heated with hot pokers from the hearth. Spent cassette batteries were laid on the fire grate to warm and recharge. After outings in the Welsh air, the musicians were exhausted but inspired. Gradually the songs of *Led Zeppelin III* began to take form, mostly folkish airs, acoustic and bucolic, vastly different in tone from the mechanized crunch and road frenzy of the Brown Bomber. For once, Led Zeppelin was not in motion. Later Robert summed up the Bron-Yr-Aur idyll to an interviewer: "It was time to step back, take stock, and not get lost in it all. Zeppelin was starting to get very big and we wanted the rest of our journey to take a very level course. Hence the trip into the mountains and the beginning of the ethereal Page and Plant. I thought we'd be able to get a little peace and quiet and get your actual Californian, Marin County blues, which we managed to do in Wales rather than in San Francisco. It was a great place."

By May 19 Led Zeppelin was ensconsed in an old Hampshire country house called Headley Grange, recording *Led Zeppelin III* with a mobile recording studio, away from the distractions of London. Band, management, and crew simply set up housekeeping and got to work, with Jimmy producing. Some tunes, like "The Immigrant Song," already existed. They had another track, a blues called "Poor Tom," recorded early in May at Olympic Studios in London. Other songs—"That's the Way," "Down by the Seaside," "Bron-Yr-Aur Stomp"— were brought along from Wales.

The Headley Grange sessions produced a mixed litter of hard Zeppelin rock bombs and wooden, acoustic numbers influenced by the prevalent California soft rock of the day. The hard numbers were as relentless as (and more meaningful than) the battle cries of the Brown Bomber. "The Immigrant Song" cast the band in the role of Viking invaders raping, burning, pillaging, and whispering tales of glory. Robert's wails became war cries; his moans were the north wind wailing through ruined Mercian monasteries. Obviously intended as the successor to "Whole Lotta Love," Robert goes for the gut: "Valhal-la I am coming." The song was hard to take seriously because its premise was so goofy, but Zeppelin fans adored it; the song set the tone of overwrought Dark Ages fantasy—a cross between an antiquarian edition of Beowulf and a stack of mint Marvels—that would be the standard psychic backdrop for all the heavy metal bands to come. It was followed by "Friends," a shameless rip-off of both Crosby, Stills, and Nash (in the chordal acoustic strumming) and Tony Visconti's string arrangements for T. Rex, the big English band of 1970. With its morbid orchestration and chanting, it was Jimmy's last stab at psychedelia, and it wound down into a drone that introduced "Celebration Day," another din-of-battle number with lots of guitar overdubs and the Living Loving Maid showing up in the second verse. The drone that began it was cosmetic rather than atmospheric. The original beginning was accidentally erased by an assistant engineer, who actually fled the studio in fear for his life when he realized his terrible mistake.

"Since I've Been Loving You," Jimmy and Robert's majes-

tic new blues, was recorded "live" in the studio and approx-
imates the band's concert sound of the day. Jimmy's lines are
pretty and original, and it's obvious that Robert had been listening carefully to both Van Morrison and Janis Joplin. "Out
on the Tiles" would finish the first side with all the subtlety
of a tumbling blimp, a mindless, monumental blast of pure
Zeppelin hot air, all tough, stomping mystique that endeared
the band to a generation of young Americans tippling cheap
Boone's Farm apple wine and ready to rock.

These same hardcore fans would be mystified by the remaining tracks that would fill the second, uncharacteristically
quiet side of *Led Zeppelin III.* It was as if Led Zeppelin was
embarrassed by the truly stupefying success of "Whole Lotta
Love" and repelled by their singular identification with this
lumbering tyrannosaurus in the public mind. These musicians considered themselves *artistes.* They wanted to make a
respectable album after the storm trooping of the first two, a
record they could play for their families at home, the way the
members of Led Zeppelin listened to Fairport Convention or
Joni Mitchell.

The side starts with "Gallows Pole," an ancient and grim
ballad that Jimmy had found on an old Folkways album by
Fred Gerlach, one of the first white musicians to play the
twelve-string guitar as a folk instrument. It's played very "down
home," with a fiddle and Jimmy's banjo. "My fingerpicking," Jimmy later told an interviewer, "was a cross between
Pete Seeger, Earl Scruggs and total incompetence." The imagery of the song recalls the Hanged Man of the tarot, in which
Jimmy (like Crowley, who had designed his own deck) was
interested. (The divinatory meaning of the Hanged Man in-
dicates changing circumstances and the seeking of wisdom and
guidance from the unconscious.) This was followed by "Tangerine," which descended from the Yardbirds. Jimmy had
written it in a period of emotional turmoil and the Yardbirds
tried and failed to get it right. Now it was rebuilt with new
lyrics, a pedal steel guitar, and an eloquent solo that seemed

to quote Jeff Beck. "That's the Way," which followed, had a lovely, echoing guitar patterned on the moody, evocative records that Neil Young was making. The lyrics dealt with ecology, dirty water, and an oblique commentary on their bad times in the States, where they had been threatened with arrest if they played another encore, where they had been accused of perversion and drug addiction by southern sheriffs, where they had looked down the barrels of guns in their dressing rooms. The mood was lifted by "Bron-Yr-Aur Stomp," a roving skiffle with a tough rhythm, Bonzo playing lightly like a rhino in a tutu. Robert's lyric was a tribute to his dog, Strider.

All these tracks were nearly complete by the middle of June, along with two outtakes from the Welsh holiday, "Down by the Seaside" and a guitar solo Jimmy called "Bron-Yr-Aur." There was one other, still without a title: a manic, keening blues version of Bukka White's "Shake 'Em on Down" with out-of-control bottleneck guitar and electronically "treated" vocals that aimed for the loose, demented feeling of Robert Johnson and came close to capturing it. Later, after Led Zeppelin had met a brilliant, half-mad English folksinger at the Bath Festival later that month, they would title this seering English blues track in homage to him: "Hats Off to (Roy) Harper." Later Jimmy would be quoted: "As far as I'm concerned, hats off to anybody who does what they think is right and refuses to sell out."

With the new album in the can, Led Zeppelin went back to work. After two concerts in Iceland they played the Bath Festival before an audience of 150,000 on June 28. Grant had turned down a quarter million dollars to play gigs at Boston and New Haven in the States that same weekend because the band craved the same acceptance and adulation in England that they took for granted in America. Accordingly, the show at Bath was considered one of the most important in their career. (It was also their last in England for the year; the real money was across the Atlantic.)

The show was on a Sunday, and also featured the Jefferson Airplane, Frank Zappa, the Byrds, Santana, Dr. John, Country Joe, and the Flock. The weather had been mixed, with a driving rain followed by hot sun. Peter Grant wanted Led Zeppelin to go on immediately when he saw there was going to be a spectacular sunset, a perfect, back-lit natural setting for Zeppelin's *son et lumière* of drama and mystery. The only problem was that the Flock's set was running long, and their manager said they wanted to play a couple of encores. Grant wasn't having this. He ordered Richard Cole to pull the plug on the Flock, stopping the show abruptly. Then the gigantic Grant walked out amid the surprised Flock and started roadying the gear off the stage himself so Zeppelin could set up. A Flock crew member objected and Cole punched him. Grant threw a few punches as well and quickly got his band onstage via brute force. Jimmy appeared as a bewhiskered rustic in a long tweed duster, dungarees, and a floppy tweed hat, his guitar slung low across his crotch. The band opened with the martial wails of "Immigrant Song" as the sun set in the west, reddening the Somerset landscape. Then they played "Heartbreaker," "Dazed and Confused," "Bring It On Home," "Since I've Been Loving You," "Thank You" (with Jones playing organ), the acoustic "That's the Way" (which Robert announced under its original title, "The Boy Next Door"), "What Is and What Should Never Be," "Moby Dick," and a long jam on "How Many More Times," incorporating Robert's Elvis impersonation on "I Need Your Love Tonight" plus lifts from "Gotta Keep Moving," "The Hunter," "Let That Boy Boogie," "The Lemon Song," and "That's All Right." For the encores the roadies threw tambourines into the audience and Zeppelin burst into "Whole Lotta Love," followed by "Communication Breakdown." Before the final number Robert addressed the horde: "I'd like to say a couple of things. We've been playing in America a lot recently and we really thought coming back here, we might have a dodgy time. There's a lot of things going wrong in America at the moment. Things are getting a bit sticky and whatnot. It's really nice to come to an open-air festival where there's no bad things happening." The encore was "Johnny B. Goode" and "Long Tall Sally."

Bath proved to be Led Zeppelin's breakthrough; afterward they were accepted at home as a major band in the same league as the Beatles, the Stones, and the Who. Peter Grant's strong-arm tactic had worked. The setting sun pulled another dimension out of Led Zeppelin's frenetic Viking sagas. (Later, during the show, he had spied someone in the audience taping the performance with a video camera; since Jimmy was always complaining about bootlegging and "those evil mikes waving on the ends of broomsticks," Grant had the taper dragged backstage, where Cole poured a bucket of water into his camera.)

Three dates in Germany followed in July. Jimmy and Bonzo had both developed airplane phobias, and the group undertook five-hour train journeys to get to Berlin, Essen, and Frankfurt, breaking attendance records in all three cities. Robert's long hair and beard cast him as a strutting Norse spear chief. Jimmy was garbed in a long crimson robe and looked like a Celtic Arch-Druid. The German kids loved it. At Essen they got so crazy that Jimmy had to stop his acoustic solo on "Black Mountain Side" so Robert could plead for the kids in front to sit down. When they refused, Led Zeppelin walked off. "Christians to the lions," Jimmy murmured to Grant.

From time immemorial to well into this century, large armies went into battle accompanied by loud bands of martial drums and trumpets. As late as 1912, the Moroccan army rode to battle with hundreds of drummers and *rhaitas*, wooden oboes blaring like massed bagpipes. As the music blared, bearers passed through the army with rations of wine or other intoxicants so that the warriors, in their late teens and early twenties, could fortify and encourage themselves into a furious, fear-deadened lust for blood and slaughter. As the troops, now dazed and confused, began to charge, the music was played even louder, faster. Bands of opposing armies had to compete against each other as well. Sometimes the best band won the day. The drum major was an important part of the battle, setting the pace of the action. The trumpets became efficient signals above the horrid, confusing, *loud* din of battle; even today bugle calls survive in modern armed forces, the last vestiges of the dreaded *din*, the cries of dying men, the clash of horses and spears, the echoes of bronze, of steel, of cannon.

Substitute the electric guitar for the trumpet. Add Robert's whispered tales of glory, of old battles and blood-lust, plus Bonzo's steady cannonade. Add 10,000 rock fans dazed and confused by grass, cheap wine, and the new soporific of choice, Quaalude (Mandrax in Europe). With their epic explosions of sound and light, Led Zeppelin seemed to be a sublimation for the din of battle, a wargasm experience for its audience. It was no accident that the young American troops in Vietnam took Led Zeppelin to heart.

So began Led Zeppelin's sixth American tour on August 5, 1970, in Cincinnati, Ohio. Playing for a minimum of $25,000 a night (and often for much more), with no support band, no stage set or props other than their amplifiers and lights, opening with "The Immigrant Song," the band again drew its audience into a private web of olden time communion, ignored by the outside world.

The new show was similar to Bath's. Led Zeppelin played their best for at least two hours a night, but they often played a little better and a little longer in Los Angeles and New York, so the show at the L.A. Forum in early September might not have been typical. Jimmy added a new palette of riffs to the end of "Heartbreaker" as well as a new blues intro and different bowing effects to "Dazed." "What Is . . . " had nice acoustic fills under the vocals. "Moby Dick" ran a quarter hour, featuring a five-minute drum roll with Bonzo's hands; afterward Robert needlessly asked for applause for *"The Big B!"*

"Communication Breakdown" was now a medley incor-

porating "Good Times Bad Times," Buffalo Springfield's "For
What It's Worth," and "I Saw Her Standing There," followed by "Since I've Been Loving You," Jonesy's organ fanfare, a leaden version of "Thank You," and the stomping "Out
on the Tiles." This faded into Fats Domino's "Blueberry Hill"
(Plant would try *anything*). Then the encores, starting gently
with "Bring It On Home." Tambourines were thrown into
the crowd for the sacrificial rite—"Whole Lotta Love," what
the people had paid their money for. The middle section was
now Jimmy's electronic concerto; he danced and gestured at
the theramin aerial like a wizard in the throes of some magick alchemy, drawing bestial cries and scary war whoops from
the little oscillator. Then more Zepp/Elvis medley—"Let That
Boy Boogie," "That's All Right," "I'm Moving On," "Think
It Over," "Some Other Time," and "The Lemon Song."

After Los Angeles the band went to Hawaii to play a cou-
ple of shows and enjoy a vacation. While they were there,
Melody Maker, England's top music paper, published its
readers poll under the headline ZEPPELIN TOPPLE BEATLES. Only
a year after the paper had named Zeppelin as the "Third
Brightest Hope," it was announcing that Zeppelin had won
the Top Group category that had been dominated by the
Beatles for the past eight years straight. Robert had also won
British Male Vocalist, and the Brown Bomber had won Best
British Album. It was a minor sensation but very satisfying.

By September 18 they were in New York, holding a press
conference to mark their earning a flat $100,000 for two shows
at Madison Square Garden. The band bantered uneasily with
an unfriendly and skeptical group of reporters. Few had seen
the band; to them, Led Zeppelin was all hype and money,
nothing else. Relations with the press would deteriorate into
open warfare within the month.

Led Zeppelin III had been mixed by Jimmy on the road,
mostly at Ardent Studio in Memphis. It was released on October 5, with the Brown Bomber still high on the American
charts. The cover was originally supposed to resemble an

annual crop rotation calendar, reflecting the album's rustic context. Instead, as a result of a compromise, it evolved as a die-cut psychedelic wheel that revealed different faces of the band as it was spun. The huge advance order in the wake of the Brown Bomber guaranteed the new album a quick rise to the top of the charts, but it didn't stay there long. The fans didn't like it as much as the classic *Led Zeppelin II*. But the press reviews were really shocking to the musicians. The critics loathed the album, harshly putting down the rock songs as more empty bombast, the blues tunes as unprincipled thievery from real bluesmen, and the acoustic songs as lame pandering to the CS&N sound. The press actively loathed the band and resented its success. Not only was the band insulted, its *audience* was attacked. First *Rolling Stone* printed the canard that Zeppelin's fans consisted mainly of "heavy dope fiends." Other papers picked up on this. *The Los Angeles Times* sneered that Led Zeppelin's "success may be attributable at least in part to the accelerating popularity among the teenage rock and roll audience of barbiturates and amphetamines, drugs that render their users most responsive to crushing volume and ferocious histrionics of the sort that Zeppelin has dealt exclusively." In other words, Led Zeppelin appealed to Seconal gobblers and the Boone's Farmers, to field hippies and speed freaks. Led Zeppelin was *déclassé*, low-rent, sleazy cock-rock with no redeeming social virtues.

The band, especially Jimmy, was genuinely wounded. The assault continued from every quarter. British critic Charlie Gillette called their music "a tool of authoritarian control." Jon Landau, the chief American rock critic of the day, reviewed one of their Boston shows as "loud, impersonal, exhibitionistic . . . violent and often insane. Nothing was delivered." One result of this was that the band decided to ignore the press. Jimmy later explained, "The third LP got a real hammering from the press and I really got brought down by it. I thought the album in total was good, but the press didn't like it, and they also went on about this enigma that has blown up around us. I admit we may have made it relatively quickly, but I don't think we overplayed our hand in the press or anything. Yet we were getting all these knocks and became very dispirited. The result was that we left off [from giving interviews] for almost a year."

The group's last appearance that exhausting year of 1970 was at a reception at the London office of Atlantic Records, where they were presented with gold records by a Mr. Anthony Grant, Parliamentary Secretary to Trade and Industry. "The government recognizes the value of pop groups," Grant said. "If they're a success, they deserve a pat on the back."

The hardcore fans of the band, those who bought the earliest pressing of *Led Zeppelin III*, found the following unattributed maxim scratched on the run-off matrix of the first side:

Do what thou wilt. So mete it Be.

Jimmy was casting his spell.

FIVE

THE SECRET SOCIETY

. . . They sliced through the shield-wall and hacked the linden battle-targes with swords, the legacies of hammers, since it was inborn in them from their forbears that they should often, in warfare against every foe, defend land, treasure horde and homes. The aggressors yielded; Scots and vikings fell dying. The field grew wet with men's blood from when in the morning-tide that glorious star, the sun, glided aloft and over earth's plains, the bright candle of God the everlasting Lord, to when that noble creation sank to rest.

Five young kings lay on the battle-field, put to rest by swords, and seven of Olaf's earls too and a

countless number of the array of vikings and of
Scots.

—FROM "THE BATTLE OF BRUNANBURH"
CIRCA A.D. 940

Stung by the criticism of *Led Zeppelin III*, alarmed by its meager sales as compared to the ultra-commercial Brown Bomber, Jimmy handled his depression as he had always done—by driving himself as hard as he could. The third album had been given as a sign that Led Zeppelin weren't monomaniacal thugs compelled by destiny to lug hard rock like Tantalus. Its country cadences and landscapes were supposed to illustrate the band's affinity for peace, nature, flowers. Instead, Led Zeppelin had been ridiculed and advised by the press (and implicitly the fans) to play what they played best—blistering, bluesy themes of lust and carnage. If that's what their listeners wanted, Led Zeppelin could accommodate. For the next album Jimmy and Robert kept up their folkish bent, but now roared like the tide surging up a narrow fjord. Jimmy would soon discover his compromise between the two realms of music, the acoustic and the metallic. Robert would divine his own cult of ancient ruins and romantic decay to go along with Jimmy's vision. The combined alchemy would produce their masterpiece.

Late in 1970 Jimmy and Robert went back to the cottage at Bron-Yr-Aur to write new material. In Wales they began to develop the introduction and work out the separate sections of a new song, an anthem that would replace "Dazed and Confused" as Led Zeppelin's centerpiece. In November Jimmy dropped a hint of its existence to a music journalist in London: "It's an idea for a really long track. . . . You know how 'Dazed and Confused' and songs like that were broken into sections? Well, we want to try something new with the organ and acoustic guitar building up and building up, and then the electric part starts . . . It might be a fifteen-minute track."

By the time Led Zeppelin began to record at Island Studio in Basing Street, London, in December 1970, Jimmy thought they might eventually end up with enough music for a double album. Part of "Stairway to Heaven" was recorded there, the six-string intro that had been composed in Wales; but now it had mutated with the Christmas season from a rural madrigal to a song that was seasonal, solstitial, hymnlike. The group then decided to move rehearsals and recording to Headley Grange, the country house in Hampshire, preferring the laidback life of the squire to the fluorescent basements of the London studio world. After a week of intensive living and playing together, the Rolling Stones' mobile studio would arrive and the new tracks would be cut.

After the equipment had been trucked out to the country, the band gradually filtered down to the dilapidated estate. Robert and Bonzo would arrive together in one of Bonzo's twenty-one cars—maybe the Jensen, perhaps the Maserati, or the AC Cobra, the Rolls, or the powder-blue Jaguar XKE. Jimmy and Peter would be driven down. John Paul Jones arrived last. They ate, according to Richard Cole, "like million-dollar boy scouts" and drank like fish. Between rehearsals or sessions, they could shoot, take walks, or go around to the village pub (where Bonzo liked to hold court in his tweed jacket and cap).

At night the roadies or Cole built a fire and the guitars came out. One evening, after Rolling Stones road manager and boogie-woogie piano virtuoso Ian Stewart had arrived with the Stone's mobile (a truck-mounted console/recording studio), Jimmy and John Paul Jones finished and wrote down the chord changes to "Stairway." The next day the band ran down "Stairway to Heaven" for the first time. As the various sections—six-string, twelve-string, solo—began to coalesce, the musicians again began to smile at each other. It was like that same magic from the first rehearsal. They knew they had something. Bonzo had problems with the timing on the twelve-string section before the solo, and they had to run it through a few times before they got it the way Jimmy wanted it. While this was going on, Robert was listening and penciling in lyrics. "He must have written three quarters of the lyrics on the spot," Jimmy said later. "He didn't have to go away and think about them. Amazing, really."

The lyrics for "Stairway" reflected Robert's current reading. The song tells, in poetic terms, of a mythographic lady's quest for spiritual perfection. She is a paradigm of Spenser's Faerie Queen, Robert Graves' White Goddess, and every other Celtic heroine—the Lady of the Lake, Morgan La Fay, Diana of the Fields Greene, Rhiannon the Nightmare. Robert had been poring through the works of the British antiquarian Lewis Spence. He later cited Spence's "Magic Arts in Celtic Britain" as one of the sources for the lyrics to "Stairway." (The title was already familiar to movie buffs as the title of a 1946 mystery starring William Powell.) With its starkly pagan imagery of trees and brooks, pipers and the May Queen, shining white light and the forest echoing with laughter, "Stairway to Heaven" seemed like an invitation to abandon the new traditions and follow the old gods. It expressed an ineffable yearning for spiritual transformation deep in the hearts of the generation for which it was intended. In time, it became their anthem.

With Jimmy producing and Andy Johns, brother of Glyn Johns, as engineer, the recording proceeded quickly. Some tracks were written in the studio. "Black Dog," with its *fire-one* guitar pattern, was a riff that John Paul Jones had brought with him. "Rock and Roll" was a "found" composition: Bonzo was playing the beginning of Little Richard's "Good Golly Miss Molly" while the tape was running. Jimmy improvised the riff and it thudded to a halt after twelve bars, but enough had been captured to structure the track. Robert improvised the exuberant lyric at once, and Ian Stewart pounded out expert boogie piano. Bonzo's drums were placed in the hall for recording, for that ambient isolation that Jimmy liked.

"Misty Mountain Hop," with its dense blues riff, Welsh spirit imagery, and Bonzo's crisp, almost delicate tapping, also was written in the studio. Somewhat more effort went into "The Battle of Evermore," which Robert and Jimmy wrote mostly at Headley Grange. Jimmy had never really played the mandolin, but Jones had brought one along and Jimmy picked it up one night and strummed out the incantatory chords that would turn into "Battle." At first it was intended as a sort of Olde English instrumental, but Robert had been reading about the Scottish border wars, and "The Battle of Evermore" was written out as a modern descendent of the Anglo-Saxon battle sagas. "Going to California" was an acoustic guitar melody that Jimmy had brought with him. An explicit tribute and *homage* to Joni Mitchell, the Canadian singer/songwriter who was an idol of both Jimmy and Robert, "Going to California" also expressed Led Zeppelin's relentless yearning for the romantic jet-life of the road, their friends and girl friends in Los Angeles, the majesty of the mountains and canyons of California. Led Zeppelin lived in two worlds, one a secure green England of family and tradition, the other a lurid Hollywood movie of fantasy and excess. The feelings expressed in "Going to California" were the interstices between the two.

Other tracks were also recorded at Headley Grange early in 1971. These included a version of "Four Sticks," a boogie piano jam with Ian Stewart, a version of "Down by the Seaside" from Bron-Yr-Aur, and another song of travel and movement called "Night Flight." Perhaps the most interesting of all was "When the Levee Breaks," which Jimmy had gotten from a 1928 recording by Memphis Minnie and Kansas Joe McCoy. But Jimmy turned the classic twelve-bar blues completely inside out with phased vocals and studio effects like a backward echoed harmonica solo. All *blooze*, muddy harp and brain-beating crunch, different themes are developed every twelve bars and merge into Led Zeppelin's most outrageous (and yet best) take on the feeling of the blues.

Late in January, with the backing tracks in the can, Led Zeppelin returned to Island Studio in London to craft the overdubs, guitar solos, and vocals. "Four Sticks," with its chiming guitars and synthesizer orchestration, was recorded there. Sandy Denny, the bell-clear soprano from Fairport Convention, came in to sing the haunting duet/playlet in "The Battle of Evermore," playing the Queen of Life to Robert's Prince of Peace. When it came time for Jimmy to overdub the solos, the studio was closed. Jimmy liked to concentrate in solitude. His usual method was to listen to the track again, limber up for a while, and then improvise a solo. Then he would play three solos; the best of the lot would go on the album. Jimmy had been using a Les Paul guitar for the album, but wanted a different sound for "Stairway." He pulled out the old Telecaster that Jeff Beck had given him, plugged it into a Supro amp, and recorded the solo in one take. It was a guitar he hadn't used in a couple of years, but as a talisman it had a strange power of its own. When John Paul Jones had piped the song's theme on double-tracked recorders, the basic tracks of "Stairway" and the rest of the album were finished. It was the end of February. It only remained to mix the album and have it out as fast as possible to counter the continuing blasts against the last album, about which Jimmy was still sensitive. As he later told an interviewer, "After all the heavy, intense vibe of touring, which is reflected in the second album, it [the acoustic part of *III*] was just a totally different feeling. I've always tried to capture an emotional quality in my songs. Transmitting that is what music seems to be about."

But the new album was delayed when Andy Johns convinced Jimmy that they had to take the finished tapes to Sunset Sound in Los Angeles for mixing. Instead, Led Zeppelin went back on the road for a month-long tour of British universities and the small clubs that had first booked the fledgling Zeppelin; for them, the band played for its original minuscule fees. This tour would test some of the new songs for the still-untitled new album, as well as the acoustic format for some of the recent songs from *III*. It would also dispel the numerous LED ZEPPELIN TO SPLIT! headlines that had been appearing in the British music press for the past month.

These rumors were published almost weekly in *Melody Maker* during 1971. Rumor also had Peter Grant taking over as manager of Emerson, Lake, and Palmer. At one point *Melody Maker* published a cartoon depicting Grant as a bloated whale with two groups, Led Zeppelin and ELP, swimming around on rafts in his stomach. A stream of pound notes was gushing from the whale's blow hole. Grant was furious and threatened to sue the newspaper. The staff heard their legs were to be broken, and an apology was quickly printed. It didn't pay to forget that the titantic Grant was extremely sensitive about his weight.

The shows began in Ulster Hall, Belfast, on March 5. It was the band's first visit to Ireland and an increasingly rare appearance by an English band in Ulster; most groups refused to play in Northern Ireland for fear of being engulfed in the sectarian violence between Catholics and Protestants. Still leery of flying, most of the band members crossed the Irish Sea in their own cars via the ferry. And there *was* trouble in Belfast on the night of the show. A gasoline tanker was hijacked and burned near the hall, a youth was shot dead, and the usual Molotov cocktails lit up the city's mean streets. But when Led Zeppelin knocked off the rust and lit into "Immigrant Song," all that was forgotten amid Zeppelin's cryptohistoric pageant. They progressed through the slow, measured blues marathon of "Since I've Been Loving You," with its grandiloquent chord sequence. "Black Dog" from the new album was given its world concert premiere, as was "Stairway to Heaven," which Jimmy played on double-necked guitar, twelve strings on top, six strings below. Jimmy had seen Chicago bluesmaster Earl Hooker with one years before, and realized it was the only instrument that would replicate the various sections of "Stairway" in performance. But the double-neck guitar was out of production, and only a limited number had ever been made. Jimmy had to have one custom-built for him by Gibson, who turned the guitar out in record time.

Robert, in a red and black blouse, introduced Bonzo's solo:

"Here comes something that gets a little bit better every night." And when the ovation for Bonzo's hand-drumming act died down, Robert spoke up again: "A lot of those musical papers that come from across the sea say we are going to break up. Well . . . we're never going to break up." With that, the band tore into "Whole Lotta Love." No matter how jaded they were about the song, Led Zeppelin knew what was expected by those who had paid to see them. As Robert said to a reporter, " 'Whole Lotta Love' is something that I personally need, something that I just have to have. We bottle it up and when we go on stage, we can let it pour out."

In the dressing room after the show a sweet Irish lass approached Richard Cole. "Are they an English band?" she asked. "I always thought they were from America."

From Belfast Led Zeppelin took off for the next show in Dublin in separate cars. Irish chauffeurs were doing the driving, but Bonzo had brought along his own driver, Matthew, who made a wrong turn and drove through the Falls Road riot area where the IRA had been skirmishing with British troops the night before. "The street was covered in glass," Bonzo said later, "and there were armored cars and kids chucking things. We just kept our heads down and drove right through."

Richard Cole had made sure that each departing Zeppelin car had at least one bottle of Jameson's whiskey. By the time the entourage straggled into Dublin's Intercontinental Hotel late that night, they were all quite drunk. Peter Grant was ill; he and Cole stayed in his suite, drinking Irish coffee. Around midnight they received a call that there was a problem in the kitchen. According to Cole, Bonzo and Matthew had gone looking for a late supper, which had evolved into a brawl. Matthew had assaulted the hotel's chef, who in turn pulled out a carving knife. As Cole arrived to smooth things over, Bonzo started shrieking for the chef's blood and lunged at the outnumbered cook; but Cole grabbed Bonzo first and said, "Shut yer fucking mouth," and punched Bonzo hard in the face, breaking the drummer's nose and covering him with his own gore. Furious, drunk, crying with rage, Bonzo stormed up to Grant's room. "That's it," Bonzo bawled. "I'm leaving the fucking band!" But Peter Grant wasn't feeling well and told Bonzo, "Go on and fuck off; don't give me that shit at this time of night." Except for the slight crook in John Bonham's nose, the incident was quickly forgotten.

The Dublin show was held in a boxing arena. The band played an acoustic set with the folkish songs from *III*; sitting on three chairs at the front of the stage, Robert sang while Jones played mandolin and Jimmy the guitar. "Going to California" would later be introduced to the set. Bonzo sat out. (Afterward, talking to an Irish journalist, Jimmy said that negative comparisons with contemporary American bands like the boorish Grand Funk Railroad and Mountain had spurred Zeppelin to record more subtle acoustic numbers.) After the usual encores ending with "Communication Breakdown," the Dubliners still wouldn't let Led Zeppelin go. So they finished with another rock medley centered on "Summertime Blues."

Led Zeppelin's "Return to the Clubs" tour progressed through March, ending at the Marquee in London. Intended as a way of thanking the fans and promoters who had believed in them from the beginning, the tour had run into trouble when the audiences proved too big for the venues that Grant had chosen. There was enough room at places like Leeds University and the Bath Pavilion, but at Stepmothers in Birmingham and at the Nottingham Boat Club there were bad scenes when hundreds tried to jam into the small clubs, causing some bitterness. Later Robert called the tour a waste of time.

On April 4 Led Zeppelin reintroduced its new songs to the British radio audience with an hour-long concert on the BBC. "Black Dog" opened with the burp-gun riff and the trademark Zeppelin lift-off, Jimmy teleporting his repetitive riffs like a Moroccan trance musician, until the song boiled into its spectacular climax. The dueling mandolins of "Going to

California" followed, taken delicately, with Robert's echoing and soughing duplicated from the forthcoming version on the album. A letter-perfect "Stairway to Heaven" came next, all gentle madrigal and organ at first, then, with Bonzo's thumping entry, emerging as a burning concerto for the double-neck guitar. One could almost feel the youth of England holding its collective breath for the song's starry, ascending final note. Then, *bombs away;* "Whole Lotta Love" came with a brilliant re-creation of the theramin "middle section." Lasting twenty minutes, Robert grafted on "Let That Boy Boogie" and "Fixin' to Die" (a la John Lee Hooker) before the inevitable Elvis tribute—"That's All Right," "A Mess of Blues," and "Blue Monday."

Shortly afterward, Jimmy and Andy Johns flew to Los Angeles to mix the new album, which Jimmy told a reporter might be called *Led Zeppelin IV.* (Originally Jimmy had thought of releasing all the new songs on four EPs or a double album; the idea was scratched to keep prices down.) Andy Johns had raved about how Sunset Sound was the best mixing studio in the world, and he and Jimmy spent weeks working on the tracks. Then Jimmy brought the tapes back to England, played them in a London studio, and was shocked to find that *Led Zeppelin IV* sounded like it was recorded under Loch Ness. Jimmy was furious. Weeks of precious time had been wasted. "All I can put it down to," he said later, "was that the speakers and the monitoring system in that room [at Sunset Sound] were just very bright . . . and they lied. It wasn't the true sound." Andy Johns walked out, and more time was wasted while a new engineer was found to remix the album. Meanwhile, the band was *rabid* to have the record out. They knew they had done their best work and that "Stairway to Heaven" was going to take over the world.

The worst riot of Led Zeppelin's career took place that July during the annual European tour in Milan. Led Zeppelin had been engaged to play that city's Vigorelli bicycle stadium, had been paid in advance in England, and appeared at the Vigorelli to find itself scheduled, according to Cole, after twenty-eight other acts. As they entered the stadium, which held 12,000, the band could see that hundreds of riot-equipped police were massed outside and inside the stadium. When Jimmy saw their riot-shields, he remarked that they looked like centurians, like a Roman legion. Backstage, Jimmy and Peter talked to the promoter and told him that it was their experience that an armed militia would surely start trouble with the kids. Jimmy also complained about the backstage area. It was so packed with swarming rock humanity that no one could move. As long as you've got all these troops, Page said, why don't you clear out backstage? But the scene only got more compacted and dangerous. Richard Cole was feeling lean and mean; he had just been to Zurich to see guitarist Rory Gallagher (one of Peter's acts) and had beaten up three German Hells Angels who had tried to crash the club. Now Cole was annoyed at the delays and decided to get the band onstage. "It was getting very fucking hectic," he recalls. "And we said, 'Fuck this, we aren't waiting here all fucking night for you fucking wops with this fucking *madness* going on here. Bollocks, we're fucking going on when we wanna go on.' "

So, taking the stage earlier than expected, Led Zeppelin began their show and received the expected crowd response—pandemonium. Then, Page said later, "We noticed loads of smoke coming from the back of the oval. The promoter came out on stage and told us to tell the kids to stop lighting fires. Like twits, we did what he said." Robert told the kids that the police would make them stop playing if there were any more fires. This went on for another few numbers. Every time the music reached one of its thunderous climaxes and the audience responded, the band would see more and more smoke. Robert kept repeating, "Stop lighting those fires, *please*." Suddenly a tear-gas cannister was lobbed at the stage and landed amid the audience in front. The band realized all the "smoke" had been tear gas. The gendarmes were attacking the crowd. Trying to play in a thickening cloud of gas, Jimmy told the band to cut it short, and they went into "Whole Lotta Love." When all the kids jumped up for their favorite song, the police tossed off another round of gas. Somebody threw a bottle and the police charged the crowd from the rear. As the kids, frantic to get away from the police truncheons, began to climb onstage, Cole smacked a couple back until he realized that the whole audience was rushing forward. The crowd was being gassed. People were clamoring up the scaffolding to get away. "Fuck this," Cole yelled. "Let's fucking go. C'mon lads, offstage!"

At first the roadies tried to save the equipment, but when he saw the panicked crowd surging forward, Cole yelled to leave the gear and run for it. When the band got backstage, they ran down a long tunnel to their dressing room, only to find themselves lost, with choking pockets of gas blocking each end of the tunnel. They were cut off. But Cole found a locked door, kicked it open, and Led Zeppelin barricaded themselves in the medical room while waiting for the riot to be subdued. When they came out again, they found the stage wrecked and all their gear destroyed. Bonzo's drum roadie, Mick Hinton, had been badly cut on the head by a broken bottle and had to be carried to the hospital on a stretcher. Afterward, in the bar of their hotel as they were trying to calm down, Bonzo told a reporter who was pestering them for quotes to piss off or he'd get a bottle broken over *his* head.

During the plane ride home Robert Plant broke into tears while trying to describe the frustration felt by the musicians. Led Zeppelin had been formed to play uplifting hard rock around the planet. The riot in Milan was just so far from the spiritual pageants of youthful unity and friendship that Robert intended for his audience. It was all just too hard to take sometimes.

Back in England Led Zeppelin got into a row with Atlantic over the new album. The music was no problem; everyone agreed that this record would be Zeppelin's best. But the record company was aghast when told of the band's unique cover concept for the album—no title, no corporate insignia or even a catalog number, and no mention of Led Zeppelin *anywhere* on the album. The only hint that the new album had anything to do with Led Zeppelin was Jimmy's name listed as producer on the inside sleeve, which would also contain the lyrics of "Stairway to Heaven," the first time the band permitted publication of lyrics and an indication they realized the extraordinary potential of the song. Confronted with this proposal, Atlantic howled that it was commercial suicide. They begged to be allowed, at least, to print "Led Zeppelin" on the jacket's spine, but that was vetoed outright. Still petulant from the drubbing that *III* had received, still refusing to speak to the press except on an informal basis, Jimmy had decided to see if the music alone could sell itself. Page explained later, "We decided that on the fourth album we would deliberately downplay the group name and there wouldn't be any information on the outer jacket. Names, titles, and things like that do not mean a thing. . . .What matters is our music. We said we just wanted to rely purely on the music."

Atlantic Records fought the band every step of the way, especially when presented with Zeppelin's choice of cover art. On the front cover was a painting of an old peasant bent under a load of brush. The painting, when the album was opened flat, was revealed to be hanging on the broken wall of an old house amid a desolate cityscape of slum housing and new tower blocks (where no doubt the future Clash fans were growing up). The inner sleeve depicted the Hermit of the Tarot on top of a craggy tor, overlooking an Escher-like walled town in the distance. At the bottom of the cliff a young adept offers himself to the hermit. Jimmy would later explain the symbolism: "The old man carrying the wood is in harmony with nature. He takes from nature and he gives back to the land. It's a natural cycle. . . . His old cottage gets pulled down and they put him in these urban slums. . . . The Hermit is holding out the light of truth and enlightenment to a young man at the foot of the hill. If you know the tarot cards, you'll know what the Hermit means." (The divinatory meaning of the Hermit is usually interpreted as a warning against proceeding on a given course without retirement and contemplation.)

Again, Atlantic balked. The cover would be a disaster, according to their experts. Jimmy talked himself sick trying to convince them. Eventually, according to Plant, Led Zeppelin told Atlantic that they couldn't have the master tapes until they got the cover right. Eventually Jimmy got his way. Led Zeppelin had been designed to retain control of its product. The design worked.

There *were* identifying marks, however, even though they were arcane. Jimmy had each member of the group devise a symbol that would represent him on the album. Robert picked a feather in a circle. Bonzo chose three interlocking circles. John Paul Jones came up with three ovals bisecting a circle. And Jimmy chose a mysterious glyph that was interpreted by some as being close to the alchemical symbol for amber. (In fact, the untitled album would often be called "Zoso" by the fans.) But Jimmy refused to say what the symbols meant; he would only deny subsequently published reports that the symbols were Icelandic runes. Appearing at the top of the liner sleeve, the four symbols served both as an ad hoc album title and runic stand-ins for the musicians' names. Led Zeppelin was now a secret society, one that any kid with the money to buy the album could join. Led Zeppelin kept the grown-ups out.

Led Zeppelin's seventh North American rampage began on August 19, 1971, in Vancouver. Assault charges against Peter Grant, which had been pending since the busted microphone caper two years before and which had for a time kept Grant out of Canada, had now been dropped. This would be the biggest and richest Zeppelin tour yet: Twenty gigs at halls holding a minimum of 12,000 each meant that the band would gross over a million dollars. There was a palpable sense among the entourage, after the near hysterical responses to the first shows, that Led Zeppelin was now unstoppable, the biggest band in the world. Since they shared a record company with the so-called "Greatest Rock and Roll Band in the World," Led Zeppelin knew what few people outside the record business did, that Led Zeppelin was outselling the Rolling Stones three to one. Now, raiding the metropolitan stadia of the United States, Led Zeppelin began to sense that it had *the power*. It could get away with *anything*. "Once we started our momentum," Richard Cole says, "the people *knew* and we didn't give a fuck. The doors *had* to open now. If they didn't we'd break them down. And that was it. We made our own laws. If you didn't want to fucking abide by them, don't get involved."

There was now less overt violence in front of them as they barnstormed their new show through the United States and Canada. Now the violence was more subtle and threatening. Jimmy in particular began to be a lightning rod for anonymous death threats phoned to police and Zeppelin's local promoters. This reinforced Zeppelin's already fierce paranoia. Several times on that tour, in Los Angeles on August 22, in Toronto, in Rochester, New York, musicians or roadies thought they saw someone with a gun in front of the stage. But the various gun scares proved to be just that. Richard Cole doesn't think a gun was ever pointed at the band onstage.

The long show at the Los Angeles Forum on September 4 probably wasn't typical. Although Led Zeppelin still gave their all and inspired frenzy in the provinces, when they got to L.A. they were home again, occupying entire floors of their squat bunker on Sunset Boulevard, the Continental Hyatt House. At the Forum they played a little louder, a little longer, a little better. They were, after all, showing off for their friends. Miss Pamela stood just off the stage, a hippie princess in fringed buckskin, as the band stepped onto the dark stage, the kids whooping it up as shadows moved about and the amps started to hum. Then the lights came on and Jimmy lashed out red streaks of tracer guitar and Robert began to wail his Norse ax-wielder's death song: "Valhalla, I am coming." "Immigrant Song" bled right into the horrid thud of "Heartbreaker," which soon found Jimmy noodling a few Les Paul delicacies, grinding out some hard blues, segueing into a Page rendition of "The 59th Street Bridge Song" and a Bach guitar theme before counting down to a climactic missile launch of rock band and singer. This was followed by a torrid "Since I've Been Loving You," the blues showcase with Jonesy on organ.

By then the audience was anesthetized. But the new "Black Dog" woke it up and made the first "oldies" part of the show sound rote and mechanical. Playing the brand-new music, the band perked up and sounded like they were *interested*. It was the first song to really rock the audience, and ended with a proud flourish. "Good evening," Robert said, the first words he had spoken that night. He complained that the current late-summer pollution alert had cost him his voice. Then he said, "This one is from millions and millions of years ago—just when the good things were happening." And the band plowed into Jimmy's rite of doom, "Dazed and Confused." Now running almost twenty minutes, Jimmy had developed the song into a display of his avant-rock techniques. After the initial morbid chords of the theme, he launched into a fine, pinpoint duet with the hammering Bonzo. As the violin bow came out and the lights dimmed to one pure spot on Jimmy, he built delicate trellises of *pizzicato* notes, splendid Carnatic melodies, and loud blats of droning electro-murk. Later Robert joined in with his moaned oms and mock-tantric chanting, in and out of unison. It was a lunatic, totally self-indulgent performance. It got a big standing O.

As did the next number, "Stairway to Heaven." The album was another eight weeks from release and none of the kids had heard "Stairway" before; but the band's perfect, carefully plotted rendition of their madrigal/hymn *cum* anthem/quest song made the crowd stand up and roar after its rapturous, volcanic finale. "It was *such* a moment," Page said later, "because we all know how difficult it is to hear a song for the first time from a group in concert, and it really hit home. It was a really emotional moment." The sit-down acoustic set included "That's the Way" (with Bonzo playing tambourine) and the careful, quiet "Going to California." As Jimmy and Jones quickly retuned, Robert introduced their paean to California: "This song was put together . . . I was gonna say in the Scottish highlands or Welsh mountains, but it was actually some hotel on West Thirty-seventh Street." So much for ruins and the cult of romantic decay.

The show ended with the long theramin thunderstorm of "Whole Lotta Love." The Southern California youth got up and shook, and the whole building seemed to vibrate to Bonzo's vulcanism until Led Zeppelin hit its stop-time bridge to the much anticipated Elvis/Ricky Nelson/rockabilly jam. That night they ran through "Let That Boy Boogie" (Jimmy taking twenty-five choruses), "Hello Mary Lou" (Jimmy's James Burton impression), a pair of Elvis re-creations, "A Mess of Blues" and "That's All Right," and "You Shook Me," for which Jimmy threw down his ultimate blues licks of the night. And then back to the now grotesque "Whole Lotta Love": "*Woman . . . way down inside . . . (blaam, boom!) . . . You need me . . .*"

"Good night. Thank yew!"

Then back East, then Canada again, then two shows in Berkeley, and a final show in L.A. Then, in mid-September, it was time for Epic's Revenge. The Yardbirds' old label released *Live Yardbirds Featuring Jimmy Page*, a remix (with canned crowd noise and bullfight cheers) of the wretched Yardbirds show at the Anderson Theater in the spring of 1968. Jimmy was livid, feeling that the album made him and the old Yardbirds (who in this era used to play shimmering versions of the Velvet Underground's "I'm Waiting for the Man") look like arseholes and sound like a garage band. Almost at once Steve Weiss, Led Zeppelin's tough New York attorney, slapped an injunction on Epic, which had no legal right to issue an already rejected recording. The album was withdrawn after a month on the market. From California Led Zeppelin moved west toward their first series of concerts in Japan. On the way they stopped for a week in Hawaii to get some rest and spend some time with their wives who were flying in from England. Before the Zeppelin spouses appeared, however, there was the usual infantile mayhem. Occasionally Led Zeppelin would decide to devour one of its own, harassing him without mercy till the breaking point drew nigh, all in good fun of course. This trip it was John Paul Jones. When the band checked into the Rainbow Hilton, Jonesy's room was flooded out with the fire hose the very first night. Later on the wives arrived to join their husbands on vacation and the attacks on Jones temporarily ceased. Jimmy moved out of the Hilton to a rented house so he could carry on in his accustomed manner without risking the approbation of the wives. He told Richard Cole to tell the roadies *not* to give Robert his phone number because he didn't want Robert to bring Maureen to his lair.

When Led Zeppelin arrived in Japan, they found "Immigrant Song" at Number 1. Since that was their show-opener, the Japanese audience—as yet unaccustomed to seeing their British rock heroes—went totally mad. Led Zeppelin's own madness carried on unabated. At the Tokyo Hilton Bonzo threw a room service cart into a shower occupied by Phil Carson, who ran Atlantic Records in England and was traveling with the band. One evening Cole and Bonzo went out and bought samurai swords. They returned to the hotel late that night and chopped their rooms to splinters. Then they chopped down Jonesy's door and found him in bed, drunk and unconscious. They dragged him out to the corridor, left him to sleep on the floor, and committed *seppuku* to his room as well. A chambermaid found Jones asleep the next morning and tried to wake him. Jones roundly cursed the hapless maid until he realized he wasn't in bed, or even in his room. After the musicians and roadies destroyed one of the corridors in a fruit-throwing fracas, Led Zeppelin was banned from the Tokyo Hilton for life.

Even the music got loose so far from home. During the acoustic set in Tokyo, Robert essayed the old chestnut "Smoke Gets in Your Eyes" right after the rarely performed "Friends."

Then the band went to Hiroshima, where they played a benefit for the victims of the atom bomb dropped there in 1945. After the show the mayor somberly presented Led Zeppelin with a Hiroshima peace medal in appreciation. Then Led Zeppelin and entourage boarded the Bullet Train for the next dates in Osaka and Kyoto. They were accompanied by a case of Suntori whiskey, a dozen vacuum flasks of hot sake, and an official of their Japanese record company, who didn't have any inkling of what was in store for the night's entertainment.

Apparently it was Jimmy's turn to be picked on. At three in the morning, with Jimmy asleep in his canvas-sided bunk, Bonzo, Jones, and Robert decided it would be amusing to pull open the curtain and bathe Jimmy with a slimy muck of cold tea, stale sake, and old rice. Robert opened the curtain, and Bonzo threw in the muck. But they had attacked Peter Grant's bunk by mistake. Instead of the physically pathetic Page, out roared Grant, three hundred pounds of insane rage. He chased the three musicians down the corridor, caught Jones and boxed his ears. He punched Robert. Then Richard Cole appeared to see what was the matter. Grant thought that Cole had instigated the incident and drew back to punch his face. But Cole ducked, and Grant connected with Bonzo, who was standing behind Cole, bloodying his face. Grant started to scream at Cole and fired him on the spot. The Japanese whose job it was to look after the group watched in utter horror, thinking the group was breaking up in front of him. Later Phil Carson took the shaken man aside and explained that this sort of thing went on all the time. At the Festival Hall in Osaka, Bonzo felt dazed. During "Tangerine" he wandered offstage, and the band had to puzzle out the song without him.

After the Japanese shows Grant, Bonzo, and Jones flew home to England, while Jimmy, Robert, and Richard Cole decided to see Asia. After a stop in Hong Kong they landed in Bangkok and checked into the Rama Hilton. Cole then went out for a walk to look for antiques to buy. When he returned Robert and Jimmy demanded that he look after them and find them something to do. So all three moved into the hotel's presidential suite. Cole connected with a bellhop named Sammy Pong and told him that Led Zeppelin wanted some women. So the bellhop took them on a long tour of Bangkok's famous red-light district. They had all bought new cameras in Japan and ran around the red-light district, checking light meters, and taking pictures. Their outlandish long hair, still very alien to Asia, was a sensation in the street. Little boys followed them from brothel to brothel, shouting "Billy boy" (which meant gay) because of their hair. Cole remembers that at one whorehouse, the three of them were standing in line to choose their girls. The place was sixty feet long and had three tiers of women, each with a number, waiting to be picked. Cole said, "I'll have sixty-six, twenty-four, and thirty-one." Behind them they heard a rough voice speaking Liverpudlian Scouse. " 'Ere, fookin' 'ell Albert! 'Owdja like that noomber thirty-seven?" They turned around to find two young sailors from Liverpool, who recognized them. "Fookin' 'ell, Led Zeppelin! Wot are *you* doin' 'ere in a fookin' 'orhouse?" They caroused in the brothel from sunset until four in the morning. "We spent all our time on our backs in the bathhouses," Cole fondly remembers. "It was all drinking, whoring, shopping for Buddhas, and antiques. It was all to relieve the pressure that had built up on the tour. People don't realize, but the bigger the group, the bigger the money gets, it's really no fucking pleasure. It's fucking rotten. You come home with tears in your eyes afterward."

After Bangkok Jimmy and Robert went on to Bombay. Jimmy was still obsessed by the desire to record with Indian musicians, but this trip didn't produce any music. Richard Cole flew to Australia to prepare for Zeppelin's first tour there the following year. The Asian trip reminded both Jimmy and Robert that Led Zeppelin's ambition as a truly international road band was still unrealized. In Bangkok, where Led Zeppelin was unheard of, the first thing they saw was a poster in their hotel: COMING SOON—THE MARMALADE, referring to a third-division but still exotic, world-hopping English band. It made Jimmy and Robert think.

Led Zeppelin's fourth album was released in November 1971. Atlantic Records supplied the trade magazines with the fonts for the four Zeppelin symbols so the nameless, anonymous record could be listed on the charts. Nevertheless, the record was variously called *Led Zeppelin IV*, *Zoso*, and *Four Symbols* as well. Reviews were better than *III*, though still generally mixed. The critics seemed to like "Stairway," but not as much as the fans, who poured out to buy the album. Again, Led Zeppelin refused to have an edited version out as a single; in response the fans bought the album as if it *were* a single, which quickly drove the album to Number 2 in America and probably added half a million copies to initial sales. But response to the record and especially "Stairway" was gradual; it sold steadily in the beginning and stayed on the charts for years. But it would really be another two years, until after Led Zeppelin's big 1973 campaign, that "Stairway" would begin to assume its anthemic proportions. But the band *knew*. To a reporter, Jimmy said, "I thought 'Stairway' crystallized the essence of the band. It had everything there and showed the band at its best. . . . It was a milestone for us. Every musician wants to do something of lasting quality, something that will hold up for a long time."

To another writer, Robert described the "automatic" nature of the lyric: "I was just sitting there with Pagey in front of a fire at Headley Grange. Pagey had written the chords and played them for me. I was holding a paper and pencil, and for some reason, I was in a very bad mood. Then all of a sudden my hand was writing out words. 'There's a lady who's sure, all that glitters is gold, and she's buying a stairway to heaven.' I just sat there and looked at the words and then I almost leaped out of my seat."

To support their album at home, Led Zeppelin went back on the circuit of major English cities on November 11, starting at Newcastle in the north. The whole tour had sold out in twenty-four hours. When tickets were released for sale at seventy-five pence each for the two massive London shows at the Wembley Empire Pool, the 19,000 seats were gone in one hour. Most Led Zeppelin shows were rather stark affairs in that "glam" era of glitter rock. The band came on with no opening act, no stage set or props, nothing except hours of music. But the Wembley shows were designed more as an evening of rock vaudeville, like a roman circus. There were acrobats, jugglers, and a pig on a trampoline. Then the Scottish band Stone the Crows, featuring guitarist Les Harvey and singer Maggie Bell (the English Janis Joplin), played a set. They were managed by Peter Grant, who harbored high hopes for them. While waiting for Led Zeppelin, Grant himself appeared backstage, surrounded by a flock of children. Then the electrical leads were connected and Ray Thomas, Jimmy's roadie and guitar tuner, strummed a chord. Bbbbbbrrrrraaaaannnnngggggggg. The audience shuddered visibly at the realization that Led Zeppelin was going to play above the sonic pain threshold. "You feel your eardrums being pushed inward like sails full of wind," wrote the writer for *Melody Maker*. "It's painful, but it rips out an emotion common to most everyone in the hall. Excitement, and something rude, something so alive it smells. . . . Then Page attacked again. It's showmanship. He curls it all down silent, then barks out like an electric dog with loads of sharp bits of bone in his mouth. . . . He moves well, all the tricks, sneaking about. It's a gorgeous action to watch. Meanwhile, Plant is still screaming. Maybe it's too loud, but maybe its not. It's obscene." The shows had been advertised as "Electric Magic"; most of the fans who heard the Zeppelin's deafening three-hour performance agreed. They were buzzing from the contact as they filed en masse into the damp, freezing London night. The British tour ended in Bournemouth in December, and Led Zeppelin took the rest of the year off.

SIX

THE CONTINENTAL RIOT HOUSE

My sexual life was very intense. . . . Love was a challenge to Christianity. It was a degradation and a damnation.

—ALEISTER CROWLEY

The members of Led Zeppelin didn't socialize with each other much at home. After landing at Heathrow airport and sending the customs inspectors into their usual frenzy because of their flamboyant locks, their various gold and platinum albums and their treasure horde of hideous "antiques" and furniture from the Orient ("Oh no, it's the *Zeppelin* again," groaned the customs men when they saw them), the band would disperse into the countryside. Robert and Bonzo lived

near each other in Worcestershire, but Jones quickly disappeared into the bosom of his family; by then he had three
daughters. He also now had a home studio where he could
compose; soon John Paul Jones would take a greater role in
the band.

There had been floods along the Thames that year, and
Jimmy could see that his life at Pangbourne—his collections
of Crowley artifacts, *art nouveau* pieces and rare guitars—might
be threatened. So for half a million pounds he bought an
eighteenth-century estate in rural Sussex called Plumpton
Place. Set in a large green park with several lakes terraced at
different levels, surrounded by a moat, the old manse attracted him in part because its attic could be converted into
the recording studio that Jimmy wanted at home. Not long
after he left the boat house at Pangbourne, a part of the house
was washed away in a flood.

Around this time Jimmy was approached by the American
film maker Kenneth Anger, whose *Scorpio Rising* had been
one of the underground cinema classics of the sixties. Anger
had been living in England and was also an avid student of
the works of Aleister Crowley. Anger had lived in Boleskine
House for a summer before Jimmy bought the place; but he
first became aware of Jimmy's interest in Crowley when an
agent, bidding for Page, outbid Anger at Sotheby's for the
original manuscript of Crowley's "The Perfumed Garden."
Anger had a new film that he was calling *Lucifer Rising*; it
would be a ritualistic depiction of Anger's interest in satanism
and it needed a sound track. Anger listened to Jimmy's music
and felt an affinity with the morbid strains and infernal
meanings of songs like "Dazed and Confused." Since they
shared an interest in Crowley, and because, according to Anger, "the area he was working in coincided with the film," he
approached Jimmy through an intermediary, a Cockney spiritualist they both knew, and then visited Jimmy in Sussex.
Jimmy proudly displayed his priceless collection of Crowley
artifacts—books, first editions, manuscripts, hats, canes,

paintings, even the robes in which Crowley had conducted rituals. Jimmy agreed to work on Anger's sound track, but said his band took up most of his time. But the cinéaste and the musician agreed on a loose deadline and Jimmy began to work on what promised to be a fruitful collaboration.

North in Worcestershire, Robert worked on his farm and thought about buying another, a working sheep farm near the coast in Wales. (He eventually would buy it, as well as the house at Bron-Yr-Aur.) At home he and Bonzo patronized a band called Bronco, whose guitarist was a friend from Kidderminster named Robbie Blunt. Robert and Bonzo would show up at Bronco rehearsals at the village hall, and then all would repair to the pub for a pint or two (or a dozen in Bonzo's case). Because of Led Zeppelin's still-intact press embargo, all this was shrouded in *omerta*. Bonzo especially loathed reporters, so it was odd that he broke the band's silence when cornered at a bar in London by a friendly journalist named Chris Welch, who covered Zeppelin for years for *Melody Maker*. Bonzo discussed how worshipfully they had been received in Japan, still virgin territory as far as rock bands were concerned. He described the band as drained, and said that he himself was frightened before the last American tour because he wasn't sure he would still play well. He also gave a glimpse at his meat-and-potatoes attitude toward his work: "I've never tried consciously to be one of the best drummers and I don't want to be. A lot of kids come up to me and say, 'There's a lot better drummers than you,' or something. But I enjoy playing to the best of my ability and that's why I'm here doing it. I don't claim to be more exciting than Buddy Rich. But I don't play what I don't like. I'm a simple, straight-ahead drummer and I don't try to pretend to be anything better than I am."

Asked about Led Zeppelin's future, the one-time laborer rolled his eyes and sarcastically roared, "Oh, he's come out with a gem! I *knew* it! . . . We might be on top next year, or I might be back on the buildings!"

At that stage, early 1972, the beginning of Led Zeppelin's prime, the band couldn't stay off the road. Whatever charms the sedate English countryside held for the musicians on a sentimental level, nothing could equal the sexual buzz of a stadium full of rapturous young hopheads in deep communion with Zeppelin's unholy blues mass. Robert and Jimmy especially needed that feeling of pure unadulterated *exaltation*, that rock-god dream of unbridled passion and omnipotence that they felt as crowd noise washed over them like a waterfall of adulation and romantic energy. There was nothing else like it.

The band was due to go back to work in mid-February, beginning with a concert in Singapore on the way to their first concerts in Australia and New Zealand. Rehearsals and early recording sessions for their next album began in January at Olympic Studio in London and continued the following month at the late Jimi Hendrix's Electric Lady Studio in New York, where Eddie Kramer, who had engineered and mixed the notorious Brown Bomber, was in charge.

The concert in the former British crown colony of Singapore was scheduled for February 14. The day before, Led Zeppelin landed at Singapore and were summarily refused permission to enter the country because of their long hair. The arch-conservative government was in the midst of a campaign against the corrupting influence of Western youth culture—long hair, drugs, sex—on the youth of Singapore. Not only were Led Zeppelin not allowed into the country, they were even refused permission to get off their plane and had to fly back to London. So the tour began instead in Perth, Australia, on February 16 and continued through dates in Melbourne, Adelaide, Brisbane, and Sydney before the band flew to New Zealand, where they played before 25,000 potty antipodeans in Aukland. As the tour ended, before an audience of 26,000 in Sydney, New South Wales, on March 10, Jimmy and Robert decided to return to India, this time equipped with sound equipment and the name of a contact in the Indian music business. This trip to Bombay was supposed to yield real music, the vaunted commingling of Eastern and Western strains that Led Zeppelin had been dreaming of and talking about for years.

Bombay was a hot, dusty, crowded port city of twelve million Hindus and Moslems on the Arabian Sea, on India's western coast. Jimmy, Robert, and Richard Cole wandered about the streets for several days with their cameras and tape recorders, taking the odd snapshots of women and snake charmers. Jimmy had a state-of-the-art Stellavox stereo field recorder; whenever they came upon a troupe of street musicians, Jimmy would ask permission and tape their performances. But the presence of these outlandish strangers with microphones always drew a bigger crowd of the curious, as well as swarms of hustlers and beggers; the hapless street musicians, living repositories of India's five-thousand-year-old musical heritage, usually ended up fleeing to some quieter alley where they could make their living in peace.

With the help of their local contact, half of Led Zeppelin held a recording session in a Bombay studio. A call went out for local musicians, and several showed up. Most were trained in India's own classical raga modes while others played in the Western tradition and were said to be members of the Bombay Symphony. There was a guitarist who impressed Jimmy, a young man who had started on the sitar but now played classical guitar with Bach-like structures. These sessions yielded Anglo-Carnatic versions of "Friends" and "Four Sticks." But later Plant explained, "We won't be issuing any of the material. It was just an experiment, we were simply checking it out, and sussing out how easy it would be to transpose the ideas that we've got into the raga style and into the Indian musicians' minds. As it turned out, it was very hard for them to cope with the western approach to music. . . . We did find out that what we want to play, we can do successfully in times to come." Jimmy emphasized that the session was just an extension of what they had planned since the beginning of the band. "The intention was *always* to do a complete world tour," he said later, "at the same time recording in places like Cairo, Bangkok and Bombay and involving local musicians as well. . . . It would have been lovely to do that with the group, but we never got around to it and those two tracks never came out in that form."

But at least Jimmy and Robert could return to England and record their new album knowing that they had tried to make their East/West fusion dream come true. But their favorite tale from that journey concerned the jam they held at the only discotheque in Bombay. Jimmy played a Japanese electric guitar strung with piano wire through a little Fender amp before a small audience of dumbfounded customers who had never seen a Western rock musician before, much less heard of Led Zeppelin. After they played the owner gave Jimmy and Robert a bottle of Indian whiskey. He offered them another if they came back the following night.

In April 1972 Robert and Maureen Plant's second child was born, a son that Robert named Karac Plant. The name Karac was a form of Caractacus, the Welsh/Britannic general, the son of Cymbaline, who waged a long and heroic struggle against the Roman invasion of Britain in A.D. 43. When Caractacus was finally captured and taken to Rome in chains, the emperor Claudius was impressed by his defiant courage and spared his life. Robert, immersed in the ancient history of Wales and Britain, gave his son a formidable Celtic hero's name.

In May Eddie Kramer flew in from New York. A few weeks earlier Richard Cole had called and said that Led Zeppelin would begin recording the new album at Stargroves, a country house owned by Mick Jagger, again using the Rolling Stones mobile studio. Kramer found the band fired up from its travels and touring. Jimmy and Robert had been particularly inspired by their ethno-sonic field work in Bombay, and most of the songs (and the many outtakes) for the new album would be written at Stargroves in rehearsal. There were exceptions: Jimmy brought in "The Rain Song" and "Over the Hills" from home and Jones had the chords and Mellotron themes of "No Quarter" previously worked out as well. Kramer has fond memories of those Stargroves sessions. "They were great, inspiring, wonderful," he says. "It was just that everybody in Led Zeppelin was so *confident*, and so very happy about what was going on. The general feeling was excellent. For instance, I have a very strong vision, from my perspective in the mobile with the doors to the truck wide open, of all four of them dancing in single file on the lawn during the first playback of 'Dancing Days.' It was Robert, Bonzo, Jonesy and Jimmy dancing in a line on a green lawn, celebrating this incredible thing they'd just recorded.

"That Stargroves thing was actually quite an experience, because Bonzo burst into my room very late one night, extremely drunk and wearing an oversized raincoat, and flashed my girl friend and I, who were in bed. Then he ran out roaring with laughter. But the room didn't have a lock and soon he was back, even more drunk, and he flashed us again. Then a roadie ran in and threw a bucket of cold water on us while we were in bed, and the other roadies were running amok, climbing in and out of our window all night. The girl left the next morning in disgust. Can't say I blamed her.

"But they were so great to work with. Bonzo was the easiest drummer I ever recorded. I had him in a room to himself, playing inside the bay window of a big conservatory, with three mikes on the drums. His sound was so great that it facilitated a *monumental* drum sound on record. You can't describe it; you have to hear it. Bonzo sounded that way because he hit the drums harder than anyone I ever met. He had this bricklayer's ability to bang the drum immensely hard. Yet he had a very light touch. In many ways, he was the key to Led Zeppelin. You could work fast with him. The only reason Led Zeppelin ever did retakes were the extremely tricky time sequences of most of the songs. Once Bonzo mastered his part, everything else would fall into place."

Eddie Kramer recalls that Jimmy was producing and *in charge*; it was still obviously Jimmy's band. But Page's style was very loose and oblique and everybody contributed ideas. Kramer felt that Jimmy was "allowing" John Paul Jones a lot more leeway to add tonal colors and material like "No Quarter." It was tricky to work with Jimmy on an album; he used many different kinds of amps to daub his varied palette of guitar music, and was "a very demanding person." But Jimmy's style was nominally laid-back. They recorded one tune, "Black Country Woman," sitting with their guitars outside in the garden. As they were starting the take, a plane flew over, and Kramer asked over the intercom if he should take the sound of the motor out as Robert was about to lay on his vocal. Robert said no, leave it in, and Jimmy nodded his head in assent.

There was no shortage of new music; so much came out of these Stargroves sessions that Led Zeppelin would spend indecisive months remixing and obsessing over what to use on the album and what to hold. Jimmy had been working on an intricate instrumental fanfare with multiple guitar voices and personas. At first he just called it "The Overture," but in rehearsal its martial air of romance and movement earned it a new working title: "The Campaign." (Later, after Robert had added lyrics, it would turn into "The Song Remains the Same," Led Zeppelin's tribute to world music.) "The Rain Song," a bluesy dirge that Jimmy had brought with him from Sussex, was painstakingly constructed, almost too formal, drenched in John Paul Jones's synthetic orchestration via the Mellotron, that forgotten progressive rock trademark then associated primarily with the Moody Blues. "Over the Hills and Far Away" was also Jimmy's, with its folkish acoustic riff and then—*fire one*—the usual Zeppelin carpet bombing. Robert would later add his goofy aphorisms and riddles, and Jones would attach a bizarre coda with a harpsichord.

John Paul Jones was mostly responsible for "No Quarter," whose morose, pretty theme inspired Robert to write lyrics with provocative images of Led Zeppelin as a Viking death squad riding the winds of Thor to some awful satanic destiny: "Walking side by side with death/The Devil mocks their every step." But then there's an incongruous cocktail-piano solo and a jazz guitar section from Jimmy. If the subtext of "No Quarter" was that Led Zeppelin took no prisoners and fantasized human sacrifice, then the message of joke tracks like "D'yer Mak'er" and "The Crunge" seemed to be don't take Led Zeppelin too seriously. "D'yer Mak'er" (the title, a pun on "Jamaica," was from an old joke not worth repeating) was a sign of the times. Jamaican reggae was becoming big in England. Bob Marley and the Wailers were living in London, an underground sensation. Zeppelin was interested in reggae (and its technical clone, "dub" music) and Bonzo was often teased about not being able to play in reggae time. "D'yer Mak'er" started as a reggae, but ended up more as a fifties parody. "The Crunge" was also a spontaneous parody of James Brown. Bonzo started playing, Jonesy came in next, and then Jimmy whanged in, playing like James Brown's influential guitarist Jimmy Nolen. It turned into a parody of funk, with Robert grinding out Otis Redding's "Mr. Pitiful" before singing: "Where's that confounded bridge?"

Then there were the hardcore rock tracks that would anchor the album: "Dancing Days," with its magisterial, snake-like theme similar to the Indian double-reed *shenai* that Jimmy and Robert had heard in Bombay; and "The Ocean," complete with volcanoes of erupting guitar, whole *choirs* of guitars, guitars building layer upon layer of sonic power. The ocean, of course, was Robert's indelible image of the overheated young crowds that swayed and swirled in front of the stage like tidal surges of humanity. And these were only the tracks that would make it on the album. The Stargroves session also produced outtakes like "Black Country Woman," "The Rover," and "Houses of the Holy," the rollicking title

song that eventually would be left off the album named for
it. There was another track, "Walter's Walk," taken at an un-
safe speed. Bonzo sounds angry and ferocious, and Jimmy Page
arrives like a night letter. There were also a couple of untitled
rhythm tracks of varying quality. One was known only as
"Slush." Later, when the group listened to the Stargroves
playbacks at their "regular" London laboratory, Olympic Studio in Barnes, they realized that they weren't as pleased with
the sound at Stargroves as they had been with their old house
at Headley Grange. Many more months would be spent remixing in both London and New York. And the usual hassles
over Zeppelin's unusual cover art would delay the album for
almost another year.

While Led Zeppelin was recording what would be their most
popular music, Peter Grant was single-handedly changing the
way that big rock groups would do business. Traditionally, if
a big act wanted to tour, their gate receipts would be split in
half with the local promoter. If the act was really big, it would
sometimes get 60 percent of the gate. But in setting up Led
Zeppelin's 1972 summer tour of America, Peter Grant astounded the American promoters by informing them that
henceforth Led Zeppelin would be taking 90 percent of the
gate. Peter would be the real promoter and pay all the ex-
penses. The local promoters would do the detail work and receive 10 percent and the glory of being associated with "the
top grossing band in the world." Naturally the American promoters *howled*, but Grant stood firm. He told them bluntly
that 10 percent of Led Zeppelin's gate was better than 50 percent of nothing. The promoters had no choice. Led Zeppelin
would earn and keep more money than any touring rock band
before them, and Peter Grant's new formula would quickly
become standard among the big rock stars. Of Grant's audac-
ity, Richard Cole says, "He just figured that the people go to
see the artist and the artist should get the money. And he took
the risk; he hired the stadiums with his money. He said, 'I'll
rent the halls, you do the work for me.' Luckily, we got in-

Four faces of Led Zeppelin during the 1973 tour

Robert Plant, New Orleans, 1973

Jimmy plays his double-neck Gibson during "Stairway to Heaven," 1973.

Jimmy Page, with
his Les Paul, 1973

Bonzo in action,
1973

Aboard the *Starship*: Danny Goldberg, Peter Grant, and Lisa Robinson

Ahmet Ertegun and Jerry Wexler give Jimmy a platinum record for *Houses of the Holy*, New York, 1973.

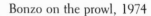
Bonzo on the prowl, 1974

Led Zeppelin in groupie heaven, the Rainbow, Los Angeles, 1974. Jimmy is in a corner behind Robert and his friends. Bonzo's roadie Mick Hinton takes a tray of drinks from a waitress, standing in front of John Paul Jones. Lori Maddox is sitting with her chum Bonzo at far right. This was typical of the kind of photograph the band didn't want their wives to see.

Bad Company, 1974

Maggie Bell, 1974

Led Zeppelin back on the road in 1975. Robert wears an Indian arrowhead on his bare chest. Jimmy wears the Mark of the Beast on his trousers.

Robert Plant surveys Hollywood at the Riot House, Los Angeles, March 1975.
"I'm a golden god!" he shouted as the picture was taken.

volved with big promoters like Jerry Weintraub [who promoted Elvis Presley's papal audiences] and they said fine."

But Grant's business triumph was offset by a personal loss when Les Harvey, the guitarist of Grant's act Stone the Crows, was electrocuted while playing a concert in Swansea, Wales, on May 3, 1972. Singer Maggie Bell, Harvey's girl friend, collapsed after the accident. No one had ever seen Peter Grant, the fearsome, swashbuckling rock behemoth, break down and weep before.

But Grant had done his pre-concert work well, and the untitled fourth album was still on the American charts and selling steadily. The result was that almost every concert the band would play in North America between June and August 1972 sold out immediately, without advertising. Fans besieged ticket offices, creating the usual near-riots that later would really get out of hand. The musicians were preparing a new show and were convinced that this tour—their eighth of the United States—would be the one that would change Led Zeppelin from a successful rock band known only to its fans to a household word and cultural icon like the Beatles or the Stones. The only problem was that the Rolling Stones would be touring the United States *at the same time,* the first shows the Stones (whose album *Exile on Main Street* was reaching Number 1 on the U.S. charts) had played America since 1969. Already the Stones tour was being flacked by their Los Angeles public relations firm as the youth cultural event of the year. Amid all this hype, despite the fact that they were actually out-drawing the Stones in some cities, Led Zeppelin realized to their amazement and horror that they might not get noticed at all. Their loyal fans still went berserk and all the shows evolved into the usual Dionysiac fiestas. But other than the fans with whom they already had a private covenant of sheer mystique, no one would care. No one would even *know.*

The problem was that Led Zeppelin's relations with the press were abysmal, unlike the Rolling Stones, who actually maintained a constant publicity circus. The band felt that the British music press was carrying on a vendetta against them. The American press was actually physically afraid of Led Zeppelin and their reputation as homicidal whipmasters; the fear was reinforced when Ellen Sander's memoir of her assault by Zeppelin during the halcyon (and much more violent) weeks of 1969 was finally published in her book, *Trips*. Robert was offended by this ill-treatment by the media. "I must admit it does annoy me," he told a writer. "I must have an ego because I have to go onstage partially to satisfy it." Elsewhere, Robert was quoted: "We knew full well that we were doing better business than . . . a lot of people who were glorified in the press. So without being egocentric, we thought it was time people heard something about us other than that we were eating women and throwing the bones out the window."

Led Zeppelin hadn't even employed a press officer for years. Back in 1968 they had used Bill Harry, the former Beatles publicist and *Merseybeat* editor who then worked for Mickie Most's acts. But they fell out with Harry rather quickly, and the story went around that Grant and Cole had pushed Harry out of an upper-floor window overlooking Oxford Street and dangled him above the traffic by his legs.

So Led Zeppelin hired another press agent, the diminutive B. P. "Beep" Fallon, who had done publicity for T. Rex and other English acts of the glitter era. In the past reporters who wanted to interview Led Zeppelin usually received no reply from Peter Grant's office. If an interviewer managed to penetrate within actual speaking distance of the band, he was usually snarled at by the large and menacing Richard Cole and bluntly told to piss off. At least Fallon would try to get the press to Jimmy and Robert unmolested. And Fallon himself was a strange personality, beloved of Jimmy and Robert, roundly loathed by Bonzo, Richard Cole, and the roadies. He spoke in his own hip argot. Everything was a "vibe." If it was time to eat, Fallon would chirp, "Eating vibe." If it was time to leave, Fallon announced, "Limo vibe." Whenever he rang up a reporter to plug one of his acts, he always prefaced his conversation by saying, "I wanna lay a verbal on ya, man." He was a scream.

When Led Zeppelin hired him, Fallon was working as press agent for a group called Silverhead, whose guitarist was Robert's friend from Kidderminster, Robbie Blunt. The singer in the band was a handsome, aristocratic blond called Michael des Barres, who first met Jimmy when Beep brought Led Zeppelin to a Silverhead gig in a little club in Birmingham. Since Robert and Robbie were friends, both bands and their entourages returned to Robert's place after the gig and jammed all night. Michael des Barres was fascinated with Jimmy from the moment they met.

"Beep and Jimmy were much alike," he says. "They were both visionary imps. And they were in love with what I was in love with in rock and roll, which was the atmosphere of it all. It had nothing to do with the songs or the lyrics, any of that. The only really important thing was the right earring, the right album cover, and looking right getting off the plane and climbing out of the limo. That, and being the stonedest person in the room. The vibe was everything. And it still is. The attitude was *everything*. That's why I love Jimmy so much.

"I mean, Jimmy was *incredible*," he continued. "Because he was the classic rock star with the moated castle, the velvet clothes, the fabulous cars that he couldn't drive and the eighty thousand rare guitars. And, like an idiot, I was dabbling with the Crowley thing at the time. I used to go down to see Jimmy at Plumpton and he'd pull out Crowley's robes, Crowley's tarot deck, all of Aleister Crowley's gear that he had collected. I thought, 'This is *great*.' It was all so twisted and debauched, their whole thing. That's what Jimmy represented to me.

"I don't know what I represented to Jimmy," Michael concluded. "I always thought that Jimmy liked me because I happened to say 'Rimbaud' at the right time."

Led Zeppelin's eighth tour of North America began on June 21, 1972, in Denver. Their new show, which ran from two and a half to four hours, depending on Jimmy's health on any given night, leaned heavily on the newly recorded material that was unfamiliar to the fans, on the new standards from the untitled album, and on veteran Zeppelin artillery pieces—"Since I've Been Loving You," "Dazed and Confused," and the inevitable "Whole Lotta Love." The show now opened with "Rock and Roll" and segued into "Over the Hills and Far Away," "Black Dog," and "Misty Mountain Hop" before Robert bade the fans his customary low-key "good evening." From the beginning Robert was having trouble with his gravelly voice, which suffered from constant changes in the summer climate. In the desert climates of Texas and Arizona, Zeppelin would step out of their air-conditioned plane into oppressive heat, then into the air-conditioned limo, then more heat, then more air conditioning. Robert's voice cracked early; for the rest of this tour he lived on a diet of hot tea with lemon and honey. He compensated with his raw sexual energy. He'd lean back and his body would *quiver*, drawing huge shrieks.

Early in the tour they played two shows at Madison Square Garden in New York. On the first night, a Friday, the air conditioning had malfunctioned in a heat wave and the vast auditorium was a steambath. That night the fans went mad from the instant they heard Bonzo's thrashing intro to "Rock and Roll" and Jimmy's all-time power chords. It was Mardi Gras, Saturnalia, and Chinese New Year in one rock show, no stage sets or props, just Led Zeppelin, the music and a few spotlights. Three hours later, as the band lurched into "Whole Lotta Love," the fans started climbing onto the stage. Richard Cole tried to do his grim reaper routine, kicking the fans back into the mire with karate blows, but to no avail. As the kids poured onto the stage, Led Zeppelin played on, roaring obliviously until the front half of the stage literally caved in down the middle under the weight of dancing fans. As people tumbled back into the pit and the monitors fell after them, the band walked off and stayed backstage until it was obvious that no one in the crowd of 20,000 had any intention of leaving. The band walked back on and played "Louie Louie" and "Long Tall Sally" without their stage monitors.

In New York the band hung out at rock clubs and drank. They worked at Electric Lady with Eddie Kramer, mixing tracks like "Houses of the Holy," the supposed title song of the next album. They played lucrative shows at Nassau Coliseum on suburban Long Island, with kids coming hundreds of miles to see the band. Balcony tickets were being scalped outside for $200 each. After a four-hour show that ended with "Boogie Mama" and "Peggy Sue," Led Zeppelin waited in their dressing room while the vast concrete parking lot cleared of the thousands of Pontiac Cutlasses and 427 Camaros as New York's suburban youth entangled itself in a typical post-Zeppelin traffic jam. Backstage, an English writer told the band that one of the music papers had just named the flaccid Moody Blues as the top English band in America. Robert, lapping honeyed tea, shook his head in disgust. "That's been going on for four years," muttered Jones.

When he did give interviews, Robert consistently complained that the press coverage of Led Zeppelin was missing what was really going on between the musicians and the fans, on a spiritual level. They were missing the energy exchange that was the core of Zeppelin's success. "It isn't just a musical thing that takes place," he told one reporter, "it's a rapport that takes it away from being an earthly thing to almost a little bit above it . . . that's the way I like to think it is. This is where you go out on a limb and become King Arthur. This is really where strength lies in popularity, by saying, 'Look, there's no strings attached.' " There was no real way to explain to the press the magical sense of telepathy and empathy the members of Led Zeppelin felt for each other, but Robert tried: "Anyway, it isn't just a teenybopper thing with swinging the mike around. There's something else going on. Even numbers we've been doing for years can get changed every night."

As the tour progressed, through Syracuse after the New York

shows and then on through the United States before winding up in Los Angeles, the band noticed that "Stairway" seemed to be the audience's favorite song (though Bonzo's solo, "Moby Dick," usually drew the loudest cheers). There was something about "Stairway to Heaven"—the chiming acoustics, the primal images of the goddess, the din-of-battle finale—that had hooked into the youth of America. "It took like Islam in the desert." Jimmy had discovered that if he left the upper twelve-string neck wide open, the strings would vibrate in sympathy with the melodies being played on the six-string neck, similar to the sympathetic overtones of the sitar and adding to the overall tonal display. This tour also marked a change of role for John Paul Jones. In the past he had been the faceless bassist, languishing in the dark, maintaining an even strain while Jimmy and Robert cavorted in the spotlight. Jones was a gifted musician who had chosen the steady anonymity of the bassist, and his features were usually masked in concentration. But on this tour Jonesy was stretching out, playing electric piano, organ, and Mellotron, joining the band as an equal. "I don't mind being in the background," he told reporter Ritchie Yorke. "I wouldn't like to be out front playing like Jimmy. To be any sort of artist, you have to be a born exhibitionist. . . . I believe you should do what you have to do, and if I'm bass, rather than try to lead on bass and push myself, I prefer to put down a good solid bass line."

When Led Zeppelin hit Los Angeles, they moved into the Continental Hyatt House on Sunset Boulevard and settled into now familiar routines, rehearsing (one recorded rehearsal featured dozens of Elvis tunes) and hanging out at Hollywood rock clubs like Rodney's English Disco and the Rainbow Bar. Jimmy linked up with his friend Miss Pamela and all seemed normal until Jimmy started to chase a fourteen-year-old teen model named Lori Maddox.

Lori was a pretty girl, tall and dark like Jimmy, with prominent features and giant eyes. She reminded people of Bianca

Jagger. Her picture had been in *Star* magazine, and earlier in the year she had met B. P. Fallon, who had been in L.A. with Silverhead. Fallon had taken some pictures of Lori, which he now showed to Jimmy as representative of the new, younger generation of rock groupies. Jimmy was smitten. According to Lori, Beep gave Jimmy her number and Jimmy called her from Texas and said, "Hi, this is Jimmy Page and I wanna meet you." Lori thought it was a crank call and said, "Yeah, right buddy, sure," and hung up on him. But Lori was intrigued. When Led Zeppelin came to town Lori and some of her girl friends went over to the Hyatt House to hang around the roof-top pool, where Jimmy began to hit on her. But her friends told her that Miss Pamela would beat the shit out of her if she caught Lori messing with her man.

"I was still like a virgin then," Lori says. "And I said to him, 'Look Mr. Page, I really can't talk to you, like I don't want to get beaten up.' But Jimmy said, 'Honey, if you come with me, nobody'll *touch* you.' "

Lori says that Jimmy chased her all over the city, following her to Rodney's, then to the pool at the Hyatt House, then to Robert Plant's suite to dry off. There she and the other new girls on the scene—Sable Starr, Lynn, and the others—spent the evening throwing empty champagne bottles out the window, trying to hit the big rock and roll billboards across the street. Jimmy, she says, was never involved in the insane antics that Led Zeppelin perpetrated in the Hyatt, causing the locals to rename the place the Continental Riot House. Jimmy, instead, was quiet and reserved, an amused observer of the brainless carnage rather than a participant.

The next night Lori was again at Rodney's English Disco with her girl friends, when Jimmy came in with Miss Pamela. Lori went to the powder room and Jimmy followed her in and started groping and kissing her "in front of everybody. And I'm going, 'My God! You can't *do* this. Stop, you're gonna get me *killed*.' Of course I really liked him, but I was afraid of him. I was only fourteen, and this was a much older man.

I didn't really know who he was and I was like too young to understand. And my girl friends were begging me to stay away. They told me that Jimmy would beat me up if he got me alone."

Lori then left Rodney's and went to the Rainbow Bar, the main watering hole for English rock stars in Los Angeles. Jimmy showed up soon after, without Miss Pamela, trying to find Lori. Jimmy was *determined*. He sent Richard Cole over to her table, and Richard said, "Jimmy told me that he's going to have you whether you like it or not."

"All of a sudden," Lori continues, "Jimmy's party left the Rainbow in a hurry. Jimmy jumped in his limo and roared off, after telling Richard Cole that if he let me out of his sight Jimmy would fire him. So Richard grabbed me and said, 'You fucking move and I'll fucking have your head.' He threw me into the back of another limo and said, 'Now sit there and shut up.' I asked him what was going on, but he just said to shut up.

"Next thing you know, we're all back at the Riot House. We're walking down the corridor of one of Zeppelin's floors and suddenly I got snatched—*kidnapped*—into the room. It was dimly lit by candles and at first I couldn't really see. And then I saw Jimmy, just sitting there in a corner, wearing this hat slouched over his eyes and holding a cane. It was really mysterious and *weird*. He was just sitting there, tapping this cane on the floor, in a chair in the corner. He looked just like a gangster. It was *magnificent*. Can you believe it? It was just like right out of a story! Kidnapped, man, at fourteen!

"Then we were finally alone. Nobody could beat up on me and I wasn't too afraid. So we peeked out a crack in the door until we were like sure that nobody was in the hall, and then we disappeared into this other room that Jimmy had. And that was the beginning of our romance. We like fell in love. From that day on we were like together. He'd come to town and he'd station himself in the Riot House and send a car to pick me up. Then he'd take off to do concerts and fly back the same night to be with me and we were *together*. We were madly, madly in love. It was like a fantasy or a fairy tale.

"But the others were really against me at the time. They were concerned because somebody warned them that if Jimmy was discovered with a fourteen-year-old girl, he'd be deported immediately. So Jimmy kept me locked in the room at all times. Both Peter Grant and Richard Cole insisted that I be kept locked up. They didn't let me go anywhere because I was so under-age. Nobody ever said anything to Jimmy and me, but I just vibed it. Eventually, we all became friends. Jimmy met my mom and everything. He called her one day and said, 'I hope you don't mind that I'm seeing your daughter.' He was a real gentleman, and she knew that he was a really respectable guy and that he had money and, I mean, *what is she gonna say*? You know, she knew I was doing it anyway, so she figures if I'm gonna be doing it, who better with?

"I mean, he was a real *romance*. He's the most romantic person in the world. He's so sweet and gentle, like the perfect man—almost feminine in his way . . . and like really sensitive, super-sensitive. When he came to town he'd send a car for me and I'd like go meet him at the airport. And then we'd get back to the hotel and we'd run straight to our room and we'd sit on the floor and we'd start crying because we were so happy to see each other again. He'd give me presents, like an old scarab necklace to keep away evil spirits, and I'd give him like an antique music box or something. It was real sweet. And it was really an innocent, beautiful perfect love, you know? Like he knew I just loved him for himself and nothing else. . . .

"Well, you'd hear a lot about Jimmy being a sorcerer or wizard and like that. But the only evidence I saw of that was just what I felt over myself. That's it. I mean, I can't explain it, but I think he's got a lot of *power* in his own little way . . . I always felt like I was under his spell. Honestly. Sometimes when we were making love and it had been going on for *hours*, honest to God, it was like being in a magic spell; dizziness, going into different places, not even taking drugs, and just feeling . . . feeling like you're in space somewhere. He was the most amazing lover in the world, a lot of power, but really soft and sensitive. I'm just sure that every girl he ever touched has fallen in love with him. . . .

"After that first year, Jimmy took me along to all the shows. Sometimes they would dedicate a show to me! And if I wasn't with him, he would call me every day from wherever he was. Especially at the time he was in his prime, '73 to '75, that was the *prime* of Zeppelin. After that, he got kinda smacked out."

The tour ended in August, a great artistic and financial success, but a sullen failure for Led Zeppelin because they were totally ignored by the media while, as forecast, the Rolling Stones upstaged them completely. Celebrities battled for entry to the Stones' dressing room. Andy Warhol followed them with his camera while Truman Capote, with Princess Lee Radziwill in tow, dogged the Stones tour from city to city. Hip authors like Terry Southern wrote serious "think pieces" for respectable journals. Meanwhile, Led Zeppelin was ignored by all but the most crass and shameless teen-age press. While Mick Jagger's stunning, glamorous Nicaraguan wife was courted as an *avant-garde* sultana, Jimmy Page was trying to hide his fourteen-year-old concubine from the law. It was ridiculous. Led Zeppelin was *bigger* than the Stones. Led Zeppelin outsold the Stones and even played better and hotter than the Stones, who were then burdened with an unwieldy, under-rehearsed horn section. But while Stevie Wonder opened shows for the Stones, sometimes warming up the crowd so much that the Stones didn't feel like even playing, Led Zeppelin was out there alone with their goony young fans, isolated from the rest of the music business and the world beyond. It was Led Zeppelin and its sleazy and freakish entourage against the world. As a result the world was afraid of Led

Zeppelin. *Rolling Stone* barely mentioned their summer tour that year.

The musicians were understandably furious. "There was always this thing," Richard Cole recalls. "They would say, 'Look at the Stones. Why haven't we got these people like Princess Radish here.' But they knew the reason why. Led Zeppelin was built around a different kind of image, a mystifying kind of thing."

And Jimmy later said, "I mean, who wants to know that Led Zeppelin broke an attendance record at such and such a place when Mick Jagger's hanging around with Truman Capote?" The answer was: nobody.

In October 1972 Led Zeppelin went back to Japan for the second time, opening at Tokyo's Budokan Hall on October 3 with a brilliant show that began with "Black Dog" and ended three hours later with the drawn-out Elvis medley from "Whole Lotta Love." In Osaka they improvised a version of "Stand by Me." But the band got bored in Japan and flew to Hong Kong for a brief vacation. "We wanted to tour the world," Cole says. "Led Zeppelin wanted to play everywhere they could. So we went to Hong Kong to see about maybe playing there." One night it was the usual fun and games. According to Cole: "We wanted to buy a snort of coke, right? So we got a bag of coke and we're having dinner and we get fucking greedy so we just start to stick our straws inside the bag. But it turned out to be fucking heroin! We didn't know what it was, and we didn't know where we were after that." The next day they went on a tour of Hong Kong harbor on a boat owned by Peter's local contact, Andrew Yu. But the boat began to take on water and seemed in danger of actually sinking with Led Zeppelin on board. Grant ordered Richard Cole over the side to swim for help, "Fuck you, ya cunt," Richard replied.

Later that month they played two shows in Montreux, Switzerland, for promoter Claud Nobs in the comparatively tiny (1,500 seats) Pavilion. The shows finished with amended

"Whole Lotta Love" medleys that incorporated Carl Perkins tunes with the usual Elvis chestnuts like "Heartbreak Hotel." Jimmy's main girl, the normally reclusive Charlotte Martin, came to Montreux for the concerts. She made her mark in the staid Swiss town by appearing for dinner at a local restaurant wearing enough diamonds to equip a royal princess.

Led Zeppelin refused to rest. On November 10 they announced that they would play the British Isles during December and January 1973; the 120,000 tickets sold out in a day. *Melody Maker* quoted Jimmy Page's reaction: "When I heard the news, I felt very humble." The tour (the biggest the band had yet attempted at home) began in Newcastle on November 30. Reviewing the show (and referring to the current David Bowie/Gary Glitter style of glam music), Roy Hollingsworth wrote in *Melody Maker*, "If you wanna hear a rock and roll band, wipe off that bloody silly make-up and go see Zeppelin." The tour progressed through Scotland (where B. P. Fallon was beaten up in tough Glasgow by ticket scalpers outside the hall) and Wales. In Cardiff the group stayed at the aging Angel Hotel, which Bonzo soundly trashed. At the Brighton Dome on December 20, Led Zeppelin played Christmas carols during the encore. The tour broke for the holidays with two nights at the cavernous Alexandra Palace, the "Ally Pally" on Muswell Hill in north London. After the second show Robert gave the entire road crew his Christmas present: one bottle of whiskey. Jimmy Page wasn't the only Led Wallet in this band.

PART
TWO

LED ZEPPELIN! THE BIZARRE OCCULT RUMOURS! A HUNDRED EXCLUSIVE PICTURES! WHY JIMMY PAGE FEARS LOVE! GROUPIE TELLS WHY SHE GETS OFF ON ROBERT PLANT! WHAT MAKES LED ZEP THE GREATEST HEAVY METAL BAND EVER! LED ZEP: THEY'LL SPACE YOUR BRAINS OUT! ALEISTER CROWLEY'S CURSE! ALL NEW HOT SCOOPS ON ZEP! LED ZEPPELIN VERSUS KISS! HUNDREDS OF RARE PHOTOS OF THE GIANT ROCK MONSTERS! JIMMY PAGE: WILL BLACK MAGIC KILL HIM? BIG PHOTOS TO FRAME! THE TRUTH ABOUT LED ZEPPELIN REVEALED! THE EVIL CURSE THAT HAUNTS THEM! WILL THE SONG REMAIN THE SAME? HAVE THEY FINALLY BEATEN THE CURSE? LIFE ON THE LED ZEP JET! EXCLUSIVE! THE LED ZEPPELIN STORY IN WORDS AND PICTURES! EVIL OMEN! CAN LED ZEPPELIN SURVIVE?

—FAN MAGAZINE HEADLINES
1973–1984

SEVEN

THE STARSHIP

And if you take your pick, be careful how you choose it . . .

—"ROYAL ORLEANS"

In 1973 Led Zeppelin reached the apogee of its flight. For the next three years the band would be in its prime, at the peak of its artistic and physical strength. Although Led Zeppelin had released no recordings the previous year, their previous four albums were selling so well that the group accounted for 18 percent of Atlantic's total sales in 1972. In years to come that figure would grow to almost 30 percent. The group had a formidable internal power and confidence as well. Led Zeppelin's creative energy was still focused on the band, undissipated by the usual solo albums, ego trips, and personnel changes. Plenty of other heavy metal rock bands had surfaced, but none could match Led Zeppelin's glamorous mystique, its style, its *duende*. Best of all, Led Zeppelin was still a secret society. Its popularity wasn't just confined to the world of rock, but to a despised segment of the rock audience—young, mostly male, mostly working class, cannon-fodder youth who identified with Led Zeppelin in a mytho-poeic fashion *beyond the music itself*. Led Zeppelin was a mystery cult with several million initiates. In the high school parking lots of every suburban American town in the 1970s, Led Zeppelin *ruled*, high priests of Album Oriented Radio.

But by 1973 Led Zeppelin didn't want to be a cult. The musicians wanted true stardom and fame beyond the confines of rock music. Even the hated music press, which had accused Led Zeppelin of stupidity and cultural fascism—capturing its sedated young audience through demagogic hectoring—was now to be courted. If Led Zeppelin was now the biggest band in the world, the group's proprietorial instincts demanded that the public should know it. B. P. Fallon's attempts to publicize Led Zepplin had been small time. So Peter Grant began casting around for an American press agent, someone to get Led Zeppelin on the front pages.

The tour of England continued through January 1973. On January 2 the Bentley that Robert and Bonzo were riding in broke down on the way to a gig at Sheffield. They hitchhiked the rest of the way and made it to the show, but Robert caught a bad cold and several dates were postponed. On the sixteenth they played a bizarre date at Aberystwyth, the nearest large town to Bron-Yr-Aur and Led Zeppelin's other Welsh haunts. They played in the 800-seat Kings Hall for an aghast, formal audience that never left their chairs and politely applauded an abbreviated performance. The tour wound down in Scotland at the end of the month.

The band took February off, resting before a month of shows

in Europe in March and then the big tour of the United States that would begin in May. The new album was about to be released after months of delay because of problems printing the cover. This was the first Led Zeppelin album to have a proper title, *Houses of the Holy*, although the title song itself had been left off the album and wouldn't surface for another two years. The album jacket, which again bore no mention of Led Zeppelin, depicted naked blond children scrambling up a neolithic stone formation in Staffin, in the Western Isles of the Hebrides. The inside of the jacket portrayed a powerful naked man holding one of the blond children over his head before a ruined fortress in a posture of submission and sacrifice. It was the color separation process that had caused the delay. At first the children had come out purple. But when the color had been corrected, the album glowed with a strange, burnt-orange luminescence. Inside, the lyrics to the songs were printed on the record sleeve, the first time Zeppelin had done this except for "Stairway to Heaven." (Some of the lyrics were mistranscribed or deliberately distorted, as in Robert's reference to hell in "The Ocean," which was changed on the lyric sheet to appear nonsensical.)

In March Led Zeppelin played to audiences in Denmark, Norway, Sweden, Austria, and Germany. In Japan and England, "The Song Remains the Same" had been introduced under its original title of "The Campaign." Now it had its proper name and earned ovations for its multiple guitar voices and chiming, mystical aura. From their audience's reaction to the unfamiliar numbers from *Houses of the Holy*, the musicians knew their new album was going to be very big.

On March 26 Led Zeppelin began a five-city tour of France at Lyons. As the roadies were setting up the gear, Peter Grant had discovered to his horror that the French promoter had neglected to provide any security. So Peter asked Benoit Gautier, a French employee of Atlantic who had known the band since the beginning and was traveling through France with them, to set up some kind of security net. The crowds had been very Teutonic in Germany, and Peter was expecting more trouble in France. Like many people who worked with Grant, Gautier had a sort of grudging admiration for Led Zeppelin's brute of a manager. "Within the record business," Gautier says, "he had the reputation of being a tough motherfucker. He'll give you a hard time, beat you down, call you names. But Peter never gave you a problem until you gave him one. I saw him *behave* many times, breaking things, breaking people physically, but every time he did it to somebody it was because they deserved it. He was very professional, a gentleman, incredibly loyal to his acts and to the people who worked for him, and especially to people who went out of their way to help Led Zeppelin."

The first gig in Lyons was at a 12,000-seat basketball stadium with four tiers of seats. There was trouble even before the show began when a large crowd of gate-crashers arrived, chanting for free music; they were, Gautier recalls, the "remnant of 1968," when an alliance of French students and workers almost brought down the government in a wave of strikes and demonstrations. Standing together, Grant and Gautier saw the gate-crashers knock down the elderly ushers who were collecting tickets in the hall, and Grant ordered the Zeppelin roadies into action. "They weren't afraid to fight," says Gautier. "That's how it was with Peter. If something's unfair, he gets furious. I would say that he could be furious enough to actually kill someone, because he's a strong guy and he's big. But he's fair, and his word meant something." Trouble continued after the show started. The stage was under one of the seating tiers, and toward the end of the concert a kid started dropping wine bottles on the group from the highest level, sending shards of broken glass shooting across the stage. Gautier ran up to the balcony and caught the youth who was dropping the bottles, and dragged him down the stairs and into the backstage area by his long hair. Between the end of the show and the first encore, the roadies whacked the boy unmercifully before throwing him out. Peter Grant asked Benoit Gautier to handle security for the rest of their stay in France.

Gautier recalls that Led Zeppelin was unlike any of the other rock bands that came through France. They had an unapproachable ganglike fraternity about them. And they looked, he says, like the cast of *Robin Hood* as performed by the inmates of the asylum at Charenton, with Jimmy as Robin, Robert as Maid Marian, burly Bonzo as Little John, and the dour John Paul as Alan A' Dale the minstrel. That left Peter Grant as the dissipated Friar Tuck and the sinister Cole as the Sheriff of Nottingham. The maniacal, out-of-control road crew filled out the cast as Robin's band of Merry Men. And there *was* something decidedly medieval about Led Zeppelin, with their velvet clothes, the lizard boots, the fur jackets, their pointed English noses, and long flowing hair.

After the Lyons show the group decided to drive to the next dates at Nantes. So Benoit Gautier rented a couple of cars. Peter Grant took off in a big Volvo with Robert and Jimmy while Gautier had Bonzo and Patsy Collins, a security goon, in a Mercedes. (Patsy had split someone's jaw in two the night before in Lyons and was considered one of the more psychopathic security guys on the circuit of English bands. Later, after wreaking much havoc with Zeppelin, he would perish in an elevator shaft in Djakarta while working for Deep Purple.) On the way to Nantes Peter Grant decided *he* wanted the Mercedes, and stole it while Gautier was parked at a rest stop. So Bonzo decided to drive the Volvo and catch up to the others. "'I'm still surprised we didn't die," Gautier says. Bonzo would spend five to ten minutes in the passing lane, against on-coming traffic, doubling every car. When they stopped for a picnic an hour later, Benoit got Bonzo drunk on heavy red wine and resumed driving.

When they got to Nantes they drove right to the hall for the sound check. But the backstage gate was slow to open and kids started to gather around the car, so Peter Grant floored the Mercedes, ramming it through the gate and ripping off

the car's fenders. After the first night's show their French promoter had disappeared, leaving the band to fend for themselves. After the show at Nantes Bonzo decided he didn't like
the food and drink offered backstage, so he took the big mal-
let he used to pound his thirty-eight-inch symphonic gong and
destroyed the three trailers being used as dressing rooms backstage. The group then went back to its little hotel, which they
decided looked more like a shelter for homeless vagrants.
Robert tried to get some milk for his tea and was told the hotel didn't have any. So the road crew was summarily un-
leashed. They took doors off their hinges and moved them
around. They flooded two floors with the fire hoses. They
plugged up the toilets and destroyed the furniture. They ter-
rorized the other guests. They were just having fun.

Benoit Gautier had sneaked out with Jimmy and Robert to
get something to eat at the only restaurant in Nantes that was
open all night. Half an hour later Bonzo staggered in with
Cole and the roadies, all drunk, looking for a meal. Bonzo
hurled insults at Jimmy for not waiting for him and sullenly
sat down to eat. When drunk, Bonzo would actually growl
like some wounded and dangerous pit bull, so Gautier referred to him as Le Bête—The Beast. Jimmy and Robert
thought this was hilarious. The Beast—of course! The nickname stuck.

After dinner Gautier, Jimmy, and Robert climbed in the
Volvo and prepared to leave. But suddenly Bonzo and the
roadies piled in as well. Gautier had to drive back to the hotel with sixteen people hanging out of the car, screaming and
singing through the deserted streets. As they went, the roadies
started demolishing the car, prying off the trunk lid, the sun
roof, all four doors, the tool kit, jack and spare tire, throwing
them all in the street. Suddenly a police car began to follow
them, followed by several more. Gautier began to panic. As
the only Frenchman, if arrested, he alone would be held liable for this English riot. So he swerved down side streets and
alleys, trying to dodge the police as the musicians and roadies

laughed hysterically, and somebody kicked in the dashboard with the heel of his boot. They were finally stopped at a roadblock by the entire local *gendarmerie*. Everybody tried to run, but they were surrounded and arrested and taken to jail. "Don't let them know I'm French," Gautier begged in a whisper.

The police had already been to Led Zeppelin's devastated hotel and were not amused. Gautier tried to explain and was locked into a cell for his troubles. Then everyone was locked up. But Richard Cole wasn't intimidated by French cops; he made everybody sing soccer chants at the top of their lungs. Soon the police were confronted by sixteen drunken British musicians and roadies singing pub songs and football cheers at the top of their voices. The police cracked in five minutes. The Zeppelin entourage was released, bused to their hotel, and locked in their rooms until morning. The Volvo was returned to the rental agency the next day a skeleton of its former self.

There were two more dates (at Marseilles and Lille) scheduled before the important Paris shows, but since the promoter had disappeared Peter canceled them and decided to head to Paris for a few extra days of wine and women. They decided to go by train. Peter paid for the tickets from a giant sack of jumbled European currency he carried around. Jimmy was late for the train, so the roadies held up the crack, obsessively on-time Nantes–Paris express for twenty minutes by jamming the doors. When Bonzo discovered that the train's bar car was closed, he again went berserk and had to be restrained from wrecking the rest of the train.

In Paris Led Zeppelin checked into the Hotel Georges V, one of the great luxury hotels of the world. Surrounded by tapestry-covered walls, Empire furniture, and their own dirty laundry, Led Zeppelin set out to have fun, shepherded by Benoit Gautier, who says that they asked him for anything except drugs. "It was obvious that some of them were using drugs," he says, "but they were very discreet. They never asked for grass or anything; they asked for legal things, mostly girls. Prostitution is legal in France. They wanted good booze, nice parties, and amusing people. Peter Grant would say, 'I want everybody to have a good time tonight, can you find six real beautiful girls?' " So Benoit would call Madame Claude, the most famous and expensive madam then in Paris, and would get back to Grant with the price. "You knew that at Madame Claude's it would cost an arm and a leg," Benoit says, "but at least you knew you would get a girl with two arms and two legs for the price." On another evening a sex show was arranged at the hotel. The boys wanted to see two girls making love to each other. The room was darkened and the girls were told to make it look real, as if the group weren't watching. Just good clean fun.

Gradually Gautier came to know the individuals in Led Zeppelin and came away with several interesting insights. Like many who knew John Bonham, he asserts that Bonzo had a split personality. "He could be the most generous guy and the worst guy," Gautier says. "Bonzo would cry talking about his family. Then the roadies would start to push him to do something, and he'd go crazy. He would throw drinks or dump food on somebody if Jimmy told him to. He had no natural defense against being manipulated, and nothing to protect him." Once Bonzo offered Gautier a big line of cocaine, and Benoit was about to indulge when he looked at the dope carefully and saw it wasn't cocaine, but heroin instead. "But it's smack!" Gautier said, somewhat amazed. Bonzo thought this prank was so funny he started to roll around on the floor. "He thought that was the funniest thing, offering you coke and giving you smack. He would take a chance on killing you!" The next day, Gautier admired a beautiful western shirt that Bonzo was wearing, and Bonzo stripped the shirt off his back and gave it to him.

Later Benoit went shopping with Robert for a fur coat. "Robert was truly a nice person," he says. "He never harmed anybody, had good manners, was always smiling. . . . He reminded me always that Led Zeppelin was two sets of guys. Two were from the music industry, who planned everything and knew what would happen. And the other two were what I call 'the fairy tale guys,' the two guys from out of town, Robert and John."

Gautier's description of John Paul Jones is perhaps the most surprising, considering Jones's reticence. "You wanted to be bright, intelligent and cultured with him. He was so smart, and could have been the most vicious and dangerous of all of them; he wasn't, but he could have been. He happened to be the act, but he could have run the record company as well.

"Of course, Jimmy was the mastermind of it all, and seemed very much in control. When I saw Jimmy doing cocaine one day I was totally shocked. He didn't seem like that kind of guy. And not only was it shocking that it was Jimmy, but that he would show that side of himself. That was the first time I ever saw Jimmy lose control.

"That's when I started to think that the wisest guy in Led Zeppelin was John Paul Jones. Why? He never got caught in an embarrassing situation. He would always show at the very last minute for *anything*. You'd never even know where he was staying. He drove himself, and was independent from the rest of the band. Peter and the band were always saying, 'Where the fuck *is* he?' It upset them that they couldn't manipulate him. He didn't give a damn. I would say that he was the most mischievous in the band. He was the kind of person who enjoyed mind games. He might say, 'Hmm, Jimmy seems tense, wouldn't it be funny if someone threw a firecracker at him.' And of course John Bonham would then throw the firecrackers at Jimmy. I thought he was *brilliant*. He could do any other job and had a great sense of a practical joke."

The European tour ended in Paris with two shows at the Palais des Sports in early April. Again there was trouble with dodgy French promoters. There were two; one held the license for the show and the other held the money, and they were arguing with each other about money at the hall. Grant wouldn't let the band leave the Georges V until he had their money in hand. While Grant was arguing with the promoters, Richard Cole was rifling a woman's handbag he had found in an unused dressing room. The night's receipts were in the handbag; Cole pocketed them and whispered to Grant that he could send for the group.

Two Americans arrived in France in time to see the second Paris show the following night. One was in his fifties, a well-dressed man in a suit and tie. The other was in his early twenties and had longer hair than anyone in Led Zeppelin. They were the band's new press agents from New York.

The older man was Lee Solters, the top show business press agent in America, who included Frank Sinatra among his clients. The young man was Danny Goldberg, then twenty-three, who had worked for *Billboard* and written for *Rolling Stone* and was now learning public relations from Solters while working for his firm. Peter Grant had been referred to Solters by Grant's new American business partners. In preparing for Led Zeppelin's upcoming thirty-three-show tour of the United States that would begin in May 1973, Grant had extended his unique musicians-take-all philosophy even further, taking Led Zeppelin away from its old booking agents, Premier Talent in New York. By self-promoting Led Zeppelin's shows himself, in association with a California firm called Concerts West and promoter Jerry Weintraub (who promoted the almighty Elvis himself), Led Zeppelin could save yet another 10 percent and keep even more of their concert fees. Again, it was a bold and innovative move, but in the short run it earned Led Zeppelin the hatred of the music middlemen—the agents and promoters who dominated the concert industry—and would later hinder Led Zeppelin's efforts to establish its own record label.

On the plane to Paris Solters asked Danny if he should take this new client, Led Zeppelin. Were they big? Were they any good? Danny explained that they were very famous to their fans, but now needed to reach the mainstream audience. The problem was that they had a negative image in the press and were regarded as wild barbarians. Even *Rolling Stone*, when it covered them at all, considered Led Zeppelin "crass" and tasteless, as well as guilty of the greater sin of actually stealing and recycling blues songs without acknowledging their sources.

So what's the *pitch*, Solters asked. Everything had to have a pitch. Danny suggested that on their upcoming tour Led Zeppelin should do a couple of benefits in aid of a hypothetical museum of the blues in some as yet unspecified southern locale. That night in Paris Led Zeppelin blasted forth with "Rock and Roll" and the Palais des Sports erupted with highly amplified hard rock. After the first song Solters leaned over to Danny and said, "You handle it." Later, during the softer, ringing acoustic set, Solters remarked that he was surprised. Jimmy Page was really a good musician.

The next day they had their first meeting with Peter Grant at the Georges V. Solters, who believed in being honest with a client, explained that Led Zeppelin had an image problem and were considered barbarians by the media. Grant thought this was a great laugh. Later, when Solters and Danny were introduced to the band, Peter Grant prompted Solters: "Tell the boys what our image is in America. What is that word? What do the press think of us?" Solters motioned to Danny Goldberg to answer the question. He gulped before answering that the press considered them mild barbarians. Much chuckling ensued, and Danny thought the band seemed pleased.

Later Robert Plant took him aside and said, "Look, you gotta realize I was young when I first went to America. I was nineteen years old, and I went crazy. I met the GTOs and my mind just snapped. I'm from a nowhere town in the Midlands and here were these girls with bare breasts blatantly coming on, and of course we went crazy the first few tours. But those days are completely over. We're *adults* now. We're successful business men. I got all that other stuff out of my system." Danny mentioned something later about Led Zeppelin's reputation for violence, and was told by Robert, "Hey, c'mon, this is crazy and very exaggerated. When we started in the sixties it was a little crazy, but since then we don't know anybody, there's been no one to tell our side of the story."

John Bonham was also quite effusive at the meeting. He wasn't drunk and impressed Danny as having a childlike quality. "You mean," he would say, "you're gonna try to reach the people that *don't* know about us? Is that the idea?" When told that was the idea, Bonzo said quietly, "Thank God you're here. We're the biggest, and we're the best, and *no one* knows it. You gotta do something about this."

John Paul Jones sat impatiently through the meeting and seemed sullen and truculent. Jimmy was quiet also, and made only a few bitter comments about *Rolling Stone.* "And he was just gorgeous," Danny says. "It was all the eyelashes and that choirboy's face. And he was just such a *star.* It seemed to radiate out from him." Danny pitched Led Zeppelin the angle of the blues museum benefits, and they seemed to like it. It was agreed that Danny would be the publicist when Led Zeppelin's ninth tour of America began in Atlanta the following month.

The 1973 American tour would be the biggest campaign Led Zeppelin had waged to date, covering thirty-three cities from May to July with a break in the middle. The tour alone was expected to gross $4.5 million. In early May London's *Financial Times* quoted Peter Grant's estimate that the group would earn $30 million that year. Accordingly, the tour was planned in style. Jimmy's fear of flying had not abated. He told a reporter that he had to be really drunk to get on a plane, and described how he once looked out a plane's window and saw gasoline pouring out of the wings. In the past Grant had chartered a small private jet for the band to jump from city to city, but Jimmy didn't like it. This time Grant chartered *The Starship,* a converted Boeing 720B jetliner owned by the former producer of the Monkees television show. *The Starship* had been redesigned as a forty-seat luxury plane decorated in Las Vegas lounge style with a long bar, video screens, plush chairs, bedrooms with fake fireplaces and showers, all the comforts. There was even an organ. The plane was fabulously expensive to charter, but to Led Zeppelin it was worth it. It allowed them to live in one city, commute to gigs in nearby towns by plane and limo, and return that night to a familiar hotel instead of the usual disorienting jump from one motel to another.

There were also major changes in Led Zeppelin's act. Arrangements were altered to accommodate Jones's new keyboards, and "No Quarter" featured dry ice to produce a creeping fog effect on stage. In the past Led Zeppelin had gone out with nothing but their music and their priapic personalities. Now they hired a Texas-based company called Showco to provide a full light show, mirrored light balls above the stage, huge revolving reflectors near the drums, exploding cannons and smoke bombs to stun the audience during the show's finale, and thirty attendant crew members to manage all this plus the sound system. In addition each musician had his own personal roadie. Ray Thomas worked for Jimmy, tuning the different guitars needed for each song. Benji LeFevre coordinated the artificial vocal effects for Robert. Brian Conliffe, who had worked for the Yardbirds, worked for John Paul Jones. Bonzo's drum roadie was a good-natured Cockney named Mick Hinton, who had once worked for Ginger Baker and now served Bonzo as valet and co-conspirator. These gentlemen were also responsible for stocking their musicians' hotel suites with creature comforts, as outlined in a pre-tour memo. Jimmy was to have fresh flowers and fruit, bottled water, an electric kettle, curtains pulled and candles lit, cold champagne, chilled orange juice, and a stereo in the bedroom tuned to the hip FM station of whatever town they happened to be in. Robert was to have the same, along with a supply of Earl Grey tea, honey, and lemons. Bonzo wanted a sheepskin rug as well. Jones wanted a piano wherever possible.

The entourage also included the English minstrel Roy Harper, who would open a few of the larger shows for Led Zeppelin. Harper was an expert guitarist and a hyper-graphic, Celt-obsessed poet who sang his urgent verses in a reedy high tenor. He was admired and coddled by Jimmy and Robert. Jimmy had even played on two of Harper's folkish albums, *Life Mask* and *Stormcock*. For both Plant and Page, Harper seemed to symbolize the innocence, sensitivity, passion, and idealism that they had sacrificed to Mammon, the god of money. To them, Roy Harper was an English lyric poet, and had to be treated with care and courtesy by the normally bestial road crew. "I personally never was infatuated with Roy Harper," Richard Cole says. "'Fucked if I know why they loved him so. He was just a pain in the ass to me." But Harper exchanged meaningful winks and enigmatic Bob Dylan quotations with Robert, and was generally considered heavy by the rest of the entourage.

Just before they left for America, there was discussion about filming the tour. A documentary crew had taken some footage during one of the 1970 tours, but nothing had come of it. Now they were approached by a film maker named Joe Massot, a friend of Jimmy's paramour, Charlotte. Massot had worked on a sort of rock western called *Zachariah*, and wanted to shoot Led Zeppelin's tour for a feature-length film. Massot had seen their triumphant show at Bath several years before, and now proposed a docu-drama of concert footage and "fantasy sequences." But Grant turned down the idea as too expensive with not enough time to prepare. Soon he would change his mind.

As Led Zeppelin was landing in Miami a few days before their first show in Atlanta, *Houses of the Holy* knocked off Elvis's *Aloha from Hawaii Via Satellite* to become the number one album in America. But that didn't prevent the press from landing on the album. *Rolling Stone* called it "a dose of pabulum" and a "limp blimp," and the rest of the press dutifully heaped on scorn and derision. Danny Goldberg, now deputized by the band as "Goldilocks" because of his long hair, had planted a tour story in *Rolling Stone* with a made-up quote from Jimmy on an impending announcement concerning "what we consider a long-standing debt to American blues musicians who have influenced our music." This was the brief-lived blues museum scheme that was quickly dropped as needless when the tour began to create its own publicity sizzle with broken attendance records and highest grosses ever.

The band was staying at the Doral Hotel in Miami. Maggie Bell was around, and the Bee Gees were dropping in and out. There were final fittings for Jimmy's black stage costume, spangled with crescent moons and silver stars. Since one of Lee Solters' clients was *Playboy* magazine, Danny Goldberg was approached to see if some *Playboy* bunnies might be available for Led Zeppelin's amusement. Danny earnestly replied that he didn't think this would be possible.

The musicians, especially Robert and Bonzo, were jittery and nervous. Robert told Danny that criticism of *Houses of the Holy* had devastated the band, and they were scared they might have lost it. But his fears were allayed on May 4 as the tour opened at Atlanta's Braves Stadium. Forty-nine thousand tickets had been sold, breaking a local crowd record held by the band Three Dog Night. From their hotel suite the musicians could see the great mass of kids filing into the stadium. Jones leaned out the window and said, "C'mon people, bring us all your lovely money!" At this, Robert Plant—high priest of rock communion and a true believer—was actually offended. "Jonesy!" he exclaimed. "How can you be so cynical. These are *our people*." Later, as the band played, Peter Grant took Danny Goldberg to the top parapet of the stadium and showed him the panorama. Inside the stadium the kids were completely bonkers. Then Grant gestured at the people on the adjacent freeway, oblivious to Led Zeppelin.

"Those," Grant said, pointing to the cars going by, "are the people I want you to reach for us."

The next night Led Zeppelin drew 56,000 people in Tampa, Florida, breaking the Beatles' eight-year-old record for the largest attendance ever for a performance by a single act. The show grossed $309,000 compared to the $301,000 the Beatles' had grossed when they had played for 55,000 at Shea Stadium in 1965. Danny Goldberg dutifully reported this to the wire services, who splashed it all over the newspapers of America. The next day Goldberg got an angry call from Steve Weiss, Zeppelin's lawyer in New York. "Where did you get that gross?" Weiss demanded. Danny explained that he simply multiplied the ticket price times the attendance, and that when you break records, the gross is part of the story, the *only* part that really meant anything to the workaday press. "Led Zeppelin *never* gives out grosses," Weiss snapped. "From now on, never give out grosses on any Zeppelin dates." A few days later Peter called Danny into his suite. Danny waited attentively as Grant snorted an unspeakable amount of cocaine into his gigantic nose. Then Grant said, "It would be really good if you could put something in the press about how Zeppelin was the biggest thing to hit Atlanta since *Gone with the Wind*." Danny gulped, and stammered, "Well, somebody has to say that. Do you want me to say that you said that?"

Grant scowled as if he were speaking to a dullard. "No, *I* don't want to say that. I just thought it would be good for the *press* to say that." Unsure of whether this was a moment of stoned dementia or a deeply desired wish, Danny threw caution to the wind and attributed the quote to Atlanta's mayor, who had requested backstage passes for his relatives. Two key New York rock journalists, Lillian Roxon and Lisa Robinson, picked up the quote, and Grant was satisfied. When Danny got Led Zeppelin on the front page of the *Atlanta Constitution*, blanket coverage by the wire services and a feature in the New York News syndicate, it was received with a grunt and a shrug. It was really the British press they cared about, because it was the British press that had slagged them the most in the past. When another laudatory *Financial Times* article appeared, Robert excitedly put his arm around Danny's shoulder and rasped, "My dad finally believes I'm a success. He's read that paper ever since I can remember. Now he finally thinks I may have done the right thing not to become a chartered accountant." When London's *Daily Express* reprinted verbatim one of Danny's statistic-filled press releases (the press in general was lost as to what else to write about these uncouth musicians) under the headline BELIEVE IT OR NOT—THEY'RE BIGGER THAN THE BEATLES, Danny's job as publicist was assured. Gradually he was accepted into the tight Zeppelin entourage. Since he was physically present at many of the concerts, the band came to think that Danny "believed" in them, and he was initiated into their boisterous locker-room intimacy. Bonzo would grab his crotch and ask, "How's yer nob?" Jimmy would joke with him and engage in civilized conversation. Jones took his frustrations out elsewhere. Initially, Danny had trouble convincing journalists to even come to Led Zeppelin's shows. Finally he persuaded Lisa Robinson, the New York correspondent for the British music paper *Disc*, who was initially terrified to meet them. But Led Zeppelin turned on the charm, and Lisa began to file complimentary *Disc* columns in which Led Zeppelin's friends and families could read about their American conquests. Lisa had been impressed by Led Zeppelin's St. Petersburg show and said so in her other outlets, *Hit Parader* and *Creem*. She was also willing to file innocuous items in her column that mattered to the band, usually self-righteous remarks about how much they missed their wives, which fooled no one including most likely the wives themselves.

As the tour progressed through eighteen more cities before the break, the group grew to love the comforts and amenities of *The Starship*. There was no more waiting in airline terminals, ogled by leering provincials. Now the limos pulled right up to the waiting plane in a private corner of the airport. There was hot food so the band could eat, and the booze flowed ceaselessly. Thai beer was served. "It was a fucking flying gin palace," Cole says. On the way back from gigs, Jones would play the organ and the band would sing old songs.

In New Orleans they stayed at the famous Royal Orleans Hotel and cavorted with the French Quarter's rampant drag queen population. By day, Robert would hold court at the Royal Orleans observation deck overlooking the Mississippi, dressed in a skimpy red bikini. At night, Richard would take the band out to gay bars, where they caught the attention of the Bourbon Street drag queens. One fell for Robert and lavished him with silver and turquoise bracelets. Another came on to Jones, who took him back to the hotel not realizing it was a man. Late that night Peter Grant got a call from the Royal Orleans night manager, who said that "Mr. Jones is all right and so is his friend." Grant called up Richard Cole and told him to go have a look. So Cole went to Jones's room and found the door broken off its hinges. Apparently, according to Cole, Jones and a drag queen called Stephanie had smoked a joint and then passed out drunk. The joint had caught the bed on fire, and the fire department had broken down the door to discover Jones and Stephanie unconscious, "with her dick hanging out." Cole duly reported back to Grant, and Jones was teased relentlessly about his *faux pas.*

"Nothing ever went on," Cole says of Led Zeppelin's penchant for gay bars. "It was a fascination that all of us seemed to have, gay clubs and all of that. Anyone who travels knows that the gay people seem to have a better fucking time than the straight people. They don't bother you or pester you. They didn't give a fuck who Led Zeppelin were, and they always had the best music. Whereas you go to other places and people want this and that. When the group's done a show, it takes a lot out of everybody. Everybody who participates is fucking *drained.* You just wanna be left alone. I don't want people coming up to Jimmy, because then I have to throw people away, or kindly ask them to move and sometimes they won't move and I give 'em a flick of the foot to the jaw and someone *carries* them out."

After their show at New Orleans' Municiple Auditorium, during which Jimmy had suggestively bowed Robert's bum during "Dazed and Confused," the band went to the Gateway, at the corner of Bourbon and Iberville, to see Frankie Ford. Robert Plant, dressed in a glittery silver blouse open to the waist, asked Ford to sing "Sea Cruise," his big hit from the fifties. Later they went to a club called the Déjà Vu, whose owner asked Led Zeppelin to imprint their hands in the fresh cement outside. "Why don't you get them to put their cocks in," Grant suggested. Robert said he didn't think his would make an imprint. From New Orleans the band flew out to other southern concerts—Jacksonville, Tuscaloosa, St. Louis, and Mobile. Lisa Robinson reported: "And there were no gimmicks. No tuning up, no intermissions, no mandatory opening act, no platform shoes, no stage show, no dancing girls, no spaceship, no rhinestones, no bullshit. Just four boys and two and a half hours of their music . . ." To Robinson, Robert expressed his philosophy: "I like to think that people go away knowing that we're pretty raunchy and we really do a lot of the things that people say we do . . . this is what we're getting over: it's the *goodness*. It's not the power, revolution, put your fists in the air. I like them to go away feeling the way you do after a good chick, satisfied and exhausted. . . . Some nights I just look out there and want to fuck the whole first row."

Before they left New Orleans Led Zeppelin was given a party by Ahmet Ertegun at a studio called Jazz City. The menu was soul food, with entertainment provided by the cream of the Crescent City's R&B masters—Ernie K. Doe, Professor Longhair, Snooks Eaglin, and Willie Tee. The Meters also played, as did the Olympic Brass Band and the Wild Magnolias. John Paul Jones played organ while a stripper mimed wild love to a tabletop. Standing together in the crowd, Jimmy and Robert watched in awe as the elder statesmen of rock and roll strutted their stuff.

As the tour headed toward sweet California, the repertoire

and collective Zeppelin improvisation got much hotter and wilder. Only the opener, "Rock and Roll," was played to the exact same number of bars every night, which somehow kept the rousing fanfare fresh for the band. The concerts invariably finished with the traditional flame-up of thousands of lighters and matches, which looked like a sparkling galaxy from the band's perspective. The shows in both Dallas and Fort Worth were sold out, and Jimmy was impressed that a trio of rich Texas groupies had hired their own jet to follow the band around.

When they finally arrived in Los Angeles, Jimmy managed to injure his right hand, badly spraining it on an airport fence. The May 30 concert was postponed for a few days later, but Jimmy made it to the Forum the following night, May 31, after immersing his swollen hand in ice water all day. "Good evening," Robert said to the audience after Zeppelin's initial bombardment. "This is Bonzo's birthday party. I met him . . . I've known him for about fifteen years and he's been a bastard all his life." Then they went into "Misty Mountain Hop," "The Song Remains the Same," and "The Rain Song"; during the slow Mellotron sections, the restless fans started to hoot for boogie. "Dazed and Confused" was now clocked at an easy half hour on self-indulgent nights. It featured eccentric bluegrass runs over funk, "Crunge"–type guitar, and a quiet, folkish guitar prelude to Robert singing a snatch of "San Francisco"—". . . be sure to wear flowers in your hair . . ."—before the obligatory bow section now reminiscent of the Ligeti modal choirs of the *2001* sound track and various horror movie themes. As Jimmy splayed out great washes of doomy sound, Robert would join with orgasmic grunts—"*Push! Push! Push!*" Bonzo would bash away murderously and then Jimmy might play a little "Purple Haze." Led Zeppelin threw in everything *and* the kitchen sink. After "No Quarter," Robert announced that Jimmy had sprained his finger, which drew an appreciative round of applause. "Here's a song about you," Robert said, and they went into the thud-boom riff of "The

Ocean." Then Robert led a sing-along of "Happy Birthday" to Bonzo before beginning "Whole Lotta Love," two choruses only and right into the middle section, which that night was Jimmy's James Brown riff sliding into the whooping and screeching theramin threat display. Gesturing wildly with his arms at the theramin, the black-clad Page posed as a wizard, drawing dread, sirenesque wails from the little black box.

After the show the band went to a birthday party for Bonzo at the Laurel Canyon home of a local radio station owner. Also at the party were George Harrison and his wife. Harrison had been observing Zeppelin quite closely, hanging out backstage at some of the Southern California gigs. One night he had asked one of the roadies, "Who goes on first?" He was told that there was no opening act; he asked if there was an intermission and was told no. "Fuck me!" Harrison exclaimed in disbelief. "When the Beatles toured we were on for twenty-five minutes and could get off in fifteen." Led Zeppelin was always thrilled when one of the Beatles came around to see them. They were of that first golden generation of English rock heroes, to whose universal fame and acceptance Zeppelin aspired.

As Bonzo was about to cut his huge cake, a drunken George Harrison rushed forward, picked up the cake's top tier, and heaved it at Bonzo, who apotheosized into The Beast. He picked up the rest of the cake and threw it at Harrison, who was trying to beat a retreat. Later Bonzo picked up George and Patti Harrison and threw them into the pool, followed by the rest of the party except for Grant, who was simply too big and mean for anyone to throw in. Jimmy protested meekly that he couldn't swim, and was allowed to walk into the pool in his immaculate white suit with the "Zoso" emblem embroidered on the lapel.

At the Riot House there were the usual outrages. Led Zeppelin had the eleventh floor to themselves. At slack moments Richard Cole would roar down the corridor on a big Honda motorcycle that he had sneaked in via the freight elevator.

On the plane to L.A. Jimmy had been shown a copy of *Star* magazine by Danny Goldberg. "Jimmy went out of his mind," Danny said. "He said, 'Look! There's a new generation of groupies in L.A.! Do you know them? Do you have phone numbers?" Led Zeppelin's ground-zero in Los Angeles was the Rainbow Bar. There they were given their own cordoned-off section and were treated like royalty. Women knew where to find them. The whole entourage could go, so Led Zeppelin had safety in numbers and no chance of the rejection they had suffered during leaner years. They could get loaded, hold court all night, and go home with whomever they wanted. Their only worry was that the stray girls would get into the photographs and alarm their wives back home.

Jimmy was locked into his suite with Lori Maddox, who had now achieved the matronly age of fifteen. There had been several death threats against Jimmy, and private security guards were posted outside Jimmy's suite in shifts around the clock. At the same time Bonzo and the Zeppelin roadies observed their annual ritual of wanton hotel destruction. Entire suites of furniture went over the balconies. After the lads had been upbraided by the owner of a Lincoln convertible onto which they had been pouring their drinks and then their glasses from the eleventh floor, someone threw a table over the side and demolished the car. The televisions went next. Watching a big color TV exploding on pavement from a great height was a favorite Zeppelin pastime. The previous year at an old battleground, the Edgewater Inn in Seattle, Led Zeppelin had thrown all their televisions into the sea below. As Peter Grant was paying the bill, the hotel manager wistfully remarked that he had always wanted to chuck a TV out the window himself. "Have one on us," roared Grant, and peeled off another $500 bill. The manager went right upstairs and heaved a big Motorola off the balcony.

But it wasn't always like that, despite all the legends of nonstop mayhem. Danny Goldberg remembers a greater reality: "My take on this period was that it was really boring. They were *tired*. One of the stories that doesn't get told was how many times there *weren't* wild parties, and how lonely and exhausted they would get, and how they would be so worried about what they looked like in a picture and would their wives be mad at them."

On June 2 Led Zeppelin flew into San Francisco to head-line an all-day show at Kezar Stadium promoted by Bill Graham. After Roy Harper had opened the show and the Tubes and Lee Michaels had played, it was 2 P.M. and Zeppelin was supposed to go on. But Led Zeppelin was in the air aboard *The Starship*, still en route from L.A. After a wild limousine dash from the airport, Led Zeppelin went on at three thirty. They played so loud that the leftover hippies along the fa-mous Haight-Ashbury "Panhandle" could hear them clearly a half mile away. Three blocks away, patients at the Univer-sity of California Medical Center complained they couldn't sleep. Zeppelin played until six and then went backstage to confront Bill Graham, who was angry about the delayed show. Peter Grant and Bill Graham were like King Kong and God-zilla in terms of their personalities. They were two truly tough guys. And Graham couldn't believe he had to pay that kind of money to Led Zeppelin. So there were bad feelings and arguments about money all day, and Graham's people wouldn't let Zeppelin's photographer onstage. In tricky situations Led Zeppelin would think of humiliating pranks and get Bonzo to perform them. So after the show Bonzo poured a bucket of cold water on Bill Graham, who was not amused. Bill Graham was treated like hip royalty from the sixties by every other manager, but not Peter Grant, who said, "No one gets paid a premium for being hip by my band." Graham disliked Led Zeppelin, but made a lot of money from them.

The first half of the tour ended the next day in Los Ange-les, with Led Zeppelin reviving the Yardbirds' "I'm a Man" and Freddie King's "I'm Going Down" in the encore.

During the month-long break in June, Led Zeppelin scat-tered. Robert bought a sheep farm on the Welsh coast, and Jimmy bought the landmark "Tower House" in London's

Kensington section from actor Richard Harris, paying £350,000 after outbidding David Bowie. Built as an eccentric home by an Edwardian architect, the house was a marvel of decoration and artisanry. Each room represented some natural theme—butterflies, the sea, astrology—and anyone walking its exquisite rooms and halls had the distinct feeling of being in the presence of some higher consciousness. Jimmy was still living at Plumpton Place, but the Tower House would soon become a refuge. Meanwhile, he wasn't allowed to touch his guitar for a month while his hand healed.

When Led Zeppelin met again in Chicago on July 6 for the second leg of the tour, conditions had changed. There had again been a serious death threat against Jimmy by a deranged man who had told a mutual friend to warn Jimmy that he would be killed while on tour. Jimmy claimed the man was later tracked down and put in a mental hospital. But the security guard remained outside his door twenty-four hours a day. "Led Zeppelin was always the focus of death threats," Danny Goldberg said, "because of their occult association and their big success. The '73 tour was the first time that significant death threats had been directed toward Led Zeppelin, so it was taken very seriously. Later, the death threats became routine."

Roy Harper was also back. "Jimmy and Robert considered him a great thinker and visionary," according to Danny. "So Roy Harper was treated with tremendous deference, and catered to by everybody else. But he was also getting crazier and would stand offstage holding this toy black rubber gorilla, which he would shake during Zeppelin's show as if the gorilla were some magical fetish that empowered the band." This went on for several shows until one day Robert's roadie, Benji Le-Fevre, turned to Danny and said, "I don't care what *anyone* says, this guy is six bricks shy of a full load." Suddenly the bubble burst. The crew had been treating Harper like Dylan Thomas for weeks. Soon Richard Cole started grabbing the poet by the neck and throwing him into the last barge in

Zeppelin's limo convoy, traditionally the conveyance of choice for Led Zeppelin's sleazy, unwanted entourage. The entourage was also later joined by B. P. Fallon and a film crew assembled on the spot by Joe Massot, whom Peter had called with three cities left in the tour after he had a revelation that a film of the tour might be valuable after all.

By the time the film crew arrived Led Zeppelin was headquartered at the Drake, a grand dowager of a hotel on New York's Madison Avenue. Every night the entourage would jump into a fleet of limos and drive to the Newark airport where *The Starship* waited, fueled and ready, at a private corner of the tarmac. On the first night of filming Led Zeppelin posed on the wings of the big jet, next to the huge letters of the group's name that had been painted on the fuselage, while the film crew clicked and whirred. In Baltimore the entire audience of 25,000 rose and fired their lighters as the group walked in, before Led Zeppelin had played a note, as a silent tribute to unadulterated charisma and unity. Jimmy was taken aback, stopped dead in his tracks by the honor. He later said that for him it was a moment of true magic.

A few nights later they flew to Pittsburgh. Danny Goldberg had convinced a writer from *Playboy* to come along. Also on *The Starship* were Ahmet Ertegun and half a dozen harlots in floppy silk playsuits (actually the roadies' girl friends), who chatted with Jimmy and B. P. Fallon during the flight. Magnums of excellent champagne and very cold Thai beer flowed freely. Peter Grant, his gigantic bulk wrapped in a Hawaiian shirt, glowered menacingly at the team from *Playboy* and the man from *The Daily Express* that Danny had brought along as well. Bonzo berated the male member of the *Playboy* team because Led Zeppelin hadn't done well in *Playboy*'s music poll. Robert flirted with the female reporter the magazine had sent. "See you later without your clothes on," he said. The Zeppelin limo convoy got a sirens-wailing police escort from the airport to Pirates Stadium. The twenty-foot stage platform sat in the middle of the outfield in the big baseball park.

Jimmy, in a white linen suit and a black shirt, had his red Gibson slung low along his crotch and his lips pulled into a tough pout; he did the gunfighter boogie all night, evoking noises from his theramin that sounded like Venusian police calls. Robert was in his usual skintight jeans and an open vest that revealed his bare chest. He strutted and preened, shook his hips and thrust out his breast, glistening with sweat. He bumped and ground, preened with exaggerated braggadocio and threw his hair back like some hippie Jesus. The thick July heat turned the concert into a delirious steambath. Stage lights glowed in hues of saffron, cerise, indigo, aquamarine, and emerald. At the show's climax, "Whole Lotta Love," Led Zeppelin's Old Testament and standard edition of Freud condensed into one volume, two hundred white doves were released. Backstage, Richard Cole jostled the reporter from *Playboy* and then threw him off the stage. And by the time the show had finished and the first fans were reaching their cars in the parking lot, Led Zeppelin was aboard its *Starship*, flying to New York.

The pace picked up even faster as the long, exhausting tour wore to its conclusion. In Boston the Zeppelin roadies went into action against a Teamsters Union goon squad that had appeared backstage at Boston Garden in an attempt to shake down Led Zeppelin. Peter Grant and his private army bloodied their faces and sent them away.

The tour ended with three shows at Madison Square Garden in New York. The Drake Hotel was plunged into the chaos. Richard Cole's suite was a madhouse of friends wanting tickets, publicists, hangers-on, groupies, people selling rare guitars, and dope dealers. The telephones were ringing off the hooks with interview requests. The media were paying attention, at last! *Rolling Stone* had finally offered Led Zeppelin its cover if Page and Plant would do interviews, but was turned down flat. All the television offers were turned down as well. Led Zeppelin was proud of turning down those.

Robert would occasionally wander into Cole's suite, look-

ing for Burmese beer and tickets for friends from Birmingham. Then Jimmy would materialize, pale, white and
wraithlike in a black velvet suit. He was by then something
of a basket case. His wounded hand was still bothering him,
and it took a concerted effort of pure will to get it to play the
guitar every night for three hours. Also, the past two weeks
had been deadened by death-threat paranoia. Jimmy hadn't
slept for a fortnight, sustaining himself on dope, booze, and
room service hamburgers. On the night of the first New York
concert, his limo had pulled up to the freight entrance of the
hall when a long-haired kid threw himself on the car and
shouted, "Jimmy, Jesus is here!" The police dragged him off
and beat him. It was unnerving. To a reporter, Jimmy whispered, "We're all terribly worn out. I went past the point of
no return physically quite a while back."

Meanwhile, the film crew, which had been put together
on three days' notice, had to keep shooting over and over again.
They were, for some reason, unable to film a whole sequence of "Whole Lotta Love," and couldn't persuade the
truculent John Paul Jones to wear the same shirt for three
nights for the sake of continuity. It was madness.

It got worse, though, when Led Zeppelin was robbed of
approximately $200,000 on its last night in New York.

When the band had first checked into the Drake, Richard
Cole and lawyer Steve Weiss deposited an undetermined sum
of cash (which has been estimated at between $180,000 and
$203,000) in the hotel safe. Led Zeppelin always carried large
amounts of cash, according to Cole, "in case we wanted to
buy a guitar in the middle of the night, or a bit of blow." But
since the tour was over, even more cash was on hand to pay
for the airplane and the film crew after the last show.

"I went down to the safe at two or three in the morning
after one of the concerts," Richard Cole says, "to get some
money for a guitar that Jimmy wanted to buy, and the money
was there then. Then we slept all day. Then, on the night of
the last show, when I went to get the money to work out the

accounts at the Garden, when we were just about to get into the limousines, I opened the thing and there was *fuck-all* in there. There was no money, just the passports. I fucking screamed."

Cole said nothing to the band, who were already keyed up for their last show. He sent the limousines off and stayed behind to call attorney Steve Weiss. Then he let himself into the musicians' rooms and "sanitized" them for what he knew would come. Two hours later the rooms were thoroughly searched by the FBI. Richard Cole was interrogated, fingerprinted, and asked to take a polygraph (lie detector) test, which he passed to everyone's astonishment.

At Madison Square Garden the band went on not knowing it had been robbed of a substantial fortune. Because the band had been hamming it up for the film crew, none of the New York performances was very effective. "Dazed and Confused" ran more than a half hour, as Jimmy used the violin bow to emit noon whistles and cybernetic death rattles before descending the purple haze into a jam on "Route 66" as Robert yelled "Oh, *suck it!*" and came in mock orgasm. While the band plowed through "No Quarter," there was consternation backstage. Danny Goldberg noticed something was wrong. The omnipresent Cole was missing and Peter Grant was in heated conference with Ahmet Ertegun. When the rest of the band came offstage during Bonzo's solo, they were told about the robbery. Strangely, they didn't seem that disturbed. As Jimmy Page later said, "It had reached a point where we really couldn't care that much."

Onstage, Bonzo played on, crashing out his brainless rhythms, drumming with his hands to create startling tabla-like inflections with dub-style pedal effects. He played bluesy little melodies on his ride and crash cymbals and the big thirty-eight-inch symphonic gong. When he came offstage and was told of the robbery, he blew up and turned into The Beast.

When the band got back to the hotel, they were grilled by the FBI. The robbery was a mystery. Cole had been officially cleared, but was still under suspicion. Either someone had a duplicate key or Cole had taken the money. (Later a hotel employee resigned under a cloud. But the money was never recovered.) The next morning the robbery made headlines in New York and the hotel was besieged by the press. Peter Grant slugged a photographer from the *New York Post* and was arrested and charged with assault. Danny wanted to set up a press conference, but nobody in the band wanted to do it. Bonzo was more upset than anyone had seen him. "If we do the press conference," Bonzo stammered, "we'll bloody well lose both ways. If we make like we care too much, they'll say we're only in it for the money. If we say we don't care, they'll say it's because we're too rich. So don't talk to the press." Eventually there was a press conference at which Peter Grant answered reporters' questions. Jan Hodenfield from the *Post* asked if the robbery was a publicity stunt. Grant looked like he wanted to devour Hodenfield's intestines. Asked why the band was carrying so much cash, Grant said they had to pay for their airplane. Asked if they were insured, Grant said no. Asked if Led Zeppelin now hated America, Grant protested, "No, we love America!"

Led Zeppelin flew home to England the following day. When Jimmy's family saw the state he was in—exhausted, malnourished, sleepless, raving—they tried to get him into a sanitarium for a rest. Jimmy himself told a journalist that he thought he belonged either in a mental hospital or a monastery. "I was thinking, 'What the hell am I going to do?' because it was like the adrenaline tap wouldn't switch off. During those concerts to that many people, there was so much energy being stored up. I felt like a kettle with a cork in the top. I'd stay up for five nights at a trot. It didn't seem to affect my playing, but I'd come offstage and I was not levelling off at all, not turning off the adrenaline. I couldn't. I felt I needed to go somewhere where there was a padded cell so I could switch off and go loony if I wanted. I was quite serious about it."

* * *

Again the band members scattered to their homes. In September Robert was voted the Number 1 male vocalist in the world by the readers of *Melody Maker*. The following month, Joe Massot's film crew began to film the individual members of Led Zeppelin around their homes; this footage would be intercut with the previously shot tour footage as well as costumed vignettes that were supposed to signify symbolic representations of the band and its entourage. Jimmy was filmed playing guitar on the shores of Loch Ness at Boleskine. His vignette involved the film crew building large camera scaffolds to shoot multiple retakes of Jimmy climbing up a rocky mountain. At the top, at night under a full moon, Jimmy appeared as the Old Man of the Mountain, holding the lantern of the Hermit of the tarot. Robert was filmed at his farm in Wales and at Raglan Castle, where an archetypal Celtic hero-myth was enacted by Robert, a lovely blond actress, and a horde of extras posing as medieval churls. Bonzo's bit was more straightforward. The drummer shows off his farm, the prize bulls, the massive car collection, and drives down to the pub for a few pints. Jones was shot at home in Sussex, reading *Jack and the Beanstalk* to his daughters. Dressed as the Phantom of the Opera, he posed playing a giant organ and night-riding through the Sussex countryside. Eventually Jones got bored and told the crew to go away. And Peter Grant and Richard Cole were dressed up as twenties gangsters, given machine guns and an old roadster, and were filmed shooting up a house. All of these sequences would later be matched to the appropriate music in the film. But the whole band harbored strong doubts about the film. Grant, who was financing it himself at an astronomical cost, derided the footage as the worst, most expensive home movie ever made. Later in the year, when Led Zeppelin had screened some of the footage and realized how mediocre their filmed, end-of-tour concerts had been, they decided to scrap the whole project.

Jimmy Page, meanwhile, was back at work. Rehearsals had begun for the next album, which he was planning as a double album with six or seven new tracks added to the band's outtakes from as far back as Bron-Yr-Aur. He was also under some pressure from Kenneth Anger, who wanted the sound track Jimmy had promised for *Lucifer Rising*. The music was coming slowly, emerging as chilling, spine-tingling synthetic chants and mantras overlaid on one another. Jimmy was frequently asked about his interest in the occult. Once he was asked what historic personage he most wanted to meet. His answer was Machiavelli, the author of that ultimate text on manipulation, *The Prince*. "He was a master of evil," Page said. ". . . but you can't ignore evil if you study the supernatural as I do. I have many books on the subject and I've also attended a number of séances. I want to go on studying it.

"Magic is very important if people can go through it," Jimmy was quoted. "I think Aleister Crowley's completely relevant to today. We're all still seeking for truth—the search goes on." In the same conversation Jimmy was asked his opinion of women, and his answer was quite telling: "Crowley didn't have a very high opinion of women and I don't think he was wrong."

Elsewhere Page was quoted as having feelings of exaltation mixed with foreboding. "I know what my musical direction is now," he said at the end of 1973, "and at those times when I've hit it, it's just like I'm a vehicle for some greater force." But he also spoke of a race against time, and a feeling of things closing in on him. Asked about the future of the band, Jimmy Page spoke prophetically: "We'll be together until one of us punts out."

EIGHT

AN ANGEL WITH A BROKEN WING

Technique doesn't come into it. I deal in emotions.

—JIMMY PAGE

Led Zeppelin's original five-year contract with Atlantic Records had expired at the end of 1973, and the price of renewal would be high for Atlantic. After an all-night negotiating session between Peter Grant and Ahmet Ertegun, the normally poised Turkish diplomat's son staggered out of the room muttering, "Peter, you're taking me to the cleaners." In January 1974 the two held a joint press conference in London to announce the launch of Led Zeppelin's yet-unnamed record company, to be distributed by Atlantic. Most artist-operated labels, like the Rolling Stones', were basically vanity operations catering to its stars. But Led Zeppelin's label was planned as an active company run by Peter Grant with an eye to breaking new acts. The endless capital would come from Led Zeppelin's bottomless pot of gold at the end of the rainbow, located somewhere in the American Midwest. There was already talk of who would be on the label besides Led Zeppelin; Maggie Bell, trying to launch a solo career under Grant's direction, already had an album (with Jimmy on two tracks) in the can. A new group called Bad Company was fronted by Paul Rodgers, the great young rock singer from the band Free, and guitarist Mick Ralphs from Mott the Hoople. Bad Company played compact, terse, hard rock and Grant was convinced they would be very big. Jimmy and Robert were also keen to sign Roy Harper and the Pretty Things, which had been one of the main London R&B bands of the early sixties, along with the Stones and the Yardbirds, and had now regrouped under original member Phil May. Robert was particularly keen on the Pretties. "We're going to work with people we've known and we've liked," Robert said. "It's an outlet for people we admire and want to help . . . people like Roy Harper, who is so good and whose records haven't even been put out in America. People there have yet to discover the genius of the man who set fire to the pavilion at the Blackpool Cricket Ground. Roy is not too happy at the thought of approaching stardom." So unhappy, in fact, that he set many strange preconditions and was never signed to the label.

In New York Danny Goldberg received a phone call summoning him to meet with Peter Grant in England. The young publicist caught a plane to Heathrow and was met by a limousine, which took him to Grant's moated estate in Surrey. Danny was shown up to the bedroom, where Grant received him in an enormous bed, clad in nightgown and sleeping cap. "Jimmy likes you," Peter said, which was his way of stroking people. He told Danny that the new label needed "an ambassador" to America and asked if he wanted the job. Danny said he'd think it over. Back in New York, he debated his move. "I agonized over it because of their bad reputation," he says. But it felt right. Friends like Lisa Robinson said, "Do it, they're the biggest group in the world." Others said that Steve Weiss, Zeppelin's lawyer, could be very tough to deal with. But Goldberg accepted the job and was installed as a vice-president of Peter Grant's holding company, Culderstead Ltd., on the top floor of the Newsweek tower on Madison Avenue in New York. In London the new label set up shop on the King's Road in Chelsea.

Recording for Led Zeppelin's sixth album had begun back in November 1973, at Headley Grange with the mobile studio owned by Ronnie Lane, the former bass player of the Faces. But John Paul Jones had become ill, and the sessions were postponed until early the next year. But Jimmy and Bonzo made a guitar and drums demo for a song in a vaguely "Eastern" key that grew out of Jimmy's cheesy Danelectro guitar solo on "White Summer." It would be the third in a series of layered, harmonized guitar pieces that had begun with "Stairway to Heaven" and continued through "The Song Remains the Same."

The sessions resumed in February 1974, again with Ronnie Lane's mobile. With Robert's epic travelogue lyrics ("Oh father of the four winds, fill my sails . . .") the Page/Bonzo demo turned into "Kashmir," complete with Dravidian guitar vamps and Jones's synthesized Arabian orchestra in the bridge. Monumental and melodramatic, "Kashmir" would become the next major Zeppelin theme. But its incantatory invitation ("Let me take you there . . .") was only rhetorical. Nobody in the band, they were later quick to say, had actually *been* to Kashmir.

Led Zeppelin was hot, and the new songs came quickly, drawing on the usual, traditional sources. "Custard Pie" was Led Zeppelin's second raid on Bukka White's "Shake 'Em on Down," with chainsaw guitar, wailing harp and an ambience of unrepentant raunch that was as fresh as new dung. "In My

Time of Dying" was an old spiritual that had been revived by
Bob Dylan years before. Jimmy covered it with his weird, ec-
toplasmic slide guitar before blasting in hard, up-tempo Zeppelin rock. The track ended with Robert calling on Jesus (an
anomaly in a Zeppelin recording) and dissolving into a comic
coughing fit. "In the Light" looked east again, replicating the
drone of the harmonium (with overdubbed bowed guitars) and
the Indian *shenai*; the lyrics again described a spiritual quest
before another of Jimmy's multiple guitar choirs. "Trampled
Underfoot," one of the undeniably great rock songs, started
as a Jones clavinet riff related to Stevie Wonder's "Supersti-
tion." Like Robert Johnson's "Terraplane Blues" and Chuck
Berry's "Maybelline," the song described a woman in terms
of car parts.

Other songs were more purely Zeppelin. "Ten Years Gone"
described Robert's regrets over his first girl friend, who demanded that Robert choose between her and his music. The
parting had been a sad one. "Sick Again" and "The Wanton
Song" were basically reprises of "The Rover" and "The
Crunge" respectively; both related to the ever-younger flock
of teen-age girls who besieged Led Zeppelin in California after
the legend of Lori Maddox had filtered down to the high
schools. To these eight new tracks, seven older Led Zeppelin
outtakes would be remixed and added to produce the double
album that Jimmy had wanted to do for years. The guitar
breakdown "Bron-Yr-Aur" and the shimmering seascape of
"Down by the Seaside" both dated from the 1970 sessions for
Led Zeppelin III. "Night Flight" (which could have been a
Rolling Stones track) and the jam called "Boogie with Stu"
(Ian Stewart) were both from the 1971 sessions that had produced the untitled fourth album. The remaining three tracks
were from the year-old Stargroves sessions. "Houses of the
Holy" was supposed to have been the title track of their last
album. "Black Country Woman" had been recorded out in
one of the gardens and was a loose, informal jam, compared
to "The Rover," a taut, intricate hunk of leaden bump over

which Robert declaimed his most visionary plea for unity and friendship, the old ideals of the sixties now forsaken in the so-called "Me Decade" of the seventies.

Although these fifteen tracks would be mixed by June 1974, it would be another year before Led Zeppelin's double album would actually be released.

During the sessions Jimmy, Robert, and Bonzo came down to London to help Roy Harper with his Valentine's Day concert at the Rainbow Theater. Robert and Bonzo took the train from Birmingham, got quite drunk, and giggled all the way to town like schoolboys. In London Led Zeppelin usually stayed at Blakes Hotel in south Kensington, where Bonzo could usually be found roaring in the hotel's small basement bar. Robert hosted the concert in leopard skin drapes and a slicked-back duck-tail hairdo, and was barely recognized by most of the crowd.

While in London the band had a meeting to decide the name of their new company. At first, deliberately crude names like Slut Records and Slag Records were projected and rejected. Then they wanted Eclipse Records, but the trademark lawyers discovered that one already existed. Several other names were suggested, and the meeting broke up with no decision. Subsequently Maggie Bell's first album for the label, *Queen of the Night*, came out on Atlantic instead because Led Zeppelin couldn't come up with a suitable name for its own label. Eventually they settled on Swan Song. It was originally the name of a twenty-minute acoustic guitar piece that Jimmy had recorded. Then it was going to be the name of their next album before finally turning into the name for the label. Since the term *swan song* usually referred to somebody's last gasp, there was some concern about possible negativity, which Jimmy brushed off to Danny Goldberg: "They say that when a swan dies, it makes its most beautiful sound." The subtext seemed to be that if Led Zeppelin was on some kind of death trip, at least the music sounded great. Choosing such a morbid name would prove prophetic. In a year circumstances would change for Led Zeppelin in unforeseen and uncontrollable ways.

Led Zeppelin had incredibly high expectations for their label. Having known instant success themselves, they assumed that their new label-mates would as well. "We didn't want to get bogged down in having to develop artists," Jimmy told a reporter. "We wanted people who were together enough to handle that kind of thing themselves, like the Pretty Things." So the band was disappointed that Maggie Bell didn't sell as well as they'd hoped. In America Danny Goldberg orchestrated an expensive press crusade on her behalf. She got great reviews, was hailed as the English Janis Joplin, but the records just wouldn't sell.

It had been decided to launch Swan Song Records with elegant receptions in New York and Los Angeles in May 1974. The parties would also introduce Bad Company, whose first album was about to be Swan Song's first official release. In New York there were other problems to be taken care of. A new movie, *Phantom of the Paradise* (directed by Brian de Palma), contained a fictitious record company called Swan Song. But when Zeppelin's lawyer had filed for a protected trademark, he had also bought out an old label called Swan Records, which gave Led Zeppelin a back-dated trademark. One day Steve Weiss and Peter Grant were screening the film to note how many times the offending "Swan Song" would have to be deleted. Suddenly, a rock star in the film was electrocuted onstage. It was too much like what had happened to Grant's client Les Harvey, and he began to weep. He ordered Weiss to have de Palma cut the electrocution out of the film as well, and Weiss had to gently explain that this probably wouldn't be possible.

Back in England the musicians were restless and looking forward to the parties and ensuing mayhem in America, which they hadn't visited in almost a year. Jimmy was isolated in Sussex with Charlotte and their daughter Scarlet. The former owner of Plumpton Place had raced horses; now his stables provided shelter for goats and chickens, Jimmy's Range Rover, and a rare, classic Cord automobile. Inside, Jimmy lived amid his art collections, Crowley artifacts, and considerable archives of rock and roll ephemera. Thousands of records littered the floors. A nearly complete collection of the Sun Records catalog occupied a special case. Robert's farm, meanwhile, was overrun with children and family and Robert's old cronies. Bonzo and John Paul Jones were stir-crazy as well.

The problem was that Zeppelin's wives didn't like their husbands going off to America to play. Whenever they saw "Los Angeles" on the typed itineraries the musicians were sent by the Swan Song office, their wives got very nervous. They knew full well what L.A. represented to Led Zeppelin—an open-armed Babylon of dope and very young girls. So for this trip, Danny was ordered to prepare *fake* itineraries that Led Zeppelin could show their wives. These documents showed that the launching parties for Swan Song in America would take place in Denver and Atlanta. Look, the musicians could say, look how *horrible* this is! We have to go to Atlanta and Denver on boring business, be back in a few days, what a drag!

In New York the musicians moved into the St. Regis Hotel. At night they hung out at the *au courant* Club 82. Lori Maddox was flown in from L.A. to attend Jimmy. The Swan Song luncheon was held at the Four Seasons, a tasteful business restaurant on Manhattan's East Side. Peter Grant had suggested that swans be rented for the restaurant's small pool, but Danny Goldberg had only been able to find what a New York animal purveyor had called "swan geese." When Grant saw these birds he lashed out at Danny: "We all fucking live on *farms*! Who are you trying to kid? *Get these geese out of here!*" Two hundred writers, radio people and assorted industry types had been invited and were eating cream pastries shaped like swans. "Current good taste being what it is," observed the *New York Post*, "the four-man British group sequestered themselves in a corner and no one lowered himself by actually making an announcement." The highlight of the party came when Paul Rodgers, the twenty-five-year-old singer of Bad Company, threw food at Steve Ross, the head of Warner Communications, the parent corporation of both Atlantic and Swan Song Records. But Ross took the good-natured insult in stride. "It was OK because Peter Grant was the *street*," Danny Goldberg says. "Peter Grant could deliver rock and roll that was guaranteed to make money."

After the party, Bonzo kept drinking. That night he blundered in backstage at the Uris Theater on 54th Street, where Mott the Hoople was playing. Bonzo wanted to sit in on drums and jam, and was told to piss off, no arrangements had been made. No English roadie could tell Bonzo to piss off, and suddenly there was a violent fight backstage. Mott's road crew thumped Bonzo soundly and threw him out of the theater on his arse.

The next day Jan Hodenfield of the *New York Post* showed up at the St. Regis for an interview with Jimmy that had been set up by Danny Goldberg. As recorded in the *Post* (with expletives deleted), the reporter was waiting in one of the Zeppelin's suites. "A press agent is frazzling, a lawyer pacing, young ladies grouping, a photographer is clutching his equipment and various roadies are swerving in and out. From the next room lunges Led Zeppelin manager Peter Grant, a 300-lb. former wrestler who looks to be en route to a Genghis Khan look-alike contest.

" 'Where the fuck is Danny Goldberg?' bellows the manager to a suddenly silent assemblage. The prospective interviewer, to mitigate the silence, volunteers that Mr. Goldberg the press agent had departed for another suite. 'Who the fuck are you?' inquires the manager of the highest grossing rock and roll band in the world. 'Why don't you get the fuck out of here?' "

Danny was discovered supplicating outside the door of Jimmy's suite. Inside, all that could be heard were Lori's giggles. Finally Danny arrived at the correct password and the door was opened. Hodenfield and Danny found Jimmy eating french fries as Lori watched him in rapt attention. "Interview?" murmurs Jimmy. "What interview?" "The one you promised yesterday," Danny replied. "Ummmm," Jimmy mumbled. "Well, I'm eating breakfast you know."

Hodenfield continues:

" 'Oh no, wait,' sighs the star, eyelashes rising from position of parade rest on pale cheeks. 'I suppose I could talk to you. For a little while. I do have to pack. And I do have to shave. And I did promise the photographer he could take some pictures. But I *suppose* I *could*.'

"He bangs the bottle of ketchup onto the potatoes and, with thumb and index finger, daintily lifts another potato to his mouth. His companion continues her vigil of attentive adoration. The press agent rings his hands.

"The star tosses his curls winsomely and plucks another potato drenched in ketchup.

"The hush is cathedral-like.

"The prospective interviewer tabulates his prospects and beats it to the street where, with crowds rushing through the afternoon sunlight, he stands wondering why he's staring at a manhole."

In Los Angeles, where the Swan Song party would be held a few days later at the Bel Air Hotel, Led Zeppelin hunkered down at the Riot House on Sunset. There, Lori Maddox lost Jimmy Page to Bebe Buell, an older woman of nineteen. And Led Zeppelin got to meet their main inspirer, the King of Rock and Roll, Elvis Presley himself.

The meeting with Elvis took place in a hotel suite across from the Forum, where Elvis was appearing. Led Zeppelin had been at one of the shows when Elvis turned to his band, which included Jimmy Page's early idol James Burton on guitar, and told them that they'd better play their best because Led Zeppelin was in the audience. Since Elvis shared a promoter, Jerry Weintraub, with Led Zeppelin, Elvis knew that the English band was outselling him. He would say to his own entourage, "Well, I may not be *Led Zeppelin* but I can still pack 'em in." Before Led Zeppelin was allowed into the presence of the King, they were sternly warned not to speak to Elvis about music. After they were introduced and had been given drinks, Bonzo got into a conversation with Elvis about cars. After half an hour Elvis's bodyguards motioned that it was time to go. As they were leaving Robert gushed, "Elvis, you're my idol. Thanks for letting us come." The King responded by singing the beginning of "Treat Me Like a Fool." Robert sang the second line: "Treat me mean and cruel." Together Elvis and Robert Plant sang the last line: "But *love* me." For Led Zeppelin the best part of the visit had been when Elvis *asked for their autographs.* He said they were for his daughter, Lisa Marie.

Back at the Riot House, the scene was ridiculous. Dozens of pretty and barely pubescent young girls were camped in the lobbies and corridors, throwing themselves at anyone vaguely connected with the band. Despite the security guard standing watch, half a dozen teen-age girls were sleeping outside Jimmy's door every night. In his suite Jimmy kept two refrigerators stocked with cold beer. One was for him and his guests; from the other he would extract cans, open his door with the chain on, and throw cold beer to the feral girls out in the hall. Lori Maddox had been Jimmy's main squeeze, but he had other girl friends on the scene as well. Chrissie Wood, wife of Ronnie Wood of the Stones, was in residence. And Bebe Buell, a beautiful model then living with Todd Rundgren and about to make her media debut as a Playboy Playmate, was due to arrive any day. A photographer for rock magazines found her way into Jimmy's bed as well.

One evening the band decided to dress up in drag and take some snapshots for their next album cover. Lori, Chrissie Wood, and Miss Lucy from the GTOs plastered makeup all over Robert, Bonzo, and John, while Jimmy was given a

striking bouffant coiffure. George Harrison was waiting in a
suite downstairs to go to dinner with Led Zeppelin, and so
the boys decided to give George a surprise. "But what they
didn't know," Lori remembers, "was that Stevie Wonder had
come along with George Harrison and was down there too.
All the guys came traipsing into the suite in makeup and dresses
and there's *Stevie Wonder* sitting there! Can you imagine? Can
you just *imagine*? There's Led Zeppelin all in drag and Stevie
Wonder thinks the guys are doing it as a *joke* on him because
he was blind. They almost died from embarrassment."

Shortly before the Swan Song party, Bebe Buell arrived at
the Riot House with her coatimundi, a South American mar-
supial that the Zeppelin entourage thought was a raccoon. Bebe
was living with Todd Rundgren, but had met Jimmy a couple of times with actress Patti D'Arbanville and was infatuated with him. So when Jimmy sent her a plane ticket to Los
Angeles, she packed up the coatimundi and flew west. "Todd
was always in the studio or on the road," she says. "I loved
him, but I just didn't see enough of him." Jimmy welcomed
the beautiful girl with his usual gallantry. "He was a charismatic devil, and we're all looking for that knight in shining
armor," she says. "And he played that role very well, only
instead of a horse he had a jet." At the Riot House Jimmy
put Bebe's pet into a closet with a bunch of fruit baskets that
fans had sent.

The reception for Swan Song was held on one of the lush
patios of the Bel Air Hotel. Led Zeppelin had ticked off a big
list of Hollywood celebrities for Danny Goldberg to invite.
They wanted only the biggest names—Robert Redford, Warren Beatty, Gloria Swanson, Bette Davis, Jane Fonda. In the
end, only Groucho Marx was persuaded to come, as well as
actor Lloyd Bridges and a few visiting English rock stars, among
them Bill Wyman of the Stones and Bryan Ferry from Roxy
Music. Bonzo asked Ferry for an autograph for his son, Jason.

As usual, the musicians sequestered themselves into a corner and avoided the rest of the party. Too shy to just go over

and introduce themselves to Groucho Marx, they kept sending Danny over to get his autograph. Groucho was frail and
old, but still radiated stardom. Finally Boz Burrell of Bad
Company wandered over and got a splendid autograph.
Groucho traced his own hand on a piece of paper and signed
it. Then Maggie Bell went over to speak with him. When
Groucho heard her heavy Scots burr, he started to sing "I Be-
long to Glasgow."

Although Miss Pamela and most of the other girls in Jimmy's past and present were there, Bebe Buell was Jimmy's
designated escort. Lori Maddox was in a state about this. She
had taken a Quaalude and wandered about the party looking
dazed, beautiful, bruised. Somehow she had bloodied her nose
and her snow-white dress was stained red. As Jimmy and Bebe
were leaving, Lori jumped out from behind a statue, crying
to Jimmy, "Why are you *doing* this to me? Why won't you
talk to me? How can you *do* this to me?" Jimmy tried to ignore her and jumped into the limo. He later told Bebe that
Lori was too young to know how to mix fantasy with reality.

Later, after the party, they all went to the Rainbow. Jimmy
had an emotional public row with Bebe, who told him he
was being cruel to poor little Lori. Inside the bar, a drunk
tried to impress his girl friend and started to hassle the Zeppelin table. Usually when this happened Richard Cole would
take the offender outside and thrash him. This time Cole gave
the particularly obnoxious drunk what Cole calls "the flick of
the foot." Cole's karate kick caused the man's jaw to break
and his teeth to fall on the floor right in front of the Zeppelin
entourage.

The next morning Lori showed up at the Continental Riot
House, as she always did, to have breakfast with Jimmy. But
before she could get to the elevator, Richard Cole grabbed
her. Just then one of her teen-age lookouts ran up and said,
"Lori, Bebe's up in the room with Jimmy!" And Cole was
saying, "Aah, Jimmy just went down to Hollywood Boulevard to get some books and wants me to have you wait in my
room."

But Lori said, "I'm not waiting in your room; I have the key to *our* room." But Cole was adamant, and Lori followed Cole to his room. But after Cole left, she slipped out and followed him up to Jimmy's suite, where she says she found Jimmy and Bebe in bed.

Jimmy looked at Lori and said, "Oh my God, I can't believe this is happening."

"And I'm like *crushed*," Lori remembers. "It was just *awful*." She ran out. A few hours later she waded through the crowd of girls camped outside Jimmy's suite and knocked on the door. Bebe opened the door with the chain on to see who was there, and Lori attacked her, grabbing Bebe by the hair and trying to drag her out of the room, encouraged by the corridor girls who hated Bebe Buell as a rival interloper from back East. Sitting calmly in his suite, watching as two of his girl friends tried to tear each other's hair out, Jimmy was amused. Later he told friends that the whole thing was incredible, *hilarious*.

A couple of weeks later in England, *Melody Maker* filed a report about the glamorous Swan Song party in Los Angeles and the uproar at the Rainbow later. There was a picture of Robert and his glittering young date. This was seen by the wives and there was hell to pay. The fake itineraries had said the party was in Denver! Peter Grant called Danny Goldberg in a rage, demanding to know how this got into the press. Trying to suppress his fear, Danny suggested that if Led Zeppelin wanted privacy, they shouldn't hang out at a notorious groupie saloon like the Rainbow Bar on Sunset Strip.

The summer of 1974 passed uneventfully, as various members of Led Zeppelin rested and played an occasional gig. John Paul Jones played bass behind Roy Harper at a free concert in Hyde Park. Joe Massot had been fired from Led Zeppelin's film project; he was accused of mixing up the group's priorities with his so-called "fantasy sequences" and of having missed too much when filming on the road. His greatest sin appears to have been that he didn't shoot a complete "Whole

Lotta Love." Later, when the film was resurrected by necessity, Massot would be replaced with an Australian named Peter Clifton.

On September 14 the whole band attended Crosby, Stills, Nash, and Young's mammoth concert at Wembley Stadium. Bonzo arrived dressed in country squire tweeds and plus fours. Jimmy and Robert were still infatuated with California country rock. In interviews that year both spoke incessantly of their deep love for Joni Mitchell and her then-current record *Court and Spark*. At a party after the Wembley show, Jimmy jammed with Stephen Stills and Graham Nash until well after dawn. A week later he flew to the States to jam onstage with Bad Company in Austin, Texas, and Central Park in New York. Bad Company's tough, spartan album of hard rock, with hit songs like "Can't Get Enough," had performed as expected. By the end of September it was the number one album in America. It was rare enough that an unknown group had made it to the top with a debut album; but it was unheard of that it was done on another rock group's vanity label. The Led Zeppelin magic was definitely holding fast. Around the same time, Jimmy, Robert, and Bonzo flew to L.A. to jam with Bad Company. Everybody stayed at the Beverly Hills Hilton. On the drive from the hotel to the Forum, as his limo was jammed by traffic near the arena, Plant opened his sun roof and stood up on the seat to look out. He was instantly recognized by fans milling about, and he began to beat his chest and shouted "*My people*" at the fans before cooler heads dragged him back into the car.

At home in Sussex Jimmy was increasingly restless and itching to get back on the road. His various relationships with women were getting confusing. At the same time, the whole band decided that Led Zeppelin would join many of its successful friends in a year's tax exile abroad. Britain's onerous tax laws meant that its most successful pop musicians were sometimes taxed for most of their royalty income. Other British rock stars like the Stones and Rod Stewart were living out of the country, in France or America. Though they were tied to their families and homes for emotional sustenance, the musicians decided that a year's tax exile would be in everyone's interest.

Jimmy prepared for this by running off with Chrissie Wood. One day Ron Wood and his pretty blond wife had driven out to Sussex to visit Jimmy and Charlotte. Sometime during the visit Jimmy and Mrs. Wood walked off the grounds and disappeared. They never came back, according to Bebe Buell, who had flown to London under the impression that *she* was going to run off with Jimmy.

For a time, Jimmy moved into Tower House, his London abode in Kensington. Amid the surreal, breathtaking artisanry of the house, he tried to put his life together. Bebe came to visit him and was awestruck by the house itself and its thematic rooms. The bedroom was covered with paintings and carvings of butterflies, and there were stained glass butterflies in the windows. There was an ocean room, with a spectacular mermaid holding a mirror that seemed to rise out of the fireplace. The astrology hall had the entire zodiac painted on the ceiling, while in the dining room a catholic confessional disguised a dumbwaiter. Down in the basement Ken Anger was trying to finish *Lucifer Rising*, working on the expensive German editing table that had been bought for Zeppelin's film. Jimmy had loaned Anger the basement of what the film maker called "that evil fantasy house" in which to work. But because of Jimmy's paranoia about the house's furnishings, Anger was literally locked in the basement, unable to go upstairs to make a cup of tea without setting off the burglar alarm. Jimmy, working in his attic studio at Plumpton, had completed only thirty minutes of music for Anger's film. "I had asked him for intimacy and strength, rhythms and counter-rhythms," Anger says. "But he gave me a short fragment of chanting voices and sounds that I thought were quite somber and morbid. He didn't seem to pay attention to what I wanted and seemed very out-of-touch all the time."

Earlier, Jimmy had financed an occult bookstore in Kensington for his astrologer. Jimmy had stocked the shop himself with various rare and antique books on magic and the occult that he picked up on buying trips to rare book dealers. The bookshop was named the Equinox, after Aleister Crowley's own occult magazine. When Jimmy ran off with Chrissie Wood, Charlotte moved into the bookshop for a while. Chrissie was installed at Tower House. One day, when Jimmy was out, a crazy American girl broke into the house, setting off the burglar alarm. When arrested, she explained to police that the ghost of Jimi Hendrix had ordered her to go to London and marry Jimmy Page. Describing the incident later to Danny Goldberg, Jimmy expressed horror at what might have happened. Danny thought Jimmy was concerned about possible harm to Chrissie Wood, but no. "What if she had slashed the tapestries?" Jimmy asked.

Around this time Jimmy made some informal recordings with Keith Richard and Ron Wood at Wood's house, "The Wick," which had been owned by actor John Mills. When Jimmy and Chrissie ran off, Jimmy had been concerned about Wood's reaction, but his fears had been allayed when Wood rang him one day and blithely inquired, "How's our bird?" The session with Keith and Woody produced a song called "Scarlet," named after Jimmy's daughter.

Swan Song's first release in England was the Pretty Things' album *Silk Torpedo*. The album was launched at a blasphemous Halloween party at the Chislehurst Caves on October 31. Naked women lined the recesses of the cave and reclined before altars in the style of the black mass. Strippers dressed as nuns doffed their black habits and swung their pendulous bosoms. Fire-eaters and magicians walked through the crowd, and everyone got roaring drunk. The party ended with Bonzo and the roadies throwing gelatin at each other.

Silk Torpedo was a good album, and Led Zeppelin presumed it would enjoy the same success as *Bad Company*. Peter Grant's instincts, it seemed, were infallible. He had forced

Atlantic to release Badco's "Can't Get Enough" as a single, and the song had gone to Number 1.

Led Zeppelin flew out of England and into tax exile in the beginning of 1975. They were planning to stay on the road for that whole year, playing America, Australia, and perhaps South America. Rehearsals for this mammoth tour began in late November 1974 at a converted theater in Ealing, west London. It had been almost eighteen months since the band had last played in public as a group. Reeling from the vagaries of his love life, Jimmy remained stoical. "1974 didn't really happen," he was quoted. "1975 will be a better year."

NINE

NOBODY'S FAULT

By remaining calm at the center of a disintegrating culture he is providing an example for its future development. If we need heroes, then rather Jimmy Page than political buffoons or licensed jesters or sporting apes; rather the shy, nervous, steely youth whose songs are inspiring a generation.

—TONY PALMER
The Observer

Two days after the thirty-first birthday of "the shy, nervous, steely youth," Led Zeppelin went back to work. They did warm-up shows in the Low Countries for the immense tour of North America scheduled to begin in Minneapolis on January 18, 1975. The tour would be the band's most ambitious campaign to date. The forty shows in twenty-six cities would gross over $5 million. And since Led Zeppelin had been starving its slavish audience for two years—no television, no tours, no albums—the audience responded to tickets sales with an unexpected, maniacal frenzy. In New York a mob overran a Ticketron outlet on Long Island and had to be dispersed with fire hoses. In Washington fans threw bottles at police trying to control the ticket lines. In Boston the management of Boston Garden had taken pity on several thousand kids camped outside in subfreezing temperatures to get tickets the following day, and allowed them to sleep in the unguarded arena, which the fans then proceeded to sack. The mayor of Boston canceled the show the next day, which saddened the band since Boston had been a Zeppelin hotbed since the earliest headbanging orgies at the Tea Party.

Aside from these minor acts of rebellion, the 700,000 seats available for the Zeppelin shows sold out in one day. At the same time, *Physical Graffiti* was released, a year late. Advance sales for Led Zeppelin's sixth album—a double set with the eight recent Headley Grange songs and seven outtakes—totaled $15 million. The album debuted on the *Billboard* chart at Number 3. Incredibly, at the beginning of 1975, Led Zeppelin had *nine* albums on the American charts. The excitement of the impending Zeppelin visitation had brought all six Zeppelin albums on the chart, and the three Swan Song LPs (Bad Company, Maggie Bell, and the Pretty Things) held respectable chart positions as well. The nine was the apex of Led Zeppelin's business career and an unprecedented coup. *Physical Graffiti*, perhaps the hardest hard rock album ever made, quickly climbed to Number 1 and stayed there for weeks. The intricate die-cut cover depicted a brownstone tenement through whose windows various cultural iconographs could be interchangeably viewed. Pictures of W. C. Fields and Lee Harvey Oswald alternated with the snapshots of Led Zeppelin in drag, taken the night they had grossed out Stevie

Wonder. Demand for the album was so high that one New York store reported selling 300 an hour.

In Swan Song's New York office atop the Newsweek building, the staff frantically tried to keep pace. Danny Goldberg was on a sofa in the corner of his office, which was decorated with various images of the blue Hindu god Krishna. "Goldilocks" had now been re-baptised by Robert Plant as "Govinda," after one of the blue god's legendary incarnations. Govinda was on the phone: "What can I tell ya, Max, I *can't* give you a job bodyguarding Jimmy Page because you're exactly who Jimmy hires security to protect himself *from*. I can't talk, I'm busy . . . I'll be busy for about a year, six months at least, call me later, God bless you, good-bye." Danny Goldberg's routine was being destroyed by hundreds of calls, most of them requests for tickets, interviews, photo sessions, any available piece of the hottest band in rock and roll. The logistics of the tour alone were crushing. *The Starship* had been leased again for an even higher fee. Forty-four roadies would deploy 310,000 watts of sound amplification, 150 lights (including 3 krypton laser beams), 5 light towers, plus the standard explosives, smoke machines, and dry ice makers. The sound system had been computerized and programmed with a then new digital delay function that could spew out torrents of feedback, howl like the furies, or synchronously provide harmonic effects on anything Zeppelin played or sang.

But the usual calamities and bad luck began even before the musicians had left England. Getting out of a train at Victoria Station, Jimmy injured the ring finger of his left hand in the train door. The tour was too big to be postponed by anything less than a fatal accident, so Page adopted what he called his three-fingered technique and dropped the arduous "Dazed and Confused" from the opening dates of the tour. There were other maladies. Robert was getting a bad cold and Bonzo had stomach problems, mostly cramps and loose bowels. For these and other reasons, a young doctor was hired to travel with Led Zeppelin aboard *The Starship* for the duration of the tour. The doctor had worked for the Rolling Stones and carried two enormous medical valises with him. He could treat any emergency from severe gunshot to depression and sobriety. The musicians snickered to friends that he gave them sexual stimulants and noticed that he had a sweet tooth: He was attracted to many of the younger girls who wantonly loitered in the lobby of Chicago's Ambassador Hotel and the other Zeppelin base camps along the tour.

Led Zeppelin landed in Chicago unprepared for the arctic gales of the Midwest in January. Robert stepped off the plane in a blouse and leather jacket, and his cold turned into a flu. Fur coats were hurriedly bought before the band flew north to Minneapolis to rehearse and open the tour. The new show again began with "Rock and Roll" and alternated unfamiliar numbers from *Graffiti* ("Sick Again," "Kashmir," "Trampled Underfoot") with older Zeppelin standards. "In My Time of Dying" was prominently featured as a morbid blues with a slide guitar that slithered like a languid cobra. There was a long acoustic set and all the other hyperkinetic blasters before the set ended *not* with "Whole Lotta Love," which now only existed as a vestigial eight bars leading into "Stairway to Heaven." By 1975 "Stairway" had taken its place as a pop anthem that had an ethereal, spiritual meaning for its fans. American FM disc jockeys of the era reported that the song was constantly requested by housewives during the daytime and by teen-agers at night. Radio stations often received requests that "Stairway" be played at a specific time to coincide with a teen-ager's funeral. Led Zeppelin's song of spiritual quest had taken root. Years later, more than a decade after its release, American radio programmers still considered it the number one rock song of all time.

Led Zeppelin then went back to Chicago and played a dismal three nights at Chicago stadium. Page's injured finger was soothed with constant oral applications of Jack Daniel's. Robert was performing with a high fever. But somehow they pulled it off. The special effects, especially the pencil-thin laser beams,

obscured some of the band's mistakes. These early shows also
included "The Wanton Song" and "When the Levee Breaks,"
which were then cut out. And of course the kids had come
not only to hear music, but to see mystique on the hoof. Jimmy's silk stage costumes were rampant with embroidered
dragons, wickedly crimson poppies, stars, crescent moons, and
esoteric symbols—the "Zoso" emblem, the sign of Scorpio,
and the stylized "666," the biblical *mark of the beast* that
Crowley and now Jimmy Page adopted as a dangerous personal emblem. The one number that consistently held the
shows together was "Moby Dick," Bonzo's drum solo. When
nothing else worked, when Jimmy was spaced out and Robert
couldn't get it up, Bonzo could still get a docile and restless
stadium full of white youths up and shaking. Offstage, he was
the monster Grendel, laying waste beyond the ramparts. Onstage, Bonzo could do no wrong, dressed in his current costume of mindless terrorism, the white boiler suit and black
derby of the *Clockwork Orange* droogs. He had been furious
when he arrived in Chicago to learn that he had placed below Karen Carpenter in the drummer's category of the *Playboy* music poll. To Lisa Robinson, Jimmy said he was
despondent about his injured finger and the less-than-killer
Zeppelin shows. Everything was going wrong, he said, and
he thought he was "reaping my karma, now, heavily." He
complained that he was still terrified of flying and had developed newer phobias such as vertigo and claustrophobia. After
the show Richard Cole dragged the band back to the hotel for
some of the old tarting-up before the obligatory visits to local
discos. But everybody felt sick or homesick or both. The tour
was slow getting started.

In Chicago both Robert and Jimmy spoke to Cameron
Crowe, a young reporter from *Rolling Stone*, who had a reputation for filing complimentary stories about the bands he
covered. Robert spoke somberly of growing older and the
changing scene in Los Angeles, where all their old playmates
had moved on or died of overdoses. Accused of writing "dated

flowerchild gibberish," Robert bridled and said, "The essence
of the whole trip was the desire for peace and tranquillity and
an idyllic situation. That's all anybody could ever want, so
how could it be dated?" Jimmy also dismissed any criticism
of the band. Asked what he would be like at the age of forty,
Jimmy answered that he didn't expect to see forty, but then
he hadn't expected to see thirty either. "I had this fear," he
said, ". . . I'm not afraid of death. That is the greatest mystery of all. That'll be it, that one. But it is all a race against
time. You never know what can happen." Asked about his
hopes, he replied, "I'm just looking for an angel with a broken wing."

From their base in Chicago Led Zeppelin flew on to shows
at the Cleveland Coliseum and the Indianapolis Arena. The
only rehearsals for this tour had been the two shows in Rotterdam and Brussels, and it showed, especially in the newer
songs from *Graffiti*. Finally Robert's flu became so severe that
a show in St. Louis was canceled on January 27. The doctor
put Robert to bed in Chicago and the tour was off for four
days. Rather than hang around in subfreezing Chicago, the
rest of the band and Peter Grant rode *The Starship* to sunny
L.A. Since they were paying a minimum of $2,500 a day for
the plane anyway, why not take a three-hour flight to California? It was Robert's hard luck.

Up in *The Starship* en route to Los Angeles, Jonesy was
sulking because he had suggested taking the plane to the
warmth of the Bahamas; but Jimmy's ardent desire to visit his
girl friends in Los Angeles had won the day, and the plane.
Bonzo had drunk an entire bottle of Scotch whisky by himself and had passed out in one of the aft bedrooms for two
hours. When he awoke, he was in his guise of the Beast.
Emerging blearily from the bathroom, wearing only his touring robe, he grabbed one of *The Starship*'s pretty stewardesses
as she passed him in the aisle. At first the unsuspecting girl
thought it was only a joke, but Bonzo suddenly bent the girl
over forward with an arm lock, pulled up her dress, and told

her that he was going to have her from the rear. Bonzo had thrown open his robe, and it felt like a rape, so the terrified stewardess began to scream. Richard Cole and Peter Grant immediately appeared from the other bedroom and quickly dragged Bonzo away from the girl, who was gently led off by a solicitous Jimmy Page, who took but ten minutes of soothing talk to calm the shaking girl's nerves.

There were several journalists on the plane as it flew west that night, including Chris Charlesworth from *Melody Maker* and tour photographer Neal Preston. As *The Starship* began its descent, Cole came up and demanded, quite sharply, "I don't want to see *one fucking word* of this in print. Understand?" Cole glowered at them. The journalists understood.

In L.A. they headed straight for the Rainbow. Most of the other English bands that passed through L.A. were fairly discreet (Elton John, the other big English rock star of the day, excepted). But Led Zeppelin publicly cavorted with the trashiest hardcore groupies around, as if they were spiritual sisters. And the scenes would get very crazy. Some drunk staggered up to Zeppelin's enclave and started screaming at Jimmy: "*You can't fucking play guitar!! Fuck you!*" Jimmy actually got up to whack the man but was restrained by Peter Grant, who warned that he had to remember his frail hands. The drunk persisted, so Grant rose and took the fellow outside and kicked him. Grant was about to whack the fellow when a slender young thing approached and sweetly asked, "Mr. Grant, can I please have your autograph?"

There was more madness two days later at the Greensboro Coliseum in North Carolina. Richard Cole was famous for his quick post-concert limousine escapes, but after this show hundreds of kids stormed the backstage area before Cole could get the limos out. The local drivers, more used to funerals, were quickly overwhelmed by the stampeding kids. Suddenly a windshield cracked on a Cadillac, then another. The roof of the band's car started to cave in on top of them. All they could see was a writhing mass of faces and bodies and *they weren't going anywhere.* So Peter Grant threw the driver out of the car by his throat and yelled, "I'll drive!" Behind them the second limo was taken over by a Deep Purple roadie called Magnet, Robert's childhood friend who had come along for the ride. Grant started to bump the police car stalled in front of him. The cop told Grant to stop and Grant yelled, "If you don't go fucking fast enough I'll drive right over you." Once the cars finally cleared the full-scale riot going on around the hall, they noticed they were being shadowed by carloads of hopped-up southern kids matching their eighty mph speed and even inching a little *closer* so their girl friends could look inside the limos. When they arrived at *The Starship*, wet and ready and gleaming under klieg lights, Grant was so relieved that he drove an extra "lap of honor" around the parked plane.

In New York, their next base camp, Led Zeppelin settled into the grand dowager Plaza Hotel. Before the hotel even let Bonzo check in, it demanded a $10,000 deposit for damages. The usual compliment of pianos and stereos were carted up to their suites; Bonzo demanded a billiards table so he could practice his snooker. Jimmy complained about his suite, which he said looked like fake Versailles. Robert made several forays to an Indian restaurant called Nirvana on Central Park South, where he continually reminded the waiters that he was married to an Indian woman.

Danny Goldberg had arranged a dual interview between Jimmy and the writer William S. Burroughs; the tape of the interview would be the raw material for a piece of Led Zeppelin to be published in *Crawdaddy* magazine. Page was of course thrilled and apprehensive. Like Crowley, Burroughs was an urbane and genial human Lucifer, a modern magus, a legendary addict, and an artist whose influence extended far beyond literature to music, painting, and film. Burroughs attended Led Zeppelin's first show at Madison Square Garden and sat in the thirteenth row, refusing cotton wadding for his ears even though Led Zeppelin was again playing as loud as the equipment could crank. Later, in his article, Burroughs was struck by how Led Zeppelin's audience was "a river of youth looking curiously like a single organism: one well-behaved clean-looking middle-class kid." He compared Led Zeppelin's loud music to the trance music of the Master Musicians of Jajouka in Morocco, who also played loud blaring themes with horns and thundering drums. Just as Moroccan music is used as psychic hygiene, Burroughs suggested, so Led Zeppelin's music was used by its audience for astral travel and spiritual regeneration. Later, when they met over dinner, Burroughs spoke effusively of Morocco and shamed Jimmy into admitting he hadn't yet visited there. Like everybody else, Burroughs was quite smitten with the retiring Page, and nattered on about the negative and positive effects of ultra-sound and famous incidents of fatal crowd stampedes in Peruvian soccer stadiums. Jimmy was outmatched and in awe, emitting his usual muttering strings of "hmmmm, yeah, uh-huh."

Back at the Plaza, Jimmy had set up a projector and was showing prints of *Lucifer Rising* to friends, trying to get more ideas to complete the sound track, now years overdue. He couldn't watch television because candle wax had dripped into the back of the set. There were lots of parties, including an all-night affair Atlantic had for the band at the Penn Plaza Club. The night's show had gone well—the band was finally sounding the way Jimmy wanted it to, and the only hitch had come during the limo escape when they were coming out of the hall to find a line of flaming garbage cans blocking their way. Several of the Rolling Stones were in town and came to the party. They would tour later in the year and Mick Jagger came to one of the Madison Square Garden shows so he could observe Peter Grant's methods firsthand. Ron Wood introduced the band to a middle-aged pharmaceutical heir who liked to give parties for British rock stars. The refreshments were unlimited quantities of apparently legal pharmaceutical cocaine. Later Robert went around showing off a telephone message slip saying that Mick Jagger had called him.

All this time Led Zeppelin was jetting to gigs around the East Coast. On *The Starship* Jimmy and Peter huddled in one of the bedrooms, off limits to the entourage. Bonzo usually rested or bullied those up front, while Jones was occupied with his floating high-stakes backgammon tourney. Robert, too full of adrenaline to sit still, bopped around the plane, chatting with Danny's media entourage, or watching the plane's supply of videos, including *Flash Gordon* and *Don't Knock the Rock*. Occasionally Bonzo would go out of control. On a flight to Detroit he was drunk and sullen. For no apparent reason, he grabbed the eyeglasses off the face of a startled Atlantic Records regional manager and crushed them with his bare hand, grinding the glass into the carpet. Without a word, Bonzo got up and walked to the back of the plane. The rest of the band was mortified. Richard Cole was immediately dispatched to soothe their very ruffled passenger. Each concert had its own incidents. Death threats were now ubiquitous, and two armed bodyguards, both former FBI agents, went everywhere with the band.

At the Philadelphia Spectrum a vicious fight broke out right in front of the stage during "Stairway to Heaven." A kid had come to the lip of the stage wanting to take a snapshot. Two middle-aged security men pounced on the kid and started beating him with their fists. Jimmy stepped to the front of the stage and was about to crown one of the goons with his double-neck guitar, but stopped. The guitar was virtually unreplaceable. So Robert stepped up and swung his mike like a golf club, punishing the brute with a bad shot to the head. The show went on, but soon the wounded security thug was seen backstage, cursing Robert out and working himself up. This began to annoy Peter Grant, who was finishing his third bottle of Blue Nun. The roadies were mobilized to hustle the snarling man out of his own building.

The tour progressed through Cleveland, Pittsburgh, Montreal, and Washington. Robert's flu was cured, and he was back in form for the scaled-down shows that now ran a more reasonable two and a half hours. Ringlets flying, kimono blouse flapping, his thrust-out bare chest shining with sweat, Robert Plant projected unadulterated, wanton, hyper-masculine libido. Bonzo bulled through everything in his tough and bulky way, his hard Midlands accent cutting through the restrained politeness that was Led Zeppelin's current public stance. Jones was almost anonymous, but he and Bonzo both complained to Danny Goldberg that they weren't in the spotlights enough and weren't included when it was time for publicity or interviews. Danny mentioned this to Jimmy and was referred to Showco's lighting director, who claimed he had *strict orders* from Jimmy that neither Jonesy nor Bonzo should be spotlit. So went Led Zeppelin's internal power struggles. On February 10 the band flew to Washington for a show at the massive Capital Centre. Jimmy hadn't slept in days and was feeling weird as the group huddled at the side of a specially built sixty-foot stage. The hall was dark, the amps had been switched on and were buzzing, and the audience was setting off fire-crackers and cherry bombs. It sounded like Saigon as the Viet Cong entered the city. Jimmy was shaking like a leaf. He hated waiting backstage before a show, preferring to jump out of the limo and run onstage. Bonzo was sweating visibly as the crowd noise built to a warlike Nuremburg roar. "This is *ridiculous*," Bonzo said. And then they heard it: "Ladies and gentlemen, *Led Zeppelin!*"

After two more shows in New York the band took a ten-day break. Jimmy and Robert flew to the Caribbean island of Dominica, while the rest of the group went home to their families.

Two weeks later the tour was back on. Everyone was rested, and Jimmy and Robert brought back vague tales of the Dominica Rastafarians, of eating hallucinatory boiled jellyfruit, of having had nothing to smoke. Led Zeppelin was now touring Texas and the South. At a show in Austin another drum kit was set up for the encore and Simon Kirke, the powerful Bad

Company drummer, joined in for a tumultuous "Whole Lotta
Love." As always, Led Zeppelin's southern fans were the most
boisterous; at the Baton Rouge show the security team confiscated three pistols and twenty-odd knives. John Bonham let
some of this southern madness wash over him, and while in
Texas Richard Cole detailed one of the security men to watch
over Bonzo lest the drummer get himself arrested. So Jack
Kelly, an ex-FBI agent (who in the sixties spied on radicals
from the bureau's Boston office), drove Bonzo around Dallas
between shows. They were cruising one afternoon when Bonzo
spied a gleaming, customized 1959 Corvette parked on the
street. Bonzo's insatiable mania for hot cars took over. "Jack,"
Bonzo said to Kelly, "I want you to wait by this car until the
owner comes for it, and I want you to tell him that Mr. Bonham would like to buy him a drink. And if he won't come,
see if you can have him arrested." That afternoon, Bonzo paid
$18,000 in cash for the Corvette, then worth about $10,000
on the classic car market. Since Bonzo's British license had
been revoked and he wasn't allowed to drive in America, Bonzo
had the Corvette trucked to Los Angeles, where it was stored
in the basement garage of the Riot House while Zeppelin's
high-priced lawyer spent two days at the motor vehicle regis-
try trying to get insurance and temporary plates. Meanwhile,
Bonzo spent hours sitting in the car with Mick Ralphs of Bad
Company, just revving the engine. Two weeks later he bought
a restored Model T Ford, and both cars were shipped back to
Old Hyde Farm in Worcestershire.

Led Zeppelin had reserved its usual floor at the Riot House,
but the expected surreal mayhem failed to materialize as in
the past. No longer were the young girls hanging around the
lobby allowed upstairs. Robert wasn't even living at the hotel;
he was holed up with a girl friend in Malibu Canyon. Even
the notorious Zeppelin roadies were somewhat quieter. The
old Zeppelin sack-and-pillage mentality was dying down. One
reason may have been the narcotic presence of heroin both
around the fringes and at the core of the tour. Several of Jim-

my's musician friends were offering him heroin. One day Danny Goldberg was in Jimmy's suite when Iggy Pop, a rock singer and protegé of David Bowie, offered Danny a line of heroin. Jimmy Page was outraged. "Jimmy, he doesn't *do* that stuff," Page said (Iggy Pop's real name was Jimmy Osterburg). "How can you offer smack to someone like that? Get *a hold* of yourself." Richard Cole confirms that heroin became much more prevalent in the Zeppelin entourage during that tour.

In Los Angeles the band was tired after a pair of four-hour marathons in Texas, and somewhat dispirited because a massive show in Florida had been canceled when its financial backers had been unable to meet Peter Grant's deadline. The band had been guaranteed a half million dollars for a single show, and were disappointed. Jimmy spent his days in his suite with the shades drawn and candles lit. He gave several interviews sitting before a coffee table covered with numerous switchblades and ratchet knives. As he spoke, his hands fluttered about in the air. The phone was off the hook, Richard Cole kept the Dom Pérignon flowing, and all food was brought in. Chrissie Wood was staying in a room nearby. Records were stacked everywhere; the Wailers' *Burnin'* album played continually on the stereo. With an armed guard sitting outside his door, Jimmy had the isolation of a monk. He spent days and nights wide awake, holding his guitar and, as he told a reporter, "waiting for something to come through."

Robert was the opposite—warm, exuberant, friendly. He drove in from Malibu one day to do some interviews at Danny Goldberg's request. A pack of reporters from London and New York had been flown into Los Angeles, first class. They were met by a limo that took them to assigned rooms at the Riot House, usually over, under, or adjacent to Bonzo's suite. Bonzo's job was to keep the unsuspecting journalists awake all night with his bombastic Alphonse Mouzon drum records played at absolutely top volume. Then the weakened scribes could be dealt with more advantageously the next day. Robert's style was to greet the press with Lori Maddox on his arm.

Lori, dressed in colorful bird feathers, tended to distract the writers as well, while Robert sipped tea with lemon. Robert would introduce her with "She's an old chum." Always effusive, Robert usually started his interviews with some throwaway line like "Actually I gave up cocaine this morning." He would talk about his concept of Led Zeppelin as an Arthurian force of goodness and Celtic lore and of his various supernatural inspirations. He often remarked that he could feel his pen being pushed by some higher authority. At one interview he bounded across the room and onto the balcony overlooking the lights of Hollywood laid out beneath him like a great sparkling grid. *"I'm a golden god!"* Robert yelled into the ether, thrusting his fists in the air and shaking his locks. In the hotel room the journalist and his photographer glanced at each other. Who was this for? Was this guy for real?

The first California date was in San Diego, and Richard Cole decided to take the plane. The flight would last only twenty minutes, but the limo convoy would have taken several hours. At 5 P.M. the Zeppelin entourage assembled in the lobby, along with stray women and hangers-on hoping for a seat in one of the six limos ("slutmobiles," Cole called them) idling at the curb. Jimmy Page, looking dazed, emerged from an elevator and a fan ran up, yelling, "Jimmy, you're so far out!" Jimmy stopped and seemed to think for a second. "You mean I'm a spiraling vortex?" he asked innocently.

Quickly, Cole matched entourage members to limos. The musicians were put in a regal Mercedes Pullman 600 with six doors and smoked glass. Grant and the lawyer got in a gold Lincoln pimpmobile with crystal bar service. The doctor, the journalists, and the sluts were thrown into anonymous black Cadillacs. On the way to the airport the limo convoy was forced to pull into four different gas stations so Bonzo could relieve his terrible diarrhea. The doctor was very unhappy because Bonzo wasn't responding to treatment and was becoming annoyed. The doctor's status on tour was already in doubt. Cole hated him and grabbed him by the neck in a drunken moment for which he was almost fired. Later he would accuse Jimmy of stealing Quaaludes out of his medical bags. Bonzo's stomach and bowels continued to be a problem: From then on, Bonzo traveled to gigs in a fancy red camper equipped with a toilet.

The Starship took off from L.A. in a serious thunderstorm. The pilot, unencumbered by the safety restrictions on commercial jets, banked sharply to avoid the thunderheads, and on board drinks were spilling and passengers clung to their seats in fear. During the short flight Grant strode up the aisle in a light blue kimono top stretched over his enormous belly. On his head was a purple gaucho hat with a blue plume. (Other nights he wore a coonskin cap.) His fingers were laden with silver and turquoise. A turquoise boulder on a bracelet around his arm must have weighed a pound. He looked like an Elizabethan privateer who was home to renew his letter of marque. As he passed by Plant commented to the journalists that Peter Grant was the "true" last of the ravers. Among the journalists was Nick Kent, an English rock writer (called "Nick Bent" by the band) who had dared to write a niggling review of *Physical Graffiti* for *New Musical Express*. A few days earlier, at some rock gathering, Kent had been splashed with bloody marys by Cole and Bonzo and insulted. "Your life isn't worth piss," the two had drunkenly screamed at Kent. Jimmy had invited Kent along to San Diego to patch up the row, but Kent was properly terrified by Bonzo and stuck close to Jimmy and Robert and the long-haired cocaine dealer who was plying them with his product while trying to sell Robert a 1955 Chevrolet. Another of the journalists was the editor of *Circus*, a rock magazine based in New York. Jimmy wanted a word with the man and invited him to ride in Jimmy's limo. It turned out that Jimmy was perturbed because *Circus* had published a paperback titled *Robert Plant*.

The bumpy flight to San Diego descended amid terrible turbulence as the plane's tape deck played Elvis singing "Teddy Bear." As the plane shuddered, Robert calmly remarked that if Led Zeppelin had to die, it might as well be to the strains of Elvis since that's where it all began for them. "Aha! Dear God!" Robert screamed as the plane lurched. "We're landing in a supermarket!"

But *The Starship* came to a halt at the edge of the dark airport as another limo convoy pulled up to the ramp. As they exited through a service gate, a group of fans standing in the rain flashed their Instamatics and clutched at the wet cars as they streaked through the gate behind a highway patrol escort. Their faces were contorted and their mouths screamed silently. The musicians marveled that people thought that rock musicians were strange, when it was really their fans who led bizarre lives, spending an evening getting soaked just to touch a wet car for a second.

The dressing room of the San Diego Sports Arena was a madhouse. The band changed into its stage clothes amid a jumble of roadies, well-wishers, and local record and radio executives trying to introduce their children. Robert called for tea and honey, ignoring the mountain of fried chicken, fresh fruit, and crates of fans' gifts piled in a corner. Just as they were about to go on, Led Zeppelin piled into a washroom for a bit of blow in privacy. Then they hit the stage with "Rock and Roll" and the San Diego Sports Arena erupted. The crowd immediately flattened the seats and pressed up close to the stage like netted fish. As the show heated up, dozens of girls were hoisted on their boyfriend's shoulders. Many of the girls took off their halter tops and wiggled their bare breasts at the band, causing a stampede backstage as the roadies scrambled to get a look. Gradually Zeppelin's avowed Apollonian intent reverted to a Dionysiac bawdiness. People fainted and were either trampled underfoot or passed over the crowd to the security men in front of the stage. The sheer body heat inspired the band. Jimmy whanged into the rarely played "The Crunge" and manipulated the theramin with wild shamanistic gestures. Robert constantly pleaded for order, and the show turned into a masterpiece. As the band left the stage for the last time after an hour of encores, a huge white-hot neon sign at the rear of the stage lit up the hall with its undeniable message: LED ZEPPELIN.

The Starship then flew north for concerts in Vancouver and Seattle, where the manager of the Edgewater Inn told Peter Grant that Led Zeppelin had recently been outdone in hotel room destruction by a convention of Young Methodists who had even ripped up the corridor carpeting and defenestrated it into the bay.

Back in Los Angeles Led Zeppelin's three nights at the Forum were introduced by Linda Lovelace, the fellatrix who starred in the film *Deep Throat*. Again, Simon Kirke of Bad Company joined on drums for the encores, adding a stupendous extra rhythmic dimension to Bonzo's Stone Age meters.

Later Jimmy was aglow because he had been introduced to Joni Mitchell at a restaurant called the Greenhouse. It was just small talk, but Jimmy had at last met one of his few idols. Later Robert passed up an opportunity to meet La Mitchell at a party, saying he was too shy to talk to her.

Richard Cole, meanwhile, had become friendly with one of Elvis's bodyguards, Jerry Schilling. The year before, while Led Zeppelin didn't tour, Cole had road-managed Eric Clapton's American tour, and had taken Clapton to meet Elvis in Memphis. Now Cole had decided to visit Elvis again, and arranged to take John Paul Jones up to Elvis's mansion in Bel Air. So they took one of the limos, and when they got to the house they were told not to discuss music with the King and to leave after twenty minutes. Cole walked into Elvis's living room with a bottle of cold Dom Pérignon in each hand. They found Elvis sprawled over a couch, wearing pajamas and house slippers, watching television with his entourage. Cole was a little drunk. "Wot the fucking hell is going on here?" he asked good-naturedly. Elvis didn't like people to curse in his house. "Man," the King said, "what's all this cussing and swearing?" But Cole started to *kid* Elvis. "You're sittin' there in your fucking carpet slippers and fucking Charlie Hodge [one of Elvis's aides] is twiddling a fucking pencil over here, what kind of fucking party is this?"

Elvis could take no more. He jumped up in a karate pose and whacked wrists with Cole, who had also gone into fighting stance. On contact, Cole's gold Tiffany watch clattered to the floor. Elvis picked it up. He liked watches, so he put it on. "That's nice," the King said.

"Ahh, fucking *keep* it!" Cole said. But giving Elvis a watch set off the King's automatic gifting mechanisms. Elvis ran out of the room and returned with another watch. "Here," he said, handing it to Cole. "You *fucking* keep this!" It was a gold watch decorated with thirty-two diamonds. Then Elvis looked at Jones and said, "Whaddaya got? Gimme your watch." Jones handed the King his Mickey Mouse watch. Elvis exited and returned with a double-dial (for two time zones) Baume and Mercier watch set in lapis lazuli. Elvis wasn't through. "What else you got?" he asked. Cole gave him his Brazilian amethyst ring. Elvis took a ring off his hand and said, "You can fucking have this," throwing Cole a two-karat diamond ring engraved with "Love, Linda." Elvis finally let Cole and Jones leave three hours later. He walked them to their limo in his pajamas and opened the car door for them. The drivers and the other retainers almost dropped dead. Elvis hardly ever came out of the house, let alone open limo doors for his guests.

When the tour ended in Los Angeles at the end of February, Led Zeppelin stayed in California. The whole band was in tax exile from draconian Labour tax laws that required successful musicians to pay as much as 95 percent on song publishing royalties. This time, Led Zeppelin wasn't going home. As always, when Led Zeppelin was resident in Hollywood, they attracted a constant trickle of clearly unstable strangers, just hanging out, hoping for a glimpse of the band or something else. Years later Danny Goldberg would say, "Look, Mark David Chapman [who shot John Lennon] was

just the guy that *did it*. He was the embodiment of the consciousness of the stoned rock fans who got insane ideas." When
strangers appeared in the lobby of the Riot House asking for
Led Zeppelin, they were referred to Danny's suite. One
morning, before the Long Beach show, a girl with mousy
brown hair knocked on Danny's door. A nervous tic spoiled
her face. She said she had to see Jimmy Page because she
had foreseen something evil in his future and thought it might
happen that night at the Long Beach Arena. She swore that
the last time this happened she had seen someone shot to death
before her very eyes. The girl was frantic. She was persuaded
to write a long note to Jimmy and then left unwillingly, only
after she was assured it was impossible to see Page. The note
was burned unread. At Long Beach, hurled firecrackers came
perilously close to Jimmy Page, and he was hit in the head
by an unraveling roll of toilet paper.

A week later Danny saw the same girl on the television news.
She had just tried to assassinate Gerald Ford, the president of
the United States. Her name was Squeaky Fromme, one of
Charles Manson's old girl friends.

And Bonzo was getting a little . . . *out there*. Smiling and
good-natured when sober, he turned into a terrible bully when
drunk, which was every night. "He was very emotional,"
Richard Cole says. "He was extremely close to his wife and
son and he didn't want to be away from them, but he had to
because of the tax thing. So he'd get depressed and if anyone
said anything to him, Bonzo'd whack them." Bonzo regularly
got into minor scuffles at the Rainbow; he had a girl friend
who worked there who occasionally traveled with the band.
If there were roadies around to back him up, Bonzo would
often provoke fights. If he was alone, he was less boisterous
and just drank. Loud and unruly, Bonzo embarrassed the other
musicians. If plans were being made to go to Dar Maghreb
for dinner, someone would whisper, *"Shhh, don't tell Bonzo."*
Both Peter Grant and Jimmy Page kept secret rooms on other

floors of the hotel so Bonzo couldn't find them when he was drunk. If there was a party at some chic locale where Led Zeppelin didn't wish to offend, it was "Don't tell the Beast."

In March Led Zeppelin hosted a party at the L.A. Shrine in honor of the Pretty Things, whose new Swan Song album was trying to climb the charts. The guests included the members of Bad Company, whose first album had sold a million and a half copies in the United States alone, and several dozen invited journalists. The Pretty Things had been revived for the third time by Phil May, with six other musicians, and were clearly in trouble. The keyboard player missed key gigs and the band would fall apart. Robert had to beg them to stay together, to stick it out.

Bonzo was near the bar at this party when he was approached by Andy McConnell, a short, neatly dressed reporter for the British music paper *Sounds*. John Bonham was one of the writer's musical heroes, and at the party he had finally screwed up his courage and approached Bonzo: "Mr. Bonham, my name is Andy McConnell and I represent *Sounds* and I would just like to tell you that I think you're the greatest drummer in the world, and that I've always wanted to shake your hand."

Bonzo turned and jerked the reporter up by his lapels, so that his eyes were level with Bonzo's, and screamed into the poor man's face, *"I've taken enough shit from you cunts in the press!!!"* Others jumped in to intervene, and a crazed Bonzo had to be pried off the journalist. Late that night, back at the Riot House, Danny Goldberg was awakened at four in the morning by a loud, steady, rhythmic pounding on his door. At first he thought the place was on fire until he realized that Bonzo had gotten hold of his room number and was trying to batter down the door. *"I know you're in there, Goldilocks!"* the drummer ranted at the top of his lungs. *"I know you're in there, and I want you to call that fucking little geezer from* Sounds. *Tell him I wanna do another fucking interview! Hah hah hah hah hah hah hah!!! I'll give that horrible little fucker an interview he'll never forget!"*

Danny was frightened. Bonzo *was* one of his employers. He feigned sleep until he heard Bonzo lumber drunkenly back down the hall. Bonzo just wouldn't get on with the press. Later he spilled his drink on a man from a British daily and forced Led Zeppelin's tour photographer to walk down the aisle of *The Starship* without his clothes.

Weird vibrations surrounded them. Something was wrong. Richard Cole could feel it. "That year they went into tax exile seemed to me like the beginning of the end," he said. Even Jimmy admitted to Lisa Robinson that he could feel the vultures circling. "I'd like to play for another twenty years," he said. "But I don't know, I just can't see it happening. I don't know why, I can't explain it in words. It's just a funny feeling. A foreboding . . ."

In May Led Zeppelin brought their laser-lit "American show" back to England for the first time in two years. Under the conditions of their tax exile, they were only allowed a few days home at a time. Three nights were advertised at the huge Earls Court Arena; the tickets went so fast that another two nights were added. They played the same show they had deployed in the States, starting with "Rock and Roll" seguing into "Sick Again." Jimmy switched to his old Danelectro guitar for "In My Time of Dying" which Robert would sarcastically dedicate to Denis Healey, the British Chancellor of the Exchequor, nominally responsible for the tax codes that had sent Led Zeppelin into its regretted exile. For "The Song Remains the Same" and "The Rain Song," Jimmy switched to his cherry red double-neck Gibson. Between songs, Robert went into his charming patter at the expense of the rest of the band. Introducing "Kashmir," he mused, "One day when we were rehearsing for some album that we really didn't know that much about, Bonzo came in with a nice driving tempo. And we thought, Mandrax? No!" John Paul Jones had his long solo spot on "No Quarter" before the whole band sat down along the edge of the stage for the acoustic set. All four had started to harmonize on "Tangerine"—something they never would have been loose enough to do in America. Then they played "Going to California," "That's the Way," and "Bron-Yr-Aur Stomp," which Robert dedicated to his dog. "Trampled Underfoot" and "Moby Dick" followed. After Bonzo's solo Robert chimed in: "John Bonham, master of the skins! The only man that can play the drums and sing 'The Last Waltz.' John comes from a circus family . . . my God, how can such a heavy group be so silly! So this is a song that goes right back to the beginning of our time. Bonzo refused to join us because he was getting £40 with Tim Rose. I had eight telegrams sent to the Three Men in a Boat in Walsall. . . . Nobody would believe the New Yardbirds." From behind his drums Bonzo piped up: "Nothing's changed!" Robert went on: "Nobody would believe it. John Paul Jones had just finished a tour with Greta Garbo. Jimmy Page was coming out of the closet. So we're really having a good time back in old England . . . you know how it is with Denis Healey—private enterprise, no artists left in the country anymore. He must be *dazed and confused.*"

The para-real, pencil-thin streaks of the laser cut the air during the bow section, and Robert sang snatches of "Woodstock." The final song was "Stairway to Heaven," followed by the encore crunches of "Whole Lotta Love" and "Black Dog." They played this show for five nights straight. After the last show on Monday night the band threw a big party backstage at Earls Court for its old friends. Jeff Beck came and stayed until 4 A.M. It was a reunion. After the shows the press went wild. Led Zeppelin had to be reevaluated. In the magazine of *The Observer* critic Tony Palmer wallowed in Zeppelin fever: "There is no theater like it, no action painting which approaches the constantly fluctuating patterns of light and sound which this lethal combination of talent has managed to unleash. If the Beatles dragged popular music from the inanities of middle-class, middle-aged, business oriented pap, then Led Zeppelin have propelled rock and roll into the forefront of artistic achievement in the mid-1970s." Remarking on

"Stairway to Heaven," Palmer asked, "Can you think of another song, any song, for which, when its first chord is played, an entire audience of 20,000 rises spontaneously to their feet, not just to cheer or clap hands, but in acknowledgement of an event that is crucial for all of them?"

Of course there were dissenting opinions. After Zeppelin's return Mick Gold, a British writer, commented, ". . . what comes across most strongly in their live music is a feeling of violent emotions internalized. There is none of the spontaneity or joy of a Stones or Faces concert. There is no release. Led Zeppelin make great play of timing and dynamics, of control. Their shows are well-paced, but there is no satisfying climax. It's body music, but because it doesn't swing, it doesn't set the audience dancing; it aims for the temples, not the feet, and its total effect is one of stupefaction."

After the Earls Court shows Robert took his family on holiday to Morocco, while the rest of Led Zeppelin set up its exile headquarters in Montreux. Three weeks later Jimmy Page flew to Marrakesh, the ancient red-walled caravan terminal at the edge of the Sahara, under the great wall of the Atlas Mountains. In the great market square, the Djemma el Fna, they watched men turn themselves into goats. The original plan was to take tape recorders and make field recordings of Morocco's penetrating Berber rhythms, but this never materialized. Instead, Robert and Jimmy headed southeast in a Range Rover, toward the Atlantic coast. When they hit the Atlantic they kept on going south, heading for Essaouira, Tarfaya, and Tan Tan, trying to reach the Spanish Sahara. But their timing was off. Morocco's king had just annexed the huge, phosphate-rich territory by walking a huge phalanx of civilians over the border armed only with red and green Moroccan flags. The Spanish army had left without firing a shot, but the Moroccan army and gendarmes maintained strict security on the roads. Every few miles Robert and Jimmy rode into an army roadblock and had loaded machine guns pointed at them. They would wave their passports furiously and explain they were only going as far as the next beach. Twenty miles later the same scenario would be repeated. The closer they got to the border, the nastier the roadblocks. Finally the road gave out completely, and they turned their car around and headed north, crossing the Strait of Gibraltar by ferry and then driving up through Spain and France toward the rest of the band in Switzerland. It was a refreshing adventure, especially after the long slog through America. The year of tax exile was turning out splendidly.

In Montreux more plans were hatched. In the fall the band would do another round of thirty shows in America and then play concerts in South America for the first time. Another visit to Japan and Australia was discussed. Robert and Jimmy wanted to go back to Morocco and record in the High Atlas. Jimmy wanted to visit Cairo and record there with Egyptian musicians, and spoke of plans to check out the music in New Delhi. Led Zeppelin, with its unlimited resources and complete freedom, was at its peak of perfection. Everybody's dreams were coming true.

And that's when the nightmare began.

After the Montreux Jazz Festival in July Jimmy reunited with his family, Charlotte and daughter Scarlet, and joined Robert, Maureen, and their two children on a summer holiday to the Greek island of Rhodes. Also along was Maureen Plant's sister and her husband. On August 3 Jimmy left Rhodes to look at Aleister Crowley's old farmhouse and abbey in Sicily, which he had heard was up for sale. The plan was for Jimmy to meet everyone in Paris a few days later. The next day, August 4, Maureen Plant was driving their rented car. Robert was next to her in front and Jimmy's daughter was in the back with Robert's children. Suddenly the car skidded on the narrow island road. Maureen had swerved and couldn't regain control. The car went over a precipice and crumpled against a tree. It was a terrible accident.

At first Robert looked at his unconscious wife and thought she was dead. The impact had fractured her skull and her pelvis. Robert had a badly broken ankle and elbow. His children were badly bruised and crying. Scarlet Page seemed unharmed. There was no ambulance available, and it took hours for a local farmer to get them to the hospital on the back of his open fruit truck.

The next day, in London, Richard got an incoherent phone call from Charlotte Martin, telling him of the accident. Maureen Plant was in very bad shape and needed blood. Her blood type was unobtainable in Rhodes, and her sister was unable to donate as much as Maureen needed. Charlotte told Richard that he had to charter a plane, fly to Rhodes, and rescue them. If Maureen didn't get to a proper hospital, Charlotte said, she was going to die. Cole hung up and pondered what to do. He was used to shouting and screaming and exaggeration from Charlotte. Peter Grant and Bonzo were in tax exile with their families in the south of France. Cole started making calls, rounding up top Harley Street doctors and orthopedic surgeons. He called Swan Song's accountant to get cash for a private jet, and was told they couldn't authorize the money without Peter Grant. "You fucking cunts!" Cole yelled. "The band's families are dying!" Fortunately, one of the surgeons had also treated Robert McAlpine of McAlpine Aviation and was able to borrow his private jet. So Cole flew out to Rhodes with two physicians and fresh blood for Robert's wife. They were met by Phil May of Pretty Things, who had a house in Rhodes, and taken to the hospital. "Robert was coherent," Cole recalls, "but his wife was just about a goner and the kids' legs and arms were broken to pieces." There were other problems as well. The owner of the rental agency was claiming that Maureen had been drunk at the time of the accident, and there were Greek lawyers scurrying about on the scent of big money. Still needing cash, Cole called Claude Nobs in Montreux and got him to Telex enough to get them out of Rhodes. Cole told his pilot to get the plane ready, and then raided the hospital to avoid any complications with the law. Cole announced to the hospital staff that the patients were being taken out immediately by plane. Cole held the bottle transfusing Maureen's blood aloft on a coat hanger. Everyone was painfully piled into a rented station wagon, hauled to the airport, and flown to Rome. Finally Cole got them all back to England, where the prognosis was grave. Maureen Plant, seriously injured, would have to spend weeks in a hospital bed. Later Robert would say, "If we hadn't had the money available to fly to England right away for the best medical treatment, I'm certain my wife wouldn't be alive now." And Robert himself was told he wouldn't walk for at least six months.

There were other pressures. Under the conditions of his tax exile, Robert was only allowed a few days in England per year, and he had used his time up already. If he stayed over the limit, his residency status would change and he would be liable for an enormous fortune in taxes. So Richard Cole called British Airways and arranged to have Robert flown to the tax-haven isle of Jersey in the English Channel. Robert was conveyed to the airport in an ambulance, wrapped in so much plaster that a forklift was used to hoist him up into the plane. Richard went along, as did Robert's assistant, Benji LeFevre, who would push Robert around in a wheelchair for the next six months. At Jersey another ambulance waited at the airport and drove Robert to a friend's guest house to wait out his exile. "So we got him out of the country just hours under his deadline," Cole says, "and we got him medical attention and saved his millions as well."

The rest of the band came to Jersey to see Robert and to sulk. The lucrative American tour was of course canceled, as well as any consideration of South America and Asia for the time being. Millions, not to mention momentum, had been lost overnight. Instead, it was decided to revive their now two-year-old concert film with a new director and to record a new album as quickly as possible. They agreed to rendezvous in California in September to begin rehearsals. Early that month Robert and Jimmy caught a Lufthansa flight from Jersey to a more congenial locale—Los Angeles. At first they moved into the Riot House, but the hotel had now become stale for them; so they rented beach houses in the exclusive Malibu colony, and Robert set about writing verses and healing himself. His prized possession was a get-well telegram from Elvis.

Robert was definitely spooked. To friends, he denied rumors in the London press that he thought Jimmy's dabbling in black magic had somehow brought down his family. He hobbled about the beach as best he could in his various casts, and enjoyed watching movie stars walk by his house on Malibu Colony Drive. He was extremely superstitious and believed that negativity associated with Led Zeppelin's music might be harrowing him. When an October storm washed away a porch attached to his house, Robert asked Danny Goldberg if he thought it was because of the "bad karma" reverberating from his song "The Ocean." To other friends he expressed reservations about performing the very witchy "In My Time of Dying" anymore. It was just too . . . *negative.* All this time Robert was seeing with a New York model named Linda. One day, at the Malibu house, Robert locked himself in his bathroom, and someone had to come and break down the door to get him out. But Plant, from all accounts, was also locked into his own remorse and grieving that his family had become victims of something he might no longer be able to control.

Jimmy also had a house on Malibu Colony Drive and was being very secretive. No one was allowed to have his phone number. Meanwhile, a girl called Ro, who was staying with Peter Grant nearby, had become obsessed with Jimmy's addictive charisma and had taken to breaking into his house and just *being there* when he came home. Since she seemed to be a friend of Peter's, Jimmy wasn't quite sure how to handle it.

While planning the new Zeppelin repertoire, Jimmy was also taking care of business in his own laconic way. Swan Song had signed a Los Angeles band called Detective, whose singer was Jimmy's English friend Michael des Barres. In typical lavish Swan Song fashion, this brand new band had been given a million dollar record deal, a quarter of a million dollars to produce an album that would take longer than nine months to complete, and a ranch of its own for rehearsals. "When Bonzo owns a fifth of you," Michael des Barres says, "you know the situation is out of the ordinary. Once we signed with them, we never even *saw* any of Led Zeppelin for two years. We dealt with Danny. We were produced to sound as much like Led Zeppelin as possible, and whatever tapes we gave them, they put out."

There was a lot of heroin around. Musicians loved heroin; it made them feel secure. The bassist Charles Mingus once said, "If God made anything better, he kept it to himself." It seemed that half the musicians in L.A. were doing smack. But Jimmy was very discreet. He nodded off at a photo call for Detective and was snapped sleeping behind the group. Someone woke him up and he said, "Ummm, I've got to stop taking that Valium." The others looked at each other and rolled their eyes. Who was Jimmy fooling?

John Bonham and John Paul Jones arrived in L.A. for band rehearsals in late October. Jones was nursing a broken hand, which had happened soon after Robert's accident. Bonzo had stayed with his family after the accident. His wife had given birth to a daughter named Zoe in June, and he couldn't bear not being there. Cole remembers, "He didn't give a fuck about the money. He just wanted to be with his wife." Now separated from his family, he reverted to his role as The Beast, prowling Sunset Strip for new victims to thrash. When sober he was the same old charming John Bonham, full of Midlands bluster and confidence, a bearish and hulking man going to alcoholic fat, always smiling through his thick beard. But when drunk, which was most of the time in America, Bonzo was a loose cannon, fully loaded and banging around the deck, destroying anything in his way. When he wasn't aggressively battering his drum kit, he was often assaultive to those around him. In these rages, the other musicians avoided him, knowing that deep down he was capable of *anything*. For the rest of Led Zeppelin, the days of semi-public orgies and barroom brawls were over, but not for Bonzo. There was something about being in America, away from his loved ones, that turned him into a maniac. It was the crystallization of an attitude the whole group had, which viewed America as a fantasy land of money, sin, and excess. At home they were all cozily domesticated with country houses, antiques, children, and aspirations to privacy. In America they were treated like royalty and told they could have whatever they wanted. And Bonzo just couldn't handle this power. It was as if Jimmy Page had been a sorcerer, plucking this young musician from nowhere and making him a star and a millionaire overnight. John Bonham was the *sorcerer's apprentice*, a stolid laborer who had gotten in over his head. Bonzo's talent had been manipulated to create enormous wealth, international fame and a power far beyond his capacity to handle it. As Danny Goldberg said, "Bonzo was a huge adult with the emotions of a six-year-old child, and an artistic license to indulge in any sort of infantile or destructive behavior that amused him."

In Los Angeles, rehearsing the new album, Bonzo went on the rampage. One night he walked into the Rainbow, hunkered down at the bar and loudly ordered twenty black russians. He downed ten of the fiery concoctions before wiping his mouth with his sleeve and swiveled on his stool to survey the night's action at the Rainbow. The first person that Bonzo laid eyes on was a half-familiar face from the local rock scene named Michelle Myer, who then worked for pop promoter Kim Fowley and was a regular at the bar. Sitting quietly at her table eating dinner, Michelle looked up and saw John Bonham, the big Led Zeppelin drummer, sitting unsteadily at the bar staring right at her. Michelle smiled at him.

Suddenly Bonzo ran amok. He lurched over to Michelle's table like an angry gorilla. Towering over the frightened woman, Bonzo bellowed, *"What the fuck did you say?"* As Michelle began to protest, Bonzo drew back and punched her in the face, sending the woman sprawling to the floor. "Don't

ever look at me that way again," he said to her over his
shoulder, as he headed back to the bar to finish another ten
black russians. Another night at the Rainbow, he picked a fight
with one of the bouncers outside. Usually Bonzo was only a
bully if he was fighting with women or if there were a half
dozen beefy Zeppelin roadies to back him up. But Bonzo was
alone and thought that he could handle the bouncer, a small
man who turned out to be a karate master and who put Bonzo
in the hospital that night. Bonzo was almost arrested. The
bouncer wanted to press charges for assault—he had witnesses—but then changed his mind.

John Paul Jones was a problem too. The band was supposed to be rehearsing, and Robert had even moved to Hollywood to be close to the action. But Jones kept disappearing.
Fiercely independent of the group, he came and went on his
own schedule and Jimmy was annoyed. "If you see John Paul
Jones," he said to Danny Goldberg who was searching for the
bassist, "shoot him on sight." To a reporter, Jimmy was slightly
more discreet. "Dealing with John Paul Jones can be quite a
trial sometimes, believe me."

The rehearsals were at S.I.R. studios in Hollywood, and
the new music was hot. The effort and energy that would have
gone into the fall tour went into the new music instead, and
Led Zeppelin burned with a rubbery new funk that was taking the band to unexpected destinations. Moroccan white guitar
noise clashed with New Orleans "second-line" rhythms. Time
signatures were brutal and labyrinthine. Bonzo was as tough
as nails, and Robert was singing in his wheelchair, wiggling
inside his cast.

Led Zeppelin also had to get out of the United States or
face American taxes. So it was decided to record at Musicland Studios in Munich, Germany. On the way to Europe,
Jimmy, Robert, and Bonzo stopped for a few days in New
York. Robert was now out of his wheelchair and was almost
walking without his cane. Wearing a dozen clanking Indian
bracelets, Robert gave optimistic interviews. Since his acci-

dent, he told Lisa Robinson, "I've had time to see. Before I was always bowled over with the sheer impetuousness of everything we did, of what we are, and what was created around it. That was knocked off course, the fulcrum was tilted a little. . . . I had to sort of think everything anew, instead of just being allowed to go on with the rampaging."

He continued, "So it turns out that the [new] lyrics all come from the period of contemplation where I was wondering, 'Christ, is it all through? Is it ended?' And as such the album is full of energy, because of that primal fight within me to get back."

Meanwhile, Jimmy was hot on the trail of a black blues guitarist named Bobby Parker, who had been described to Jimmy as an undiscovered legend playing his talent away in the suburbs of Washington, D.C. Jimmy badly wanted to sign a real bluesman to Swan Song, so he and Danny Goldberg flew down to Washington to hear Parker play, after Goldberg had tracked him down through area music journalists. They found Bobby Parker playing R&B and disco hits with a lousy band in an NCO club on an army base in Virginia. Jimmy took out a cheap little battery cassette player and recorded the set, and reluctantly accepted when Parker called him up to the stage to jam on some old blues. Playing without a pick, Jimmy fared poorly. After getting Bobby Parker's hopes raised to a fever pitch—*discovered by Led Zeppelin!!*—Jimmy and Danny flew back to New York. Jimmy played the tape he had made of Parker for Robert and Bonzo, and they hated it. They could hardly even hear anything. Bobby Parker was forgotten.

The band flew to Europe separately. Bonzo always traveled with his roadie, Mick Hinton, who also served as Bonzo's valet, go-for, nursemaid, and *duenna*. Hinton was a good-humored Cockney veteran of English rock—he had worked for Ginger Baker—and was treated by Bonzo as an indentured servant. Bonzo even made Hinton dress like him. On tour earlier that year both had worn the white boiler suits, jack boots, and black derbies of the *Clockwork Orange* droogs. On the flight to Europe, Bonzo sauntered up to the first-class section of the British Airways jumbo and started on the complimentary champagne, while Hinton rode coach in the back of the plane. During the first hour of the flight, Bonzo guzzled two bottles of champagne, threatened the steward, shouted, and menaced the other first-class passengers. Then he passed out, drunk. When the steward began to serve supper, the other passengers threatened his job if he woke Bonzo up to eat.

Two hours later Bonzo woke up and found that he had pissed on himself from all the champagne he had drunk, ruining his pants and soaking his seat. Suddenly he began to bellow for his slave: " 'Inton! 'Inton!! Come 'ere!" Mick Hinton ran up to first class and Bonzo beckoned him in with a whisper. "Quick, you cunt, walk in front of me!" he rasped. He got up and walked to the lavatory, close behind Hinton, to try to avoid the ridicule of the other passengers, whose amusement was soon stifled by the stink that began to spread from Bonzo's saturated chair. Like a mother carrying spare diapers for her baby, Hinton had a change of pants for Bonzo in his flight bag. Then Bonzo made Hinton sit in his pissed seat while he took Hinton's dry seat in the rear of the plane and passed out again.

The tracks for Led Zeppelin's seventh album, *Presence*, were cut in just eighteen days in Munich that November. The studios were under the Arabella Hotel, where Zeppelin was staying. Richard Cole, who hadn't seen the group since Robert's accident, now brought the equipment to Munich and organized his usual fun and games to relieve the tension. Musicland was a very in-demand recording studio then, and all the other British tax exiles wanted to work there. Led Zeppelin had been squeezed in two weeks before the Rolling Stones were scheduled to come in and record their new album. In the past Zeppelin's recording sessions had progressed slowly, with all the grace and neurotic deliberation of a novelist with writer's block. With the Stones on his heels, the perfectionist

Page was forced to loosen up into a state of mere tightness. The sound of the new music was hard and unforgiving. It was a screaming, multilayered electric guitar album with no pretense to acoustic music. The new songs reflected the constant travel and motion of the band's year in exile. Robert's lyrics reflected his anguish and what seemed strangely like repentance.

The opening track of the album would be its centerpiece. "Achilles Last Stand" was the culmination of Jimmy's desire to build multitracked harmonized guitars into a towering structure of movement and emotion. Its predecessors were "Stairway to Heaven," "The Song Remains the Same," and "Kashmir," and its inspiration was their Moroccan travels. Jimmy deploys his myriad guitar voices over what Zeppelin connoisseurs came to consider John Bonham's greatest rhythm track. Robert evokes the din of battle, the mighty arms of Atlas, and sleeping Albion who will someday rise again. The rhythms change from epic Zeppelin pomposity to an intricate stop-time Spanish bolero. Like most of the songs on this album, "Achilles" was given strange guitar fanfares and a gloomy coda that rang its changes like chimes at midnight. "For Your Life," a slower song about cocaine and overdose in Los Angeles, is more somber in tone. Jimmy conjured up an eerie rock drone that swooped around the channels, and Robert's tale of gambling with dope and losing is buried way into the mix, almost indecipherable under Page's heavily edited guitar barrages. Equally difficult were the lyrics to "Royal Orleans," which seem to describe John Paul Jones's nocturnal adventures in New Orleans two years earlier. Playing their brains out, Led Zeppelin essayed the Meters' trademark "Cissy Strut" while Robert smirked about a man he knew who went down to Louisiana, had a bad fire, and ended up kissing whiskers. The victim was jocularly identified as "John Cameron," who was actually Jones's old studio rival in the days when he was arranging for Mickie Most.

But the most shocking words on the album were reserved

for "Nobody's Fault But Mine," adapted from an old Blind Willie Johnson blues tune. After an incredible phased guitar fanfare intro and a John Bonham lift-off, Robert delivers an amazing lyric of repentance and malaise. He identifies the devil as his pursuer and announces he will try to save his soul. He cries that he has a monkey on his back and pledges to change his ways. These stark confessions were backed by a down-and-dirty jam that was one of the most relentless pieces of pure rock this group ever mined. "Nobody's Fault But Mine" was Led Zeppelin's "Hellhound on My Trail." For Robert and perhaps the others, it was a sort of exorcism. Fans who managed to puzzle out the obfuscated lyrics were convinced that Robert was admitting that he had sold out to Satan and now wanted out.

Other tracks included the hard "Candy Store Rock" and "Hots On for Nowhere," with a great cascading riff and one of Page's most bizarre guitar solos on record. The album would be concluded with "Tea for One," a sad minor blues with Spanish overtones and crying, disconsolate guitars. "Tea for One" was the other, darker side of Zeppelin's run for the rainbow. It acknowledged the crushing loneliness and depression of a life lived on the road, for the moment, without the normal anchors that kept regular people sane and in balance.

Presence owed much of its brilliance to the conditions of panic under which it was assembled. When Zeppelin's studio time had been used up, Page estimated that they still had at least three days' work left, with all the guitar overdubs still to come. Page called up Mick Jagger, explained the situation, and asked for two extra days in Munich. Jagger said fine. Jimmy had already been working eighteen hours a day for two weeks. Now he simply stayed up for several days and over-dubbed the whole album. The innumerable guitar overdubs to "Achilles" were performed in one night. The rest of the album was done the following day. The strange solo in "Hots On for Nowhere" should be heard in that desperate context. Finally, exhausted and wrung out, Jimmy finished the album when he said he would. It was, he told *New Musical Express*, "the ultimate test of that whole lifestyle." For Jimmy Page it was all a matter of pure will. To another reporter he recalled, "Anyway, the day we finished, the Stones came in and asked how we'd gotten on. I said, 'All right. I've finished thanks to the two extra days you gave us.' They said, 'The tracks?' And I said, 'No, the whole thing'; and they couldn't believe it."

The whole album had been recorded and mixed in less than three weeks. And the only bad moment had occurred when Robert stumbled on the way to the recording booth and al-most re-injured his healing ankle. "I've never known Jimmy to move so quickly," he said later. "He was out of the mixing booth and holding me up, fragile as he might be, within a second. He became quite Germanic in his organization of things and instantly I was rushed off to hospital again, in case I'd reopened the fracture, and if I had I probably would never have walked properly again."

In December the band flew to Jersey to continue their en-forced absence closer to Britain. On December 10 they jumped onstage at Behan's pub and played some old favorites. On the day before Christmas, Robert, Jones, and Bonzo flew home to be with their families, while Jimmy went to New York to mix the sound track for the now revived Zeppelin movie. On the last day of the year, Robert Plant walked across his farm-house kitchen without his cane for the first time since the ter-rible car crash.

TEN

POWER, MYSTERY, AND THE HAMMER OF THE GODS

The essential ingredient for any successful rock group is energy—the ability to give out energy, to receive energy from the audience, and to give it back to the audience. A rock concert is in fact a rite involving the evocation and transmutation of energy. Rock stars may be compared to priests . . . The Led Zeppelin show depends heavily on volume, repetition and drums. It bears some resemblance to the trance music found in Morrocco, which is magical in origin and purpose—that is, concerned with the evocation and control of spiritual forces. In Morocco, musicians are also magicians. Gnaoua music is used to drive out evil spirits. The music of Jajouka evokes the God Pan, Pan God of

Panic, representing the real magical forces that
sweep away the spurious. It has to be remembered
that the origin of all the arts—music, painting and
writing—is magical and evocative; and that magic
is always used to obtain some magical result. In
the Led Zeppelin concert, the result aimed at
would seem to be the creation of energy in the
performers and the audience. For such magic to
succeed, it must tap the sources of magical energy,
and this can be dangerous.

—WILLIAM S. BURROUGHS
"ROCK MAGIC"

Although its reign had been mostly benign, Led Zeppelin's
empire began to crumble in 1976. It was as if the disaster that
had struck Robert Plant's family sapped Led Zeppelin of its
remarkable good fortune and the group's insatiable will for
domination. Although Led Zeppelin would release two albums and a long feature film that year, things would never
be the same again. With Zeppelin off the road, its adepts were
distracted. Into the breach stepped the Zeppelin imitators,
mostly American bands playing Xeroxes of Jimmy Page's power
chords with blond singers wailing overwrought, mystical drivel.
These Zeppitators had felt the shadow of the Zeppelin when
it passed over America in the early seventies. The group Boston pioneered the first of the many "Little Stairways"; their
anthem "More Than a Feeling" was a big hit in America that
year. A band called Heart, fronted by two sisters from the state
of Washington, played raw copies of Zeppelin material and
even opened their shows with "Rock and Roll." Lynyrd
Skynyrd's "Free Bird" challenged "Stairway" as an American
radio anthem. Another band from Massachusetts, Aerosmith,
even revived "Train Kept A-Rollin' " and had a hit. Led
Zeppelin was nominally retired, but its music lived on as played
by other musicians. (Later, the fans would joke that the two

best Led Zeppelin singles ever made were Heart's "Barracuda"—which took its bass and drum "riddim" from "Achilles Last Stand"—and "Lonely Is the Night" by Billy Squier.) And even that music would be overshadowed by the newer soft-rock that was taking over, at least in America. The year's biggest successes would be Peter Frampton and Fleetwood Mac, former English blues scholars transplanted to corporate America. Underneath the pop music structure, meanwhile, in London and New York, there was another current of young bands that reviled Led Zeppelin and its generation. Within a year, the punk bands—the Sex Pistols, Clash, Generation X—would stage a revolution, and Led Zeppelin would surrender.

After a few precious days with their families, in January 1976 Robert Plant, John Paul Jones, and John Bonham flew to New York to further conduct their affairs in exile. They settled into the Park Lane Hotel on Central Park South and complained bitterly about their fate. Robert spoke of how "the finest English talent" was in New York because they couldn't afford English taxes. He pointed out that Mick Jagger lived four blocks away on the West Side and carped, "My reward for all the things I've done should be to be able to go back and be with Maureen and the children." But Robert stayed in New York while his family pulled through alone in England. As they came to know him better, the people who worked in the Swan Song office realized that there were two Roberts. One was the Celtic visionary and spiritualist; the other was the vulgar rock star in pursuit of the normal vices of his profession.

The main order of business was the completion of Led Zeppelin's movie, now in its third incarnation and titled *The Song Remains the Same*. Its new director, Peter Clifton, had assembled Joe Massot's concert footage and fantasy sequences into a ragged occult documentary. Using makeup and special effects, Jimmy aged a hundred years as the Hermit of the tarot. Robert's damsel-in-distress, rescued after a gory struggle, vanishes before his eyes. Bonzo is shown dragging formula race

cars. Jones is depicted leading some dark mission that in-
volves a brutal rape. Peter Grant and Richard Cole are laugh-
ing gangsters tommy-gunning houses. With its less-than-magic
sound track, recorded in New York at the bitter end of the
1973 tour, the movie was musically handicapped from the start.
But it was all they had, and they were determined to release
it that year.

While the sound mixing was underway, Bonzo was on the
loose, taking care of business his own way. One night he
showed up backstage at a Deep Purple concert at the Nassau
Coliseum on Long Island. Bonzo was drunk and in very high
spirits, and was wobbling on his feet in the wings when he
noticed a free microphone during a lull in the music. Stag-
gering forward, Bonzo walked out onto the stage before the
Deep Purple roadies could grab him. The group stopped
playing, amazed, as Bonzo grabbed the mike and shouted,
"*My name is John Bonham of Led Zeppelin, and I just wanna
tell ya that we got a new album comin' out called* Presence
and that it's fucking great!!" Then Bonzo turned to leave, but
before he went he turned back and gratuitously insulted Deep
Purple's guitarist. "*And as far as Tommy Bolin is concerned,
he can't play for shit!!*"

Presence was released in April, the first album to reach
"platinum" status (one million records or tapes sold) in America
on advance orders alone. In England the previous month
Jimmy explained the record's mental landscape: "It was recorded while the group was on the move, technological gyp-
sies, no base, no home. All you could relate to was a new
horizon and a suitcase. So there's a lot of movement and
aggression. A lot of bad feeling toward being put in that situation." The title was meant to convey the sense of extra-
sensory impact that Led Zeppelin had, and was represented
on the album jacket by a small black obelisk depicted as a
normal household object used for healing, education, and
spiritual regeneration. The object was meant to be a puzzle,

another Zeppelin enigma. Reporters called the Swan Song office in London to inquire as to the nature of the object. Richard Cole would take the calls and reply that the musicians didn't even know what it was. The concept had come intact from Hipgnosis, the design firm that did most of Led Zeppelin's covers. Later, in interviews, Robert described the object as "Kubrickian," referring to the epochal slab in the film *2001: A Space Odyssey*.

As usual, the press reviews for *Presence* were niggling. Many reviewers thought (rightly) that the album was a downer. Radio programmers liked it better ("Achilles Last Stand" was played every night on London's Capital Radio for months), but sales soon fell off. Perhaps *Presence* was too "serious." Robert's cadences on "Achilles" reminded that *The Iliad* was chanted for a thousand years before it was written down. But *Presence* became the only Led Zeppelin album ever to appear in bargain bins.

That didn't mean, however, that Led Zeppelin's essential popularity had disappeared. In America in 1976, pollsters for the two presidential campaigns found such overwhelming Led Zeppelin graph peaks on their demographic charts that both Democratic and Republican candidates appeared to endorse Led Zeppelin! The daughter of the president, Susan Ford, said on *The Dick Cavett Show* that Led Zeppelin was her favorite group. Speaking at the National Association of Record Manufacturers convention, Jimmy Carter reminisced about listening to Led Zeppelin records during all-night sessions when he was governor of Georgia.

In May there were upheavals in Swan Song itself. Danny Goldberg was fired as vice-president of the company after refusing to take what he considered unethical steps in booking a tour by Bad Company. Danny was fired because *nobody* could be permitted to quit Led Zeppelin. But Peter Grant started to cry anyway. "I never thought I'd live to see the day," he sobbed, "when I'd hear myself say, 'Danny Goldberg is fired.' " The Pretty Things' career ended soon after. Led

Zeppelin knew how to produce only instant success. There was no desire to spend the long plodding years usually necessary to build, nurture, and develop an artistic career.

So Robert and Jimmy concentrated on their big success, Bad Company, whose second album, *Straight Shooter*, had done almost as well as its first. They showed up to jam at several Bad Company shows before flying back to England on May 26. Sitting in the first-class section, guzzling champagne, Robert and Jimmy got quite drunk and giddy. Half way over the Atlantic, they started harassing the other celebrity passengers flying British Airways that night. Actor Telly Savalas, who played the bald television detective on *Kojak*, wasn't amused and said so. Dudley Moore suffered in silence. The British gutter press reported that Savalas had been insulted, but in a press release, Jimmy and Robert said that "it was just a bit of fun."

That summer Jimmy was also attacked in the press by Kenneth Anger, who had finally grown tired of waiting for Jimmy to finish the *Lucifer Rising* sound track as promised. After several years Jimmy had only managed to deliver twenty-eight minutes of music that Anger considered usable. There was no denying that the music was extraordinary—morbid, hypnotic, and utterly chilling. Related to "No Quarter," "Kashmir," and the later "In the Evening," the sound track music was composed of drones and chants, flutelike melodies, and wailing bowed guitar played through an early ARP synthesizer. The general effect was like a satanic mantra crackling with the thunder of clamorous feedback and the distant sound of far-away chimes. But it was only a fragment of what Anger had asked for, and in his anger he went public. He accused Jimmy of sabotaging his film and implied that Jimmy was a heroin addict. Anger's major frustration was that Jimmy was so isolated that it was impossible to communicate with him. "I felt like my collaborator had died," Anger said later. Not only were Jimmy's phone numbers a closely guarded Swan Song secret, but Swan Song itself was half shut down, in exile with Peter Grant in Montreux. The Swan Song office in Chelsea even refused to take messages. Callers were simply told to call back later. "The selfishness and inconsideration were appalling," Anger said. And even when he spent time with Jimmy, Page seemed so spaced out that Anger couldn't communicate. "It was like rapping on inch-thick plate glass. Jimmy had more or less turned into an undisciplined, rich dilettante, at least as far as magic and any serious belief in Aleister Crowley's work was concerned." Anger felt that Jimmy was a prime example of "magic gone hay-wire, half understood, not under will." He remarked that Aleister Crowley had been a heavy user of both heroin and cocaine, but that Crowley could handle it because of his robust mountaineer's physique. Jimmy Page appeared wasted. "He couldn't handle it," Anger remarked.

In interviews, Jimmy counterattacked, seeming wounded and righteous. He explained that he had offered Anger an editing table and space to work in, and claimed that he had been waiting for Anger to finish, not the other way around. But Anger's published claim that Jimmy was having "an affair with the White Lady" implied that Jimmy was using heroin and that this was the cause of his malaise.

In September Jimmy and Bonzo were in Montreux, where they recorded a solo drum track that Jimmy intended to treat with synthetic distortion and use in some future Led Zeppelin album. Then Jimmy flew back to England to counter the Anger problem and be with Charlotte, who had been taken very ill. There was also the problem of evicting friends from Tower House, a couple who were suffering from delusions that they had become Jimmy and Charlotte. The vibes at Tower House were always very strange, as they seemed to be at all of Jimmy's residences. At Boleskine, which had now been redecorated by a renowned satanist named Charles Pierce, a caretaker had committed suicide and another had gone mad and been taken away to the hospital.

Bonzo had spent much of the summer in the south of

France, but after recording in Montreux he sent his wife and children back to England with his chauffeur, Matthew, and went to Monte Carlo for some fun with Mick Hinton and his girl friend. Bonzo's girl friend from Los Angeles also flew in for the party, which was joined by Richard Cole. "The old beast," Cole says; "someone had to look out for him."

One night Bonzo's party was at Jimmys, an expensive nightclub in Monte Carlo. "The thing is," Cole remembers, "that Bonzo really loved his wife and family and didn't want to be separated from them. And he would get drunk and do things and then be very emotional and so sorry the next day. That night he was drinking, and he started in on Hinton. And he had this gun with him—it was only a gas gun—in a shoulder holster under his white suit. And he got outrageous with Hinton and went and pulled the gun on him.

"Now, if you know Jimmys," continues Cole, "you got Onassis and Saudis and all them down there. You got these rich fucking Turks and the Mafia and the fucking heavy Corsicans, *and all of these wealthy guys have got guys with guns with them*! Now you imagine some long-hair in a white suit standing up and pulling a gun out, the whole place is gonna fucking go bananas and someone's gonna get shot to death for no reason.

"He went for the gun and started hitting Hinton, his whipping boy, kind of teasing him. I said, 'Fucking leave him alone.' He says, 'Shut up you cunt, or I'll do you as well.' "

Bang. Cole hit Bonzo on the nose as hard as he could with his fist. Bonzo went down with a broken nose, blood spewing everywhere. As the gun clattered across the floor, Cole hissed to Hinton's girl friend, "Take that fucking gun and throw it in the toilet. Hide it, get rid of it." The police arrived, arrested them all, and held them for three hours. The police kept asking about the gun, and everybody maintained that there was no gun. Meanwhile, Cole and Bonzo were hissing to each other, trying to figure out what to do with all the cocaine they were holding. Finally they were let go.

The next day Bonzo rang up his chauffeur in Worcestershire. "Matthew? Listen—fucking go to the tailor and get me another white suit. That cunt Richard's covered me in blood again!" Later, looking in the mirror, he thanked Cole for the second broken nose in five years. "I needed that," Bonzo said in amazement. "Now it's fucking straight again."

In late October 1976 Led Zeppelin flew to New York to attend the premiere of its movie, *The Song Remains the Same.* (There was boisterous behavior again in First Class—Cole threw an open switchblade at somebody—and the authorities had asked questions when the plane landed. Later, a drunken Cole picked a fight with *Melody Maker's* New York correspondent, Chris Charlesworth, and was thrown out of Ashley's, the bar they were in. The next day, Plant apologized profusely to Charlesworth, telling him that Peter Grant had slapped Cole around for abusing a friendly English journalist. Three days later, Plant again called from England to apologize once more.) Two days earlier their record company had released the movie's concert sound track as a double album. Reaction as usual was polarized. The young kids who flocked into the theaters often stood up and applauded Bonzo's drum solo, "Moby Dick." There were occasional disturbances outside theaters after late weekend shows. Even on celluloid, Led Zeppelin's power to viscerally ignite a seventeen-year-old ready to die for his favorite band was undiminished. The movie had turned out a crypto-mystical pastiche of outdated concert footage (which even the band found dull) and the Dark Ages dream sequences cooked up around the band. The critical reaction was predictable. *The Song Remains the Same* was routinely panned for its violent nightmares and relentless narcissism. In *Rolling Stone*, critic Dave Marsh thrust home: "Far from being a monument to Zeppelin's stardom, *The Song Remains the Same* is a tribute to their rapaciousness and inconsideration. While Led Zeppelin's music remains worthy of respect (even if their best songs

are behind them), their sense of themselves merits only con-
tempt." The movie was a moderate success at the box office,
and then quickly disappeared, relegated to the occasional
midnight show at some drive-in in the South. (It's ultimate
influence would be felt years later on MTV, where Led Zeppelin's clumsy film served as a model for the videos of the
heavy metal groups that emerged in Zeppelin's wake.) As always, the sound track album went platinum.

Jimmy Page did a long round of interviews in October and
November of 1976 in which he continually denied rumors
that Led Zeppelin waas dead, and in which he also slagged
his own movie, citing the concert footage as "take-it-or-leave-
it" and filled with "howling mistakes." On the other hand,
he justified the project as a worthwhile tax fiddle and an ad-
equate summing up of the era when Led Zeppelin still closed
their shows with "Whole Lotta Love."

Robert Plant, meanwhile, was back on his sheep farm in
Wales with his wife and children. They lived in an ancient
stone house on nearly three hundred acres with a big flock of
sheep and a pig called Madam. After their auto accident on
Rhodes, Robert decided to sell the family's horses. Life on a
Welsh sheep farm was idyllic and hard work, but Robert's leg
was healing, and his children were more beautiful than ever.
Speaking of his five-year-old son, Karac, Robert told a reporter, "We call him Baby Austin, after that Bionic Man. He
knows no fear, has no anticipation of danger. I envy him."

Nearly two years after Robert Plant's car accident, Led
Zeppelin went back to work. Rehearsals had begun late in 1976
on a live version of "Achilles Last Stand," which had been
built in the studio and needed an arragement Jimmy could
play in concert. Rehearsals continued in January 1977, at a
converted theater in Fulham that was owned by Emerson,
Lake, and Palmer. The tour would be Led Zeppelin's biggest
to date, fifty-one shows in thirty cities before more than a

million fans. It would be Led Zeppelin's eleventh tour of America, and anticipation was running high. The number eleven had been Aleister Crowley's favorite. Crowley even spelled the word *magick* with a *k* because it was the eleventh letter.

Led Zeppelin had been away a long time, and the climate of pop music had drastically changed. The punks, the so-called New Wave of younger bands, had crashed-landed into the middle of a demoralized music scene polarized by the 4/4 thump of disco and the dinosaur stomp of hard rock. Younger bands—The Sex Pistols, the Clash, the Damned, the Stanglers, Generation X—were taking over the club and fashion scenes, especially in England where it mattered. The older successful bands—Led Zeppelin, the Stones, Rod Stewart, Yes, Genesis—were continually insulted and derided by the punks and their spokesmen in the press as boring old farts. Led Zeppelin and Elton John were particularly reviled for their success, their wealth, their outmoded vulgarity, and for pandering to America. Worst of all, they were called junkies, drugged-out millionaires who had no relationship or rapport with the kids they were playing for. The new bands were part of their own audience—nihilistic working class youth with a kinky taste for self-mortification.

Rather than lick its wounds in silence, Led Zeppelin responded to the challenge. They chose the most scabrous and lame-brained of all the English punk bands—the Damned—and started to go to their gigs at the Roxy, then London's prime punk venue. Jimmy and Robert went together one night in late January. Two nights later Robert went back with Bonzo. The Damned played depraved leaper music at top volume and had a profoundly effective negative charisma. The drummer's name was Rat Scabies.

The eleventh U.S. tour was scheduled to begin in March, and Led Zeppelin spent February preparing for the campaign. The group's instruments and equipment were shipped to the States, and Jimmy sold off a lot of his old guitars. *The Starship* had been grounded, so now Peter Grant chartered another luxury jet called *Caesar's Chariot* from the owners of Caesars Palace, the gambling casino in Las Vegas. The Dallas-based Showco would again provide lights, sound, and special effects, including the giant overhead video screen that had been used before only at Earls Court in 1975. A few days before the band itself was scheduled to fly to Texas for the opening concert in Dallas, Robert came down with a throat ailment that was diagnosed as tonsillitis. Faced with a singer with no voice or energy, the tour was postponed for a month. So Led Zeppelin rotted for several weeks, not even bothering to rehearse since their gear was already across the sea.

The 1977 tour began on April Fools' Day in Dallas. Shows would again run over three hours through fifteen songs and the two encores, "Whole Lotta Love" and "Rock and Roll." From the beginning, it was clear that this tour was different. Jimmy arrived in the United States very weak. Peter Grant's wife had left him, which put a tremendous damper on the tour's spirit. In the past Grant had been Led Zeppelin's Jolly Roger, always keeping spirits as high as possible. Now he was angry and humiliated. "I think she went off with some guy who was working on the farm," Cole says. "I think that's what was really the fucking end of everything. It's funny, but I hated that last tour. You could *feel* it . . . something very bad. It was all the drugs, I suppose. The drugs . . . I dunno, but there was something *wrong*. It wasn't the same."

For one thing, Cole's job had expanded. With Jimmy Page and, according to Cole, most of the road crew strung out on heroin, a steady supply had to be assured. And there was no shortage. "It's like anything," Cole says. "If you want it, it's there, and all you do is follow through." In addition to the pulled curtains, lit candles, and FM stereos, Jimmy needed heroin. "By the time it came to that," Cole said, "I've got to have it as well."

After a show in Oklahoma City Led Zeppelin moved to

Chicago for four nights in Chicago Stadium. The shows were getting longer and more intense. "Good evening," Robert took to saying; "welcome to three hours of lunacy." And it was. "The Song Remains the Same" opened to pure din by those assembled. "The Rover," Zeppelin's underrated unity anthem, came next, followed by "Nobody's Fault But Mine," which was usually dedicated to Blind Willie Johnson. The opening set ended with "In My Time of Dying," which for some reason Robert Plant had decided to sing after all. "Dazed and Confused" had been banished from the set. Instead, Jimmy deployed a solo bow section that included eerie bagpipe themes and occasionally "The Star Spangled Banner." This would evolve into "Achilles Last Stand," Led Zeppelin's fast, furious time travelogue. The next set Jimmy played with his old Danelectro guitar tuned down to his Eastern mode. "White Summer" and "Black Mountain Side" segued into the monumental "Kashmir" and "Ten Years Gone." A long acoustic set followed: "Battle of Evermore," "Going to California," "Bron-Y-Aur Stomp," and "Black Country Woman." The musicians sat across the front of the stage, and Robert kept his injured foot propped on a stool for support. Jimmy hunched over his mandolin in total concentration. Bonzo banged the tambourine and John Paul Jones showed off a new triple-neck guitar, which had a little mandolin neck above the six- and twelve-string necks.

"No Quarter" had now evolved into a sardonic, kitch-laden piano recital that included "The March of the Wooden Soldiers." "Sick Again" was dedicated to what Robert called "the L.A. queens." By the time Led Zeppelin began its final bombing run with "Whole Lotta Love," its fans had been satiated.

From the start, the vibes felt negative. One night Jimmy went on dressed as a Nazi storm trooper. The band hung out at after-hours clubs with Willie Dixon's kids. Dixon was ailing, and "Nobody's Fault But Mine" would be dedicated to him while the band was in town. By the third night, Jimmy was feeling ill. He needed a chair to play "Ten Years Gone" and then staggered off with severe stomach cramps. The show was canceled. Later the problem was said to have been food poisoning.

The next day Jimmy felt better. Sipping warm Dr Pepper soda in his suite while Cole padded about in his pajamas, Jimmy gave an interview. "I always take a chance," Jimmy said about the previous night's collapse. "I can't just play safe. Dancing on the edge of the precipice—you've gotta live like that. Better to live one day as a lion than a thousand years as a lamb." Cole opened a window to let in some air. "Don't jump, Richard," Jimmy cracked. "You'll make a bad impression on Chicago." Asked about the glaring absence of "Dazed and Confused," Jimmy replied that he wasn't dazed and confused anymore. "Led Zeppelin," he said, "is a stag party that never ends. . . . This is no last tour. We're here and we'll always come back. It would be a criminal act to break up this band."

During April, Led Zeppelin invaded its own true heartland domain, the cities of the American Midwest. Their audience was starved for them and there were the usual confrontations and melées between police and Zeppelin youth brigades, including a small riot of gate-crashers in Cincinnati and minor police actions in St. Louis, Indianapolis, and Atlanta. In Cleveland for three nights, Robert dedicated "Over the Hills and Far Away" to "one of the greatest dreamers in the world, a star-quality badge-holder named John Bindon." This was an inside joke; Bindon was a chic but notorious London gangster and convicted murderer who now held the position of Master Assassin in Led Zeppelin's private strike force. "It is indeed a pleasure to be back the third night," Plant told the audience at the last show in Cleveland, "but oh, how weak the mortal frame." Two nights later, Led Zeppelin played for 76,000 raving kids at the Pontiac Silverdome in Michigan, breaking its own four-year-old record for the biggest audience for a single act. For once, even Peter Grant didn't demand

Zeppelin's fee in cash. Instead, Richard Cole picked up a check for $800,000 after the show.

In May the tour broke for two weeks of rest. Jimmy had been thinking of going to Cairo (in the footsteps of Crowley), but as always he was vascillating about the decision. But he made up his mind when he was watching television one night and saw a program on the mysteries of the pyramids. Suddenly, in some old newsreel footage, Jimmy saw a zeppelin flying over the ancient monuments, and his decision was made. Jimmy went to Cairo for four days before returning to England and his family. On May 12 the whole band convened at the Grosvenor House Hotel in London to receive a statuette as a reward for their "colourful and energetic contribution to British music."

The second leg of the long tour began again in Alabama on May 18 and progressed through the South. At Fort Worth they played Jerry Lee Lewis's "It'll Be Me" in the encore. At Tampa there was another debacle. Twenty minutes into the show, rain started to pour and the band walked off in fear of electrocution. Ever mindful of the fate of Les Harvey, Led Zeppelin was even further jolted when Keith Relf, the former Yardbirds singer, had electrocuted himself while playing his electric guitar at home the year before. Even before the Tampa show, the roadies had been sent on to check and recheck the electrical connections. When the rain got worse, Peter Grant canceled the show. He originally intended to play the next night, but the disappointed crowd of 70,000 did some damage to Tampa Stadium on the way out, and Led Zeppelin was banned from returning.

On June 7 Led Zeppelin began the first of six sold-out nights at Madison Square Garden. Jimmy Page danced with his guitar acrobatically while Robert's electronic harmonizer, which let him sing with himself, produced unexpected vocal pyrotechnics. Up till New York, Robert had been deferring to his injured foot. The once wild and dancing rock god was now more posed and statuesque. But under the harsh spotlight of Broadway, Robert came back into his own and started to steal shows again. In interviews he waved his unrepentant hippie flag in answer to doubts about Led Zeppelin's *relevance* in relation to the no-future ideology of the punks. Asked what he liked to listen to, Plant replied that he liked Robert Johnson, Bukka White, Elmore James, and Bulgarian folk music. Jimmy stayed in his suite at the Plaza and blasted the Damned's album until the other guests complained and the hotel threatened to throw him out.

In mid-June the band flew to California. On the way to San Diego, Jimmy was so wasted that he had to be almost carried onto the plane. He seemed to live in a netherworld of heroin and tranquilizers. The tour doctor accused him of lifting the Quaaludes out of his medical bags. Page told him to shut up or be fired.

In Los Angeles Led Zeppelin abandoned the Riot House and checked into the less tainted Beverly Hilton. There Jimmy received a few reporters, bantering about Stravinsky, New Wave, the tragedy of guitarist Bert Jansch's arthritis, and his favorite guitars—a Gibson Everly Brothers (a gift from Ron Wood) and a 1959 Les Paul that Eagles guitarist Joe Walsh had given him. After commenting to *Guitar Player* magazine that the untitled fourth Zeppelin album was still his favorite, Jimmy said, "My vocation is more in composition really than in anything else. Building up harmonies, using the guitar, orchestrating the guitar like an army—a guitar army. I'm talking about actual orchestration in the same way you'd orchestrate a classical piece of music."

Later Jimmy sat in his darkened suite as Neal Preston, the tour photographer, clicked through tray after tray of Zeppelin concert slides. Jimmy was looking for a certain picture of himself, but every time a new slide of him came up, Jimmy would be dissatisfied, pointing out some flaw in his physique—"Belly! Crow's feet!"—that the camera had captured. Finally Jimmy was asked what exactly he wanted. Without missing a beat, Jimmy Page answered what he was looking for: "Power, mystery, and the hammer of the Gods."

As always in the past, the Zeppelin hangout of choice was the Rainbow. This time, the scene was much more subdued. Even Bonzo had changed, according to Lori Maddox. "I loved Bonzo," she said. "When he was straight he was the nicest guy in the world, but when he was drunk, he was a maniac. The Beast, for sure. But he still cared about people and he used to lecture me when they were in town then. One night at the Rainbow in '77 he goes, 'Lori, I've been coming here for seven years.' He goes, 'For seven years I've seen the same faces.' He goes, 'I don't want to come back here in seven years and find you here.' And that was a good piece of advice, you know? That night, Bonzo changed my life in a lot of ways."

The six sold-out nights at the Forum in Los Angeles were a great coup for Led Zeppelin. Robert was unbridled again and passionate. He screamed "Jimmy, oh Jimmy" during Page's spitfire solos. At one of the shows, Keith Moon joined the band for an awesome "Whole Lotta Love." The only problem was the audience. This time around, the kids were younger, more restless, even a little nuts. Although *Melody Maker* had described Led Zeppelin's effect on its New York audiences as "a muzzy paralysis," in California the youth ran amok. Frisbees would sail onstage during the acoustic set, breaking Jimmy's fragile concentration. Firecrackers were tossed at the stage and exploded in the musicians' faces. "We've all been hit by things on stage," Robert said, "but the firecrackers are much worse. They scare the hell out of us."

After another two-week break in July, the third and final leg of Led Zeppelin's 1977 tour began at the massive Seattle Kingdome. A week later they were in San Francisco for two nights at the Oakland Coliseum, where once again the show was promoted by Bill Graham. As usual, Graham's veteran security force was at odds with the Zeppelin flying squad, corporaled by John Bindon. For ten years Peter Grant and

Bill Graham had been calling each other's bluff. On July 23, the night of the first Oakland show, there was a showdown of sorts.

It started with Peter Grant's young son, Warren, who was along for part of the tour. There was a hand-lettered sign saying LED ZEPPELIN on the door of one of the house trailers in use backstage as a dressing room, and young Grant asked one of Graham's security men if he could take the sign. According to Richard Cole, the security man shoved Warren Grant away. Bonzo, offstage for a moment, saw this and went over and cursed the man and kicked him a few times before getting back onstage. Then Peter Grant was told that someone had hurt his son, and Grant and John Bindon took the security man inside the trailer and allegedly assaulted him while Richard Cole stood watch outside. Another of Graham's people came to his colleague's aid, and was handled roughly by Cole when he tried to get into the trailer. When Graham's people finally got in the trailer, it was awash in blood and the security man was the unconscious victim of a prolonged, steady beating. The man was taken away to the hospital.

Led Zeppelin's second Oakland show took place the next night, July 24, after Bill Graham had been forced to sign a letter of indemnification, absolving Led Zeppelin from responsibility for the previous night's carnage. The document was of course illegal, as Graham had no legal right to act on behalf of his hospitalized employee. Feelings were running very high, and Jimmy Page sat down for the entire performance, an unprecedented gesture. The next day Led Zeppelin was packing for the trip to the next city, New Orleans, when Richard Cole happened to look out the window and saw police SWAT teams surrounding the building. A few moments after Cole stashed the band's cocaine, he was arrested, as were John Bonham, Peter Grant, and John Bindon. On July 25 all were charged with assault and freed on $250 bail each. A civil suit for $2 million was filed on behalf of their victim.

After this debacle, the band split up. John Paul Jones took off with his family for a camping trip in California. Jimmy stayed put in San Francisco with Peter Grant, while Robert, Bonzo, and Richard Cole flew to New Orleans and checked into the Royal Orleans.

"I remember we walked into the hotel lobby," Cole says, "and as I was checking the group in, there was a call for Robert from his wife. I said, 'Your old lady's on the phone,' and he said, 'All right, I'll take it.' He went up to his room to take the call, and two hours later he called me and said, 'My son's dead.' Like *that*. It was like . . . shit! Jesus fucking Christ!"

At that point the details were still sketchy. On July 26 Karac Plant had been attacked by a violent respiratory virus. The next day the child's condition worsened and an ambulance was summoned, but the boy died before reaching the hospital in Kidderminster. The London press were headlining the story, saying that a "mystery virus" had killed a rock star's son.

Robert was in deep shock. He asked Bonzo and Richard Cole to fly home with him that night. Cole scrambled to charter a plane, to no avail. *Caesar's Chariot* wasn't certified to fly over the Atlantic, and Atlantic Records' corporate plane was on loan to President Carter. So Cole got them to New York on a commercial flight and then to London on British Airways. From Heathrow Cole chartered a private jet to take Robert and Bonzo home. At the airport in Birmingham Robert's father was asked his reaction by a reporter. "All this success and fame," the elder Plant said, "what is it worth? It doesn't mean very much when you compare it to the love of a family."

A few days later Cole went up to Birmingham for the funeral of Karac Plant. Afterward he sat on the green lawn of the crematorium with Robert and Bonzo, the three veteran rovers saying little, mostly just staring.

At the beginning of the ill-fated tour, whose remaining dates had been canceled, Richard Cole had felt that something was going to happen. "The fucking whole thing was wrong," he says ruefully. "There was something wrong. It should never have happened. The whole thing just *went* then. That was it. It never was the same again. *Never.* The whole thing just erupted. It was like somebody said, 'Here, you fuckers, have *this!*'"

Photographs by Peter Simon

Robert Plant at the Riot
House

Robert Plant at the Riot House

photographs by Peter Simon

"Stairway to Heaven" in Long Beach, 1975

San Diego, 1975

Robert, master of
braggadocio, 1975

"Evening: Fall of Day," a colorful 1869 oil of the sun god Apollo by William Rimmer, was the basis for the 1975 Swan Song logo.

John Paul Jones, dour and watchful, Los Angeles, 1975

Robert Plant and family on the farm in Wales, 1976. Karac Plant at left.

Detective (Michael Des Barres at far right) poses for their Swan Song publicity glossy while Jimmy Page slumbers in the arms of Morpheus. The Beverly Hills Hotel, 1975.

Jimmy Page and Richard Cole aboard Caesar's Chariot, 1977.

Led Zeppelin, older and wiser, posing in a Hertfordshire meadow before the Knebworth Festival, August 1979

Robert Plant, publicity photo, 1982

ELEVEN

IN THE EVENING

What's that man movin' 'cross the stage?
It looks a lot like the one used by Jimmy Page
It's like a relic from a different age . . .

—PAUL McCARTNEY
"ROCK SHOW"

Soon the maledicta and infamous libels were flying like bats at sunset. Word on the street had it that Robert Plant blamed Jimmy Page's occult dabbling for the disasters that had landed on Robert's family. The street had it that Robert was through with Jimmy, and that Led Zeppelin had flown its last raid. And these *were* the worst of times. Elvis died of a barbiturate overdose in his home in Memphis that August. This was a real blow to Led Zeppelin, who had drawn songs and inspiration from Elvis since childhood and even considered themselves Uncle Elvis's depraved nephews. The following month Bonzo's car spun out near his home in Cutnall Green, and the drummer sustained three broken ribs and a taste of his own mortality.

In late October Jimmy Page sat for a series of painful interviews with the British music press to deny the rumors that Led Zeppelin was splitting. Visibly distressed at allusions to the now fabled "curse" on Led Zeppelin and the suggestion that the band was now reaping its bad karma, Jimmy spoke in a barely audible whisper: "All that was really tasteless. . . . It's not karma at all. I don't see how the band would merit a karmic attack. All I or we have attempted to do is go out and really have a good time and please people at the same time." Jimmy acknowledged that the vibe around the band was "heavy," but maintained that karma was the wrong term to use. Led Zeppelin didn't deserve this.

Asked about music, Jimmy said that he was auditioning Zeppelin concert tapes that he had collected since the band's first show so that a *real* "live" Zeppelin album could be released to counter what the group felt was a mediocre and expedient performance for its film sound track. He spoke about his new home studio in Sussex, complete with computerized console and memory bank. He was toying with the new Roland guitar synthesizer and had worked on an orchestrated suite for "treated" guitars that would sound like Les Paul, Django Reinhardt, and Jimi Hendrix in the same band. The lyrics, he said, would deal with the four seasons; but work had been hampered by the theft of a cassette box full of Page's demos in America the previous July. But in these interviews, Jimmy kept getting back to what bothered him the most—the charge of negative karma. "Just say," he told *Melody Maker*, "that Jimmy Page is upset by the use of the word 'karma.' I just don't know *what's* going on."

In February 1978, through their lawyers, John Bonham,

Peter Grant, Richard Cole, and John Bindon pleaded *nolo contendere* to the assault charges arising from the Oakland Coliseum brawl the previous July. All four were found guilty and given fines and suspended sentences. Bill Graham was furious that Led Zeppelin had once again gotten away with it. "So they'll never learn," he said ruefully.

Robert Plant spent that winter with his family, and by late spring Maureen Plant was pregnant and the healing process had begun. Robert spent most of his days tinkering on the village piano and drinking so much beer he was soon describing himself as obese. By April Bonzo had talked Robert into rejoining the band, at least just to rehearse. (Around this period, Roy Harper had given an interview to an English farming magazine. The interview was mostly about Harper's sheep, but he also mentioned that he was working with Jimmy Page, writing lyrics for the next Led Zeppelin album. Plant saw this interview [he also subscribed to the magazine] and reportedly exploded. As a result, he contacted Page for the first time in several months.) So Led Zeppelin reconvened in May at the rented Clearwell Castle in the Forest of Dean on the Welsh border and limbered up for a few hours after ten months of silence. By July Robert was sitting in with a local band in Worcestershire, singing R&B standards at venues like Wolverly Memorial Hall. In August he sat in with Dr. Feelgood at the Club Amnesia on the island of Ibiza. In September Richard Cole and Simon Kirke both married, and Robert attended their reception in Fulham along with Jimmy and John Paul Jones. "Everyone was looking at Percy out of the corners of their eyes, to see how he was doing," Cole says. And soon it became clear to everyone: Percy was doing fine, and Led Zeppelin would be back. That same month, September 1978, Keith Moon, the Who's great drummer, died after overdosing on a drug that was weaning him from alcohol.

In November the whole band moved to London to rehearse an album that would be recorded the following month in a Stockholm Studio owned by the group Abba. Musically,

John Paul Jones had taken over the band. Most of the new songs would be built around themes and ideas he brought with him, for which Robert wrote lyrics reflecting the emotional roller coaster he was riding. For the first time John Paul Jones would receive primary composing credit on a Led Zeppelin album. The rehearsals were sensational, and the musicians realized they still could do it. Led Zeppelin had been scornfully ridiculed as musical Goliaths and anal-retentive tax exiles by the punks and new wavers. Now they could fight back with what they realized was their best, most sophisticated music. In the next rehearsal hall, the punk band Generation X was preparing for a tour. As Led Zeppelin were leaving one night, Generation X's spike-haired young singer hurled taunts of obsolescence at them. Bonzo asked who the kid was, and was told his name was Billy Idol.

Led Zeppelin left England in early December for Stockholm. In Sweden the tracks for the group's ninth album would be recorded at Polar Studios, a comfortable and very "live"-sounding studio where Abba had achieved the echoed sound that had made it one of the top groups in the world. Led Zeppelin drank Sweden's extremely alcoholic chemical beer and once again made their album in three weeks. This time, the mood of the sessions was subdued, and Richard Cole couldn't even get a wild party going anymore. "Cold and boring," he says of the Stockholm sessions. Like much of Led Zeppelin's best music, the new tracks were recorded in December. There seemed to be something about the long solstitial nights that clicked for Led Zeppelin.

With the no-nonsense Jones in charge, recording went quickly. Many of the songs had disturbing or turbulent treated guitar overtures and codas, a reflection of Jimmy's current taste. Some of these, such as the spidery enchantment that opens "In the Evening," were taken from themes that had originated in the *Lucifer Rising* sound track. "In the Evening" was terrifying, with its infinitely redoubled guitars and Robert's convulsive screams of "I've got pain"; yet it had an equally terrible majesty, an almost symphonic grandeur that might have heralded a new kind of music. Other tracks had a similarly immense feel. "Fool in the Rain" started as pure steady Zeppelin, but under John Paul Jones the song went to Brazil for the bridge as the band mutated into a samba street band complete with whistles and shouts. The surreal time-skips and wounded imagery of the lyric set a mood of wistful melancholy that dominated the whole record when it came out. There was also some lighter material. "South Bound Suarez" (written by Jones and Plant) was a simple rhythm track over which Jimmy laid one of his typically dissonant guitar solos. "Hot Dog" was a funny parody of country hoe-down music, inspired by a girlfriend of Robert's from Texas named Audrey Hamilton.

Two tracks seemed especially strong to the band. The episodic "Carouselambra," with its multiple themes and hard-bopping synth programs, was like a ride on a fast, sinister merry-go-round. Robert's lyric, mixed so deeply into the magma of the song that the words were unintelligible, had the cadences of a funeral oration for a Norse chieftain. They were made purposely clear, however, on "All My Love," a complex song of mourning and procreation, of death and re-birth. Glistening with synthetic strings and trumpet voluntaries, "All My Love" was Robert's one concession to hope and the future on a record that otherwise dripped with a powerful dejection. The album would end with a monumental Led Zeppelin blues dirge, "I'm Gonna Crawl." After an intro that sounded like a Ralph Vaughan Williams grand landscape, over a lush synthetic orchestral river, Jimmy Page constructed his ultimate blues solo. On this album, where he seemed to have run out of ideas, Jimmy Page turned back to the blues for solace, and his solo seemed to cry with abject remorse.

At least three other tracks were recorded in Stockholm. Two of them, later titled "Ozone Baby" and "Wearing and Tearing," featured Led Zeppelin dressed in the ripped and pinned garb of New Wave, surging with raw power. The latter was really "Train Kept A-Rollin' " on leapers. And "Darlene" was a showcase for Bonzo and Jones's good stride piano, a skilled parody of the Big Bopper and old rock and roll clichés more than anything else.

The sessions for the album that would be called *In Through the Out Door* were finished a few days before Christmas, and the band flew home to be with their families. Just before they left Sweden, they got a call saying that their erstwhile security man, John Bindon, was in Brixton facing manslaughter charges, having allegedly killed a man in a nightclub with a knife. (He was subsequently acquitted of the charges.)

The regenerative surge described in "All My Love" was consummated on January 21, 1979, when Maureen Plant gave birth to another son, who was named Logan Romero Plant. The following month, Robert, Jimmy, and Bonzo returned to Stockholm to mix *In Through the Out Door*. Robert was so excited by the punky energy and sound of one of the outtakes, "Wearing and Tearing," that he wanted the group to release it immediately as a single. "We did that song," he later said, "with the intention of saying, 'OK, we're old dinosaurs and boring old farts, try a little bit of *this*.' " But Jimmy had another plan, which was to release the three spare tracks as an Ep before a big outdoor show that Led Zeppelin planned to play the following summer. In May of that year it was announced that Led Zeppelin would reform to play two massive outdoor shows in the natural amphitheater at Knebworth Park, near Stevenage in Hertfordshire, north of London. *In Through the Out Door*, with its six different covers, would be released at the same time. Led Zeppelin was attempting that rarest of show business miracles—the Comeback.

The press and the new wavers greeted this news with derisive insults. *New Musical Express* opined that "the manner in which old superfart Led Zeppelin have consistently presented themselves has made the band's name synonymous with gratuitous excess. . . . In some ways part of the reason for the venomous loathing directed at the band is not just because they've let themselves down, but also because you know damn well that Jimmy Page at least—like many of the new punk icons a former art student—certainly knows better." And Paul Simonon, the bassist of the most formidable of those icons, the Clash, summed up the visceral hatred the new bands felt for Zeppelin. "Led Zeppelin?" he was quoted. "I don't need to hear the music. All I have to do is look at one of their album covers and I feel like throwing up!"

Led Zeppelin tried to ignore all this as best as possible. Jimmy gave a series of interviews flogging the Knebworth events, and wouldn't even respond to questions about the punk attacks on the band. Instead he drank beer, chain-smoked Marlboros, and spoke on his efforts to prevent the environmental pillage of his beloved Loch Ness. Earlier he had supported a campaign to prevent the stringing of electrical pylons along the shore of the lake. And in May he was invited to cut a ribbon at the reopening of Phillips Harbour in the town of Caithness. At the ceremony the local Labour MP got up and tried to milk some political mileage out of the event. Jimmy disliked Labour and its tax laws, and when it was his turn to speak he got up and dryly noted that the fishermen who had rebuilt the harbor did so almost on their own, as most of the local council had been against spending for the project.

Robert Plant, meanwhile, was singing R&B in Stourbridge with a band variously called Melvin's Marauders and Melvin Giganticus and the Turd Burglars. All the Led Zeppelin musicians showed up at various charity functions in aid of a myriad of causes from Cambodia to handicapped children. Swan Song also had a new act, Dave Edmunds, the great rockabilly guitarist from the group Rockpile, who would release four albums for the label and would sponsor the recording debut of the Stray Cats as his backing band. Swan Song continued to release Bad Company's albums, although the Pretty Things had broken up. Swan Song also released two albums by Detective, before Michael des Barres' L.A. band finally broke up. The problem with Swan Song was that nobody ran it, and the owners saw each other so rarely that there were never any meetings to make decisions about their label. Richard Cole still answered the phones, but the inactivity was driving him mad. "They would never give anyone the go-ahead to do anything," he recalls. "People would bring tapes to the office and I would send 'em on down and nothing would ever happen. It was embarrassing to me. I said, 'What the fuck am I doing?' You get despondent and just drink."

Late in July Led Zeppelin played two nights of live rehearsals at the Falkonerteatret in Copenhagen, Denmark, using the Danish audience as litmus paper for its English comeback. The show—Zeppelin's first in two years—was similar to the 1977 Zeppelin concert repertoire, with the addition of two of the new songs, "In the Evening" and "Hot Dog." Again, "Dazed and Confused" was deleted; now the dramatic bow segment would serve as a twilight-of-the-gods prelude for "In the Evening," Led Zeppelin's new, ever more doom-laden electric guitar symphonette.

Back in England the band gathered at a film studio to work on the new lighting for the evening shows at Knebworth. The most spectacular was a curtain of laser light that would form a pyramid surrounding Jimmy during his bow segment. The next time they all met was at the sound check in the empty bowl of grass at Knebworth. During "Trampled Underfoot" John Bonham put his eleven-year-old son on the drum stool and walked out into the field to listen to his band. Jason Bonham played with his father's huge Ludwig hickory sticks ("trees" in drummer jargon) and astounded the rest of the band by how hard he hit the drums. "It was the first time I ever *saw* Led Zeppelin," Bonzo said.

The first Knebworth show was on August 4, and Led Zeppelin was terrified. It was their first English show since 1975, four years earlier. Robert said, "I didn't believe there was anything I could do that was really good enough to fulfill people's expectations. For me personally, it took half the first night to get over the fact that I was there, and over everything that was going on. My voice was all clammed up with nerves."

But when the band went on that first night, there was a monstrous roar from the hundreds of thousands of denim-clad English kids, who had earlier heard Todd Rundgren's band and Commander Cody, among others. "Celebration Day" had been added to the early part of the three-hour show, while "Heartbreaker" was added to the encores. "Communication Breakdown," that hoary progressive rock grandfather, closed the show. A week later they played again, this time after Ron Wood's band, the New Barbarians. But it rained and the show was plagued by technical difficulties—the theramin refused to work, rendering "Whole Lotta Love" rather flaccid—and was then heavily panned by the English music press as a hopeless exercise in dinosaur music. Led Zeppelin, one paper said, should be an extinct species.

In Through the Out Door was supposed to have been released prior to the Knebworth shows, but the usual delays prevented this, as well as the three-song EP Jimmy had wanted to do. Instead, *In Through the Out Door* came out in the late summer and promptly saved the American record industry from pandemic bankruptcy. The previous year, impressed by the enormous media attention lavished on the New Wave bands, the record companies had gone out and signed young musicians who barely knew how to play their instruments. Only a few of these bands—the Sex Pistols and the Clash—had enough rebellious attitude and animal magnetism to overcome the fact they couldn't really play. In America nobody bought these records. The suburban kids, who had once purchased millions of rock records and pumped up the music business into a multibillion dollar industry, *hated* the punks and detested New Wave. What they wanted was Led Zeppelin and its clones—Black Sabbath, Heart, Cheap Trick, and Foreigner (which was actually more a clone of the ever popular Bad Company). In the high schools, the New Wave fashions and the punk ideology were for losers and nerds. In the high schools of the late 1970s, Led Zeppelin and the Pittsburgh Steelers, in the words of writer David Owen, "drifted together in a vague continuum of big money, fast cars, and prestige." At a time when American record stores were empty of customers, *In Through the Out Door* brought so many kids into the shops that the badly slumped industry got a huge boost overnight as the Zeppelin customers began buying other hard rock bands as well. Trade publications like *Billboard* ran articles implying that Led Zeppelin had rescued the entire pop music business from an early oblivion.

In Through the Out Door had six different covers, each depicting a scene of "Dear John" devastation in a depressingly seedy barroom. Jimmy's solos were spectacular, but the fans recognized that it was John Paul Jones's album—subdued, dark, ominous.

Later in the year drugs again became a problem. Richard Cole was so strung out he was unable to function. "I did Knebworth," he says. "That was the last thing I did with them. I was smacked out of my mind on heroin. I couldn't even handle the money or anything." Then, a few months later, a nineteen-year-old boy, described as "a friend of the band," died of a drug overdose in Jimmy's house. Immediately, Jimmy set about looking for a new place to live, preferably near water like all his abodes.

While Jimmy Page brooded, on vacation in Barbados, the rest of the band tried to keep busy, making appearances at charity functions and concerts for UNICEF. Robert, Jones, and Bonham showed up at a *Melody Maker* poll-winner's reception to collect Led Zeppelin's multiple awards. (The staff of the music paper was not a little displeased, since they had been desperately chasing the rocketing circulation of *New Musical Express* by concentrating on the New Wave bands. Much chagrin ensued when their readers voted for Zeppelin in umpteen categories.) Robert arrived in his Land Rover, while Bonzo and Jones came in by Rolls. Later Bonzo got drunk, complained that the Police should have won the best band award, and started to sing the chorus from "Message in a Bottle" at the top of his voice. John Paul Jones wore a "Rock Against Journalism" button.

In April 1980 Led Zeppelin began to rehearse again for a short tour of Europe. The plan was to play fourteen concerts during June in Germany, Holland, Belgium, and Switzerland. It would be Led Zeppelin's first European shows since 1973. Eventually, in the autumn of 1980, the band would undertake a less demanding tour of the United States. There would be no new records to promote, no laser shows, no more epic self-indulgence. It would just be Led Zeppelin on-stage—power, mystery, and the hammer of the gods.

There would be no more Richard Cole either.

For some time that year, Cole says, the drug traffic around the Swan Song scene in Chelsea had been intense. Cole recalls that $6,000 worth of cocaine was bought one day, with the profits going to finance another trick. But in the spring of 1980 a heroin deal went bad and somebody died. Richard Cole split a small batch of heroin with a friend named Bobby Buckley, each paying ten pounds to a local dealer. The deal had taken place at a shop in the King's Road, with Bonzo also involved. "John Bonham was there with [a Zeppelin road manager] buying smack, cos Bonham was using smack as well," Cole says. That evening, John Bindon—freed from his manslaughter charge—came around to say that Bobby Buckley had been found dead with a needle in his foot. Bindon was looking for the dealer that sold his friend Buckley the heroin that had killed him. Cole told Bindon to come back the next day, because the dealer was coming back to his house.

The next day Cole and Bindon were waiting for the dealer at Cole's house when Jimmy Page came over to buy heroin from him. "He was a drug addict," Cole says of Page; "we *all* were." But Cole explained the situation to Jimmy and told him to leave since there was obviously going to be trouble.

Jimmy left right away, and when the dealer arrived, John Bindon knocked him senseless. A few days later Cole's house was surrounded by riot-equipped police. Earlier a Colombian girl had been murdered in Cole's street; someone had told the police that Cole had bragged in a pub that he had run the girl over and thrown her in a basement somewhere. Cole denied the charge. Then they asked if he knew that Bobby Buckley had died of an overdose. Cole said he knew nothing.

Richard Cole fell out with his employer, Peter Grant, before the European tour. Grant decided that Cole was too wasted to do his job, so Rex King ran the tour instead. In a stupor Cole uttered a vague threat against Grant's children, which got back to Peter Grant, who never forgave him. Richard was fired. He flew to Italy with a girl friend to try to kick heroin, checking into the Excelsior Hotel in Rome. At dawn the following morning Italian counter-terrorism police broke down the door. They confiscated two switchblades, three syringes, a spoon, a lemon, and an eighth of an ounce of what the police said was cocaine; Richard claimed it was planted. Richard Cole was charged with terrorism and sent to the maximum security Regina Coeli prison near Rome, where he rotted for six months.

The first date of Led Zeppelin's first tour since the death of Robert Plant's son was in Dortmund, Germany, on June 17 at the Westfalenhalle. The whole tour was scaled way down, with no video screen or much in the way of visual effects. Jimmy appeared painfully thin and frail in a floppy suit and skinny punk tie, and played with a new, spartan economy. John Paul Jones had short, swept-back hair and was clearly the music director of the band, playing electric clavinet and organ in addition to grand piano and his bass. Bonzo was at his heaviest, fully bearded, and played in top form when he was feeling well. Robert Plant was subdued when compared to the raving swordsman of a now bygone era, but he still danced and moved with his own peculiar graceful gestures.

He dressed for the stage in a silk T-shirt, jeans, and sneakers. The show had changed again; it now began with "Train Kept A-Rollin' " in a version the old Yardbirds would never have dreamed possible. Then came "Nobody's Fault But Mine" and the bone-chilling "In the Evening," now without the bowed, distorted fanfare. "The Rain Song" reprised some mid-period Zeppelin before the newer "Hot Dog" and "All My Love." "Trampled Underfoot" was devastating hard rock, relieved by "Since I've Been Loving You," now Robert's trenchant show-piece of loss and emotion. White light and smoke filled the stage for "Achilles Last Stand." After the "White Summer" solo (painstakingly played and sounding more Spanish now than Indian) had segued into "Kashmir," the show ended with "Stairway to Heaven," Led Zeppelin's universal hymn of teen redemption. Depending on the audience, the encores were "Rock and Roll," "Communication Breakdown," and "Whole Lotta Love."

The shows were highly erratic as the tour moved on through Cologne, Brussels, and Rotterdam. On some nights Jimmy looked "weary, unshaven, unsteady and sweaty," according to one of the few journalists who covered the tour. On other nights he jumped in the air, used extravagant wizard moves to finish songs, and actually *spoke to the audience*, even introducing songs occasionally in his peculiar, nasal voice. This had never happened before.

Offstage, the scene was as subdued as some of the shows. Without Richard Cole to goad Led Zeppelin, there were few of the usual outrages. The musicians were all well into their thirties, successful British businessmen selling long hair and progressive rock to European youth and the American soldiers who filled the ten-thousand-seat halls in Frankfurt and Mannheim, waving signs saying NUKE IRAN. At Nuremburg on June 27 John Bonham fell off his drum chair and collapsed after the third song of the night. The official explanation was "exhaustion." In Frankfurt a few days later he walked over to the side of the stage during "White Summer" to hug

Ahmet Ertegun, who had just arrived. The crowds were so furious and violent in that town that Jimmy had to stop playing, walk over to the mike, and beg, "Please, just give us a chance!" Led Zeppelin couldn't even hear itself playing.

Jimmy chain-smoked continually. He said he just wanted to play and play with his band and never stop. Offstage, he seemed more alert and sociable than he had in years. One night, in the basement bar of the group's hotel in Mannheim, Jimmy made a rare post-show appearance. He drank a little and chatted with fans, among them the editor of a Led Zeppelin fanzine called *Tight But Loose*. The editor asked for an autograph, and Jimmy took a pen and scrawled "Tight But Loose readers—Thanks for your support. Hope we can always live up to your expectations. Jimmy Page Led Zeppelin."

Led Zeppelin's last tour ended in Berlin on July 7, 1980, after Jimmy cancelled a series of concerts in France. Asked for a comment, Bonzo said, "Overall, everyone has been dead chuffed with the way this tour's gone."

A little more than two months later, Led Zeppelin reconvened to rehearse for the upcoming American tour. Later they gathered at Jimmy's new house in Windsor, a huge former mill, again alongside the Thames, protected by a high stone wall. It had been purchased from actor Michael Caine for nearly a million pounds, and fit Jimmy's two main criteria: It was on the water and it had room for rehearsal space and a studio to replace Jimmy's recording facilities at Plumpton. There, on Old Mill Lane in Windsor on September 24, 1980, Led Zeppelin gathered for the last time.

Hopes for the group's complete revival were very high. The week before, Jimmy had told a journalist, "I feel there is a lot more to do simply because this band thrives on a challenge." By then Bonzo had stopped using heroin, but he had been drinking heavily and was taking a drug called Motival, which reduced anxiety and kept his spirits up. A friend later said that

Bonzo had seemed very wound up and anxious about going back to America because the last Zeppelin tour had been such a disaster and lawsuits were still hanging over him in California.

Rex King was chauffeuring Bonzo that morning. He picked Bonham up at his place, Old Hyde Farm, but the drummer insisted that they stop in a pub before driving to the rehearsal. At the pub Bonzo drank four quadruple vodkas with orange juice and ate a couple of ham rolls. He continued to drink vodka during the band rehearsal at a studio in Berkshire, until he was almost too drunk to play. It had always been a point of pride with John Bonham that he was never too far gone to do his job. During a twelve-year career he had never missed a Led Zeppelin concert and had been careful to be on time and at his best at every rehearsal.

Later Bonzo continued his binge at a band reunion party at Jimmy's house in Windsor. He downed two or three large double vodkas an hour before midnight, when he passed out on a sofa. Jimmy's assistant Rick Hobbs had been through this scene before. He half-carried Bonzo to a bedroom and laid him on his side, propped up with pillows, and turned out the light.

The next afternoon Bonzo hadn't appeared. Benji LeFevre, who worked for Robert, went in to wake the drummer. But his face was blue and ghastly and there was no pulse. An ambulance was called, but it was obvious that Bonzo had died sometime that morning. He was thirty-one years old.

Immediately on receiving the shocking news, Led Zeppelin and its retinue scattered. Robert went north to be with Pat and Bonham's children while Jones went home and Jimmy stayed in Windsor. The story of Bonzo's death made international headlines, and soon a little cluster of fans began a silent vigil outside the wall of Jimmy's house. Immediately the maledicta and annoying rumors began to spread. A fan magazine claimed that thick black smoke had been seen billowing from Jimmy's house on the day after Bonzo died, and that the guitarist had gone on a destructive rampage upon hearing the news, cursing in strange languages. It was also blithered that Jimmy had ordered a huge supply of recording tape and had cut some sort of "tribute" to Bonzo. And the old canard about led Zeppelin's so-called *Black Album* was refloated. Kicking around for years, this rumor had it that the band had recorded an album's worth of death chants that a German writer claimed he had translated from Old Swabian. Two days after Bonzo died, the London *Evening News* headlined ZEPPELIN "BLACK MAGIC" MYSTERY. Quoting an unnamed source close to the group, it was reported, "It sounds crazy, but Robert Plant and everyone around the band is convinced that Jimmy's dabbling in black magic is responsible in some way for Bonzo's death and for all these other tragedies. . . . I think the three remaining members of Zeppelin are now a little afraid of what is going to happen next."

Bonzo's memorial was held two weeks later on October 10 at Rushock parish church not far from the Bonhams' farm. Bonzo's remains had been cremated shortly after his death. Massive security had been laid on, but only eight local youths stood in a drenching rain to witness the obsequies. The small church was packed, and several villagers stood outside, unable to get in. Local musicians from the Electric Light Orchestra and Wings supported Pat Bonham and her children, Jason and Zoe.

At a coroner's inquest sometime later, a pathologist reported that John Bonham had died of an overdose of alcohol, having drunk forty measures of vodka during a twelve-hour period, and then choked on his own vomit while asleep. Jimmy testified that Bonzo was "pretty tipsy" when he arrived at the rehearsal, and also said that it was hard to tell how drunk Bonzo was because he drank all the time. Rex King testified to Bonzo's binge after leaving Cutnall Green, as did Rick Hobbs and Benji LeFevre. After the hearing, the East Berkshire coroner noted that the police had visited Jimmy Page's house when they learned of John Bonham's death, but had found nothing suspicious. The coroner went on to record a verdict of death by misadventure—an accidental suicide.

At the Regina Coeli prison in Rome, a fellow prisoner approached Richard Cole and said, "One of your group's dead." "Poor Pagey," thought Cole, believing that it was Jimmy who had died.

But the sorcerer had survived. His apprentice had not. There were unfounded press reports that the three surviving members were divided about whether to split. Various English drummers—Cozy Powell, Carl Palmer, Aynsley Dunbar—were rumored under consideration to replace Bonzo in a reformed Led Zeppelin. But then Jimmy couldn't see going out on the road with anybody but John Bonham anyway. Nobody had the heart for it. On December 4, 1980, as the English winter days grew shorter, Led Zeppelin issued the following, typically ambiguous statement to the press: "The loss of our dear friend, and the deep sense of harmony felt by ourselves and our manager, have led us to decide that we could not continue as we were."

TWELVE

CODA

. . . we knew that if Bonham had been there, he would have done what had to be done. You know, you need a drum about that big and be able to hit it so hard. Bonham—you won't get another one of him.

—CHARLIE WATTS

After Bonzo died, the fragments of the once mighty Led Zeppelin slowly began to drift in their own currents and eddies.

Jimmy went back to work almost immediately. A neighbor of his, film director Michael Winner, commissioned him to score the sound track for the awesomely tasteless sequel to the film *Death Wish*. With a tight deadline to finish *Death Wish*

II, Jimmy reached into his old trick bag. "In the Evening" was transformed into the film's theme song, 'Who's to Blame," sung by blustery old-timer Chris Farlowe. "The Release" was a short chase theme that implied what direction Led Zeppelin might have headed had not Bonzo done himself in. When in doubt, wise sound track hacks loot the classics, and Frédéric Chopin's "Prelude No. 3 in G#" now reappeared as simply "Prelude," mournfully played on the crying, bent-note electric guitar. The most significant feature of the *Death Wish II* sound track was the really frightening sonic montage of "scary sounds" that Jimmy contrived for suspenseful episodes, dark swooping cones of droning noise that seemed to bring the icy edge of the void too close for comfort.

In September 1981 Jimmy bought a recording studio in Berkshire that had been owned by Gus Dudgeon, Elton John's producer. At that point he had been almost a complete recluse for a year, refusing to speak to anyone not an employee or a close friend. But he was contemplating an endorsement of Roland synthesizers, and told a visiting Roland employee that the reason he wasn't playing in public was because he missed Bonzo too much.

After that, with rare exceptions, it would be two years before Jimmy Page was heard from again.

John Paul Jones disappeared completely. As a pop recording artist and stage personality, that identity was retired and John Baldwin returned to his family life in the placid English countryside. Everybody around Led Zeppelin knew that Baldwin was its only real survivor. He hadn't died, or lost a child; he never got into hard drugs. Instead he retired to his farms with a great fortune and his dignity intact. From time to time, Baldwin's good luck was attributed to his refusal to join Led Zeppelin's legendary satanic pact. Even intelligent and rational friends of Led Zeppelin like Danny Goldberg and Benoit Gautier refused to discount the story completely. "At a certain time, Jimmy *might* have done it," Gautier says. "I wouldn't be surprised if it were true. They were all *very* young, and the other two guys were from out-of-town. They hadn't made it in the business and Jimmy was already a legend. I'm sure he could have persuaded John [Bonham] . . . I wouldn't be a bit surprised, if you look at who died and who suffered and who survived. You have to believe that Satan is able to do that. It's logical in its craziness. Jimmy couldn't manipulate Jonesy to the last."

As for the late Bonzo, Gautier says, "I think he's basically up there, or perhaps somewhere else, and he thinks it's a good joke. You can almost hear him saying, 'Let's drink to it and play some darts. Hey, funny, eh?' "

It took longer for Robert Plant to recover from Bonzo's death. The two had grown up together and Robert of course had brought John Bonham into Led Zeppelin. Speaking two years later, Robert recalled Bonham's death: "It was one of the most flattening, heartbreaking parts of my life. I had a great, warm, big-hearted friend I haven't got anymore. It was so . . . *final*. I never even thought about the future of the band or music."

Robert's interest was revived a few months after Bonzo passed on. In the spring of 1981 he began appearing anonymously with a northern R&B band called the Honeydrippers, led by guitarist Robbie Blunt, an old friend from Kidderminster who had played with Silverhead and Chicken Shack. The Honeydrippers pumped out vintage 1950s R&B, the music of Albert King, Otis Rush, and Gene Vincent, in nightclubs throughout the north—Sheffield, Nottingham, Derby. At the same time, Robert was recording a collection of rockabilly songs on a four-track tape recorder. Later in the year he felt ready to move up from re-created R&B. Writing with Robbie Blunt on the four-track, he began to create his own new musical persona, one he could better live with now that the days of flamboyant Percy were in his past. His new songs were also influenced by Arabic music. Before leaving on a trip to Morocco with his wife in the spring of 1982, he gave Robbie Blunt a cassette of the orchestral odes of the late Om Kalthoum, the Egyptian singer and pan-Islamic heroine, and told the guitarist he should learn to play like she sang. In Morocco Robert and Maureen visited the town of Goulimine, in the south, and heard the Berber rhythms and chants of the famous Blue Women of Goulemine. Then they went even farther south, skirting the edge of the Sahara.

Back in England Robert took Robbie Blunt and a group of Midlands musicians to a studio in Wales to record his first solo album. Like Jimmy, he raided the late-period Zeppelin masterpiece "In the Evening" for the album's main stomp, "Burning Down One Side." The Arabic classicism of Om Kalthoum was apparent on "Slow Dancer" and "Pledge Pin." When the basic tracks were done, using various drummers and Blunt's simple, bluesy guitar, Robert took the tapes to Jimmy Page for approval. "It was very emotional," he later told an interviewer. "We just sat there and I sort of had my hand on his knee. We were just sitting through it together. He knew then that I'd gone, that I was off on my own with the aid of other people and just forging ahead, and all I wanted him to do was to do the same thing." In the same interview Robert confessed his motivation at age thirty-four: "I didn't want to be written off as an old fart."

In May 1982 Jimmy and Robert joined the group Foreigner in Munich for an encore, Little Richard's "Lucille." A few months later Robert's first solo album was released on Swan Song. *Pictures at Eleven*, contrary to Robert's expressed expectation, was a success. It debuted in the U.S. Top Ten and stayed there for five weeks, reaching Number 3. In England it got as high as Number 2. Since Robert didn't want to play any Led Zeppelin songs ("It would be idiotic and heartless," he was quoted), he didn't tour to support his album. Around the same time Jimmy told *International Musician*, "It would be silly to even think about going on with Zeppelin. It would have been a total insult to John. I couldn't have played the numbers and looked around and seen someone else on the drums. It wouldn't have been an honest thing to do."

The songs Robert Plant wrote for *Pictures at Eleven* were mostly expressions of release and relief. It was as if he had at last been freed from the dark shadow of the Zeppelin.

By mid-1982, two years after the dissolution of the band, Led Zeppelin still was managing to generate public controversy. "Stairway to Heaven," now more than ten years old, was *still* the most requested song on American FM stations, and this began to bother a group of Baptist preachers in the South and Southwest. One prominent Baptist used his radio pulpit to preach that "Stairway to Heaven" carried subliminal satanic messages. On a nationally syndicated Sunday morning broadcast, he played two versions of "Stairway to Heaven." The first was at normal speed and sounded like what every healthy American teen-ager considered his personal hymn. The second version was played at a much slower speed, and the words "Here's to my sweet Satan" could be faintly discerned. At the end of the song, the same spooky voice seemed to say "It's gonna snow." The preacher claimed this as proof that rock music was a vehicle for the Antichrist. And in April 1982 a committee of the California state assembly played a *backward* tape of "Stairway to Heaven" in public session, in the belief that subliminal Devil worship had been grafted into the record via a process called backward masking. Some members of the committee claimed they clearly heard the words "I live for Satan" when they heard "Stairway" played backward. Led Zeppelin was duly denounced as agents of the Devil, luring millions of kids into damnation as unwitting disciples of the Antichrist and the forces of darkness.

Eddie Kramer, the producer and engineer who worked on four Led Zeppelin albums, says that these charges are "totally and utterly ridiculous. Why would they want to spend so much studio time doing something so dumb?" Kramer insists there is no such thing as backward masking and that Led Zeppelin never recorded any hidden messages in their songs. He also points out that any preacher can take "Stairway to Heaven" into a recording studio and overdub whatever is necessary to realize some crackpot theory.

In December 1982 Jimmy released Led Zeppelin's last album as Swan Song's last record. *Coda* was a collection of eight tracks spanning the length of Zeppelin's twelve-year flight. "We're Gonna Groove (a one-time show opener) dated from the *Led Zeppelin II* sessions in 1969. "Poor Tom" was from the Bron-Y-Aur period in 1970, while "I Can't Quit You Baby" was from an Albert Hall sound check the same year. "Walter's Walk" had been left over from the 1972 Stargroves sessions. The second side consisted of the three Stockholm out takes—"Ozone Baby," "Darlene," and "Wearing and Tearing"—plus the treated drum track titled "Bonzo's Montreux," which Jimmy had remixed in 1982 in his new studio, and credited to "The John Bonham Drum Orchestra."

The album was released with no fanfare. The jacket was almost sepulchral, with old snapshots of the band on the inside sleeve. As usual, the critics panned the record. *The New York Times* noted that *Coda* was the first new Led Zeppelin music since Bonzo's death, "and a timely answer to the prayers of record-store owners, record executives dismayed by the continuing sales slump, and America's white male teenagers. It did not have to be very good to be just what the doctor ordered, and it isn't." *Coda* entered the American charts at Number 4 the week of its release, and sold well for the next year.

During the summer of 1983 Robert Plant released his second solo album, *The Principle of Moments*. Written in Ibiza and again recorded in Wales with drummers Phil Collins and Cozy Powell, it was less adventurous than *Pictures at Eleven* and was even more successful as a result. The album was also helped by the two cool and enigmatic videos produced to promote it. The video for the FM radio hit "Bit Log" conveyed the song's lyric of on-the-road melancholy by depicting Robert stranded at a gas station in the American desert, tearing up old photographs, searching through a ruined town, and puzzling over a cat's cradle before being towed off into the sunset. In the video for "I'm in the Mood," Robert Plant is posed gazing earnestly at a lemon.

Most significantly, *The Principle of Moments* was issued on Atlantic, not Swan Song. Personal problems had brought down Peter Grant, who had never even attended any of Robert's rehearsals or recording sessions. So Robert declared his total independence of the last vestige of Led Zeppelin by abandoning Swan Song. Queried later about Grant by reporters, Robert refused to comment beyond saying that he still respected Peter Grant and their past association.

In June 1983 Robert drove his big brown Mercedes to Shepperton Studios near London to rehearse for his first solo tour, which would begin in America in September. The drummer on the American tour would be Phil Collins, while Richie Hayward, late of Little Feat, would work on Plant's English tour at the end of the year. A few days later he taped performances for *Top of the Pops* and *A Midsummer Night's Tube*, and then went to court to prevent what he felt was an inferior performance from running on the *Tube* show.

Robert went to America in September and toured for two months, playing material from both his solo albums. Despite many requests, he refused to play any Led Zeppelin music. Instead, many of his shows ended with a reggae version of Bob Marley's "Lively Up Yourself." In interviews, he confirmed that he had separated from his wife and was living alone. He said that he was happy to be a solo act because he felt too isolated with Led Zeppelin, and also said that he was pleased that his records had been seriously reviewed. Several times he specifically denied all the rumors about Jimmy Page and his occult interests, and especially discounted the stories concerning his aversion to Jimmy's preoccupation with Aleister Crowley. Robert described himself as a person who lived in the country and enjoyed tennis and good travel writing. Wistfully, he said he regretted not having kept a journal of Led Zeppelin's journeys and adventures over the years. He also slagged the new generation of young Zeppelin imitators like Def Leppard.

The American shows had mostly sold out. The Zeppelin kids turned out in droves to hear Robert's new art rock, which was described in the press as "moody, unmelodic tone poems" and "artfully melodramatic rock exoticism." Richard Cole, now living in Los Angeles, thought the show he saw was stiff. The kids, he noticed, just *sat* there, with none of the febrile, tribal headbanging that Zeppelin used to conjure automatically. Before he went back to England. Robert appeared as a guest VJ on MTV, the cable rock video channel. Smiling, relaxed, casual, with bags under his eyes from tour fatigue, he played videos by Elvis, Dave Edmunds and the Stray Cats, Visage, and Duran Duran, whose "style and elegance" he singled out for praise.

In October Robert, Jimmy, and John Paul Jones met in London to discuss formally dissolving the moribund Swan Song, which would release no more records and whose offices in New York and London were now closed. But the three couldn't manage to reach a decision about closing their company. "They haven't changed," Robert said to a friend, speaking of his two former comrades. "They still can't make up their minds."

The previous month, in late September, Jimmy Page had emerged from his veil of seclusion to play an all-star benefit at Royal Albert Hall. It came about because Ronnie Lane, the one-time Faces bassist (and proprietor of the mobile studio that Led Zeppelin had used to record), had been crippled by multiple sclerosis. Lane had received some relief from an unorthodox treatment with hyperbaric oxygen, which required expensive equipment that was beyond the reach of most sufferers of the debilitating disease. So Ronnie Lane asked Eric

Clapton to play a benefit in London so a machine could be bought that would be used by other MS victims as well. Clapton agreed to play, and began a chain of events that would culminate in the formation of a 1960's English dream band. Glyn Johns agreed to produce the show, and brought in Ian Stewart of the Stones, who in turn brought in drummer Charlie Watts and bassist Bill Wyman. Later, during a party at Jeff Beck's house, Stewart also recruited Beck and Jimmy Page. The previous summer, there had been a Yardbirds reunion at the Marquee, organized by Paul Samwell-Smith, Jim McCarty, and Chris Dreja. Neither Eric Clapton or Jeff Beck turned up, and Jimmy wasn't even invited, which he had felt was an insult. So at the party, Ian Stewart was discussing the Ronnie Lane benefit with Jeff Beck and Jimmy wandered over and complained, "Nobody ever asked me to play. Why can't I play on it?" Stewart replied, "Step this way." Soon other musicians—Joe Cocker, drummer Kenny Jones, Steve Winwood—joined as well, but the drawing card for the show would be the three Yardbirds guitars—Clapton, Beck, and Page— together on stage for the first time.

The show took place in the last week of September. Eric Clapton acted as host and opened the show with a set of his skillful blues and southern rock. Jeff Beck and his improvising fusion band (with Jan Hammer on keyboards) took the middle spot and played atmospheric electro-jazz for an hour. Jimmy had been saved for last because he had been out of the public eye for so long. He walked on under a single spotlight to an emotional storm of cheering and, deliberately, took off his jacket, removed his rings, and rolled up his sleeves as the applause washed over him. Pencil-thin and sporting a long mop of black curls, he opened with his Chopin prelude, backed by Jeff Beck's rhythm section of drummer Simon Phillips and Fernando Saunders on bass. Steve Winwood came out to do the vocals for "Who's to Blame" and other songs from the *Death Wish II* sound track. Finally Jimmy was strapped into the Gibson doubleneck, on which he played "Stairway to

Heaven" as an instrumental, without vocals, still majestic and dynamic even without Robert's voice. He finished with a twelve-string coda and a little bow display before walking off. When he came back, it was with Eric Clapton and Jeff Beck. The three guitarists played "Layla," Clapton's famous love song. They were all around forty and preoccupied with the stresses of deepening middle age, but that night they all seemed radiant and purposeful. During Jimmy's show someone looted his dressing room.

Three months later the ARMS (for Action Research into Multiple Sclerosis) benefit went on the road to four American cities—Dallas, San Francisco, Los Angeles, and New York—under the auspices of Bill Graham. To mark the occasion, Jimmy Page told friends, he ended his long addiction to heroin.

The American leg of the tour began with rehearsals and two shows in Dallas. Steve Winwood had other commitments, so Jimmy recruited Paul Rodgers to come along and sing with him. Bad Company had disbanded two years earlier, and Rodgers was making solo albums and trying to return as one of English rock's great vocalists. For some time he and Jimmy had been talking about forming a band and going on the road. For this tour they began writing a long song in four segments that remained unfinished and untitled but which they performed anyway. After Dallas the tour went to San Francisco, where Jimmy holed up in his hotel suite, so overcome with nerves that he didn't even socialize with the other musicians. After the shows, while the other stars hung around backstage and talked, Jimmy stepped into a waiting van and was whisked back to his hotel. One San Francisco paper slammed him as "the most over-rated guitarist in rock." The next night Jimmy stepped to the front microphone and said, "Good evening—it's nice to see some friendly faces out there." Responding to the pressure, Jimmy produced a superb set. After playing Chopin on his black Telecaster for two minutes, he whipped out his bow and touched it to the guitar. As the crowd began to scream in recognition—"The Bow!!"—Jimmy threw it into the audience without playing a note, as if the bow were just some meaningless gimcrack from the remote past. Then he introduced Paul Rodgers and played "Who's to Blame" and "City Sirens" from *Death Wish II*, and then went into "Mama Loves to Boogie" from Paul Rodgers' solo album. Then he introduced "a completely new number that Paul and I have been working on, and we really hope you like it." Variously titled "Midnight Moonlight" or "Bird on the Wing," the new song was like a lexicon of Jimmy's guitar mannerisms. Sitting on a chair and bending over the guitar in concentration, Jimmy played blood-boiling hard rock, folkish fingerpicking, psychedelic sustained notes, and a new style of chiming funk. As the song started to stomp, Jimmy got up and began to display all his old moves, throwing back his hair, leaning back to the floor, gesturing through sustained chords with an extended arm, strutting around the stage, smiling and waving, enjoying himself; he was uninhibited by all the crippling self-consciousness of the past. The audience response to this new song, as in all the other cities, was utter pandemonium. This was the man who turned guitar playing into an athletic event. Jimmy finished his set, as he had in London, with the instrumental "Stairway to Heaven," which Robert had refused to sing on his American tour two months earlier. This time, Jimmy invited the crowd to sing along. "Be my guest," he said. For the explosive "Stairway" finale, Clapton and Beck came onstage and played with him. After "Layla," Bill Graham introduced all the musicians, who had lined up on the stage with Ronnie Lane. When Graham got to Jimmy Page, the audience shouted for five full minutes in tribute. Jimmy was embarrassed. Once again, he had stolen the show.

When the ARMS tour arrived in Los Angeles a few days later, Jimmy checked into the Sunset Marquis as "James MacGregor." Traveling with him was a young stripper whom Jimmy had picked up in an all-night liquor store in San Francisco. When Jimmy got into town, he called Richard

Cole, who was living quietly in Hollywood, drinking away the $200,000 he had left over from Zeppelin.

Before Cole had been released from his Italian prison after Bonzo had died, he had been visited by English detectives who wanted to discuss a few unsolved murders with him. Soon after, Jimmy Page was arrested for possession of a small amount of cocaine. These unrelated events, plus the advice of friends who warned Cole that Peter Grant was after him, prompted Richard Cole to relocate to California after his release in early 1981. A little more than a year later, Jimmy visited Los Angeles and got Cole to procure heroin for him. "He was so thin then," Cole remembers, "that you could stick your fist between his neck and his collar." This time, when Richard Cole visited him at his hotel, Jimmy still looked spectrally thin, but didn't ask Richard for dope. He was clean. Jimmy also had a reunion with Lori Maddox, now twenty-five, who still loved Jimmy Page even more than ever. They met at the Rainbow, and were soon kissing each other under the tables. Later Lori tried to drag Jimmy out to the parking lot so they could be photographed together, but he fought her off. He moved Lori into his hotel and the two old lovers had a long talk. Lori told Jimmy she was hurt because she knew he had been in town over the past few years and he had never called her. "And this is what he said to me," she recalls, slipping into an endearing imitation of Jimmy's accent: " 'Lori, for the last seven years I've been so smacked out I didn't even want to see you.' He goes, 'Now I'm off the stuff. You know how long it took me to get off it? *Four days.*' "

Lori continues, "Just say our love was special. I'm the angel with a broken wing, you know. I'm embarrassed talking about it. You know, I don't tell *anybody* this, and I hope he doesn't get angry with me 'cause I still love him very much. He has such a great heart, an *incredible* heart. I'll always love him. I grew up with him, it was like the beginning of my life.

"And it was so sad to see him like that, so thin and pale," she says. "I couldn't even believe it. It just hurt me so much because he must have been so unhappy to have done that to himself. I think all the bitches drove him to it. The next thing I knew, he just went asexual for a while and kind of hibernated and went into heroin. He wasn't the old Jimmy anymore. But now he's quit and he's the same person again, as strong as ever.

"He told me he did it every day for seven years, and he says he's not doing it anymore. I believe he's not. There's no reason for him to lie. And he was worried about me. He said, 'You're not hooked on that stuff, are you Lori?'

"And when I said no, he said, 'Thank God!' "

In Los Angeles Jimmy again played well. When he pulled out the bow to tease the crowd, the Forum went berserk. Paul Rodgers, stocky, sincere, still swinging his mike like the teenage singer of Free fifteen years before, was beginning to hit his stride. Backstage, Jimmy had his own dressing room. The girl from San Francisco sat in a corner and said nothing. Because of his role in the Oakland massacre back in 1977, Richard Cole was confined by Bill Graham to one backstage corridor of the Forum, allowed in only as a courtesy to Jimmy. At one point Cole inquired about Peter Grant: "How's Fatso?" Jimmy said, "I fired the fat cunt. Fuck him, he's had it. Bollocks him."

The next night Jimmy was visited by his old friends Miss Pamela and singer Michael des Barres, now married to each other and living in Los Angeles. Michael had a new band, Chequered Past, with Steve Jones, who had been guitarist for the Zeppelin-reviling Sex Pistols. Backstage, Michael was trying to act coolly while at the same time begging Jimmy to play on a few tracks of his group's first album. Steve Jones was saying to Jimmy, "You've always been my idol," and Jimmy was going "uh-huh, uh-huh," having been awake for five days straight at that point. Later, Jimmy told Miss Pamela that he was lonely and had no friends. "Always the con man," Pamela laughed.

After Los Angeles the ARMS tour traveled to New York.

Jimmy again got the great crowd response that was now accepted by the other two Yardbirds guitarists, who had once been cast as his great rivals. (*Rolling Stone,* covering the tour, reported: "There were the tiniest intimations of tension between Clapton, who kicked a debilitating drug problem more than a decade ago, and Page, about whom such a thing has never been said.") Jimmy's reviews were again mixed. One critic said he looked "as gray as a piece of fast food roast beef." Another said that Jimmy's new collaborative song with Paul Rodgers, if edited down, could help redefine the word multiplatinum.

After the tour Jimmy went home, and then on to Singapore and Bali for the Christmas holidays. Before he left, he told the press that he might form a new band with Paul Rodgers sometime in 1984, and maybe cut a record and go back out on the road. "I've been unemployed too long," he was quoted.

When Jimmy returned from Singapore, he called Richard Cole in California and told him about Robert's December tour of England. John Paul Jones had got onstage and jammed at the Bristol show. Jimmy was scheduled to catch up with the tour when it hit London. Cole recalls Jimmy saying, "I was gonna go later on in the evening. But then Jonesy called me up and said, 'No no no.' He said, 'You gotta go right from the beginning, cos after the fourth number it goes straight downhill.'"

A few months later Richard Cole was arrested twice in one day for drunken driving and faced jail under California law. Instead, he fled the country on the night flight to London. Before he left, he mused on what he termed "that whole fucking Led Zeppelin stigma." Asked if he believed in it, he replied, "I don't think anyone's fucking benefited. I never had any fucking good luck from it after it was over. Plant's not with his wife; his son died. Pagey . . . Jones is all right. Bonzo's dead. Grant is out of it. . . . The whole fucking thing seems like it's under a *cloud.*"

∗   ∗   ∗

But gradually, Led Zeppelin's wounds began to heal. As 1984 progressed and England was gripped by labor unrest, Jimmy Page went back to work at the age of forty. He played on sessions for a Stephen Stills solo album, and joined Robert Plant and disco funk producer Nile Rogers in the studio to work on an album of classic rock and roll songs. Not only did these sessions reunite Jimmy and Robert in a recording studio for the first time since Bonzo's death, they also re-paired Jimmy with Jeff Beck for their first dueling guitar solos since the end of the Yardbirds. The first five tracks from these sessions were released anonymously in the autumn of 1984 as an Ep titled *The Honeydrippers/Volume One*, on Robert's new Es Paranza label. The Honeydrippers' material included new versions of Hank Ballard and the Midnighters' "I Get A Thrill," Phil Phillips's New Orleans classic "Sea of Love," Ray Charles's "I Got A Woman" (which Ray borrowed from an old gospel record by the Southern Tones called "It Must Be Jesus"), Ben E. King's "Young Boy Blues" (written by Phil Spector), and a raucous, big-band, dueling guitar mosh-up on Roy Brown's "Rockin' At Midnight." Although released *incognito*, Robert's voice was unmistakable and he appeared in the dreamy, romantic videos shot in the Balaeric isles. The music didn't really generate that much heat, but old fans recognized the pure enthusiasm that was familiar from Led Zeppelin's relaxed, homage-laden encores back in rock's days of yore. The album was a commercial success, staying in the American Top Ten for weeks.

Even Bonzo got into the act, from beyond the grave. In England a group from Liverpool called Frankie Goes to Hollywood had a number-one hit with a song called "Relax." But the song's hard-hitting drum track had been programmed by a New York engineer on a Fairlight digital synthesizer after "sampling" two seconds of Bonzo's drums from *Led Zeppelin II*. The ironies were murderous.

Late in 1984, Jimmy was observed by police looking dazed and confused at a London train station. When they investigated, they found a packet of cocaine and arrested him. Since it was his second cocaine arrest in two years, there were fears he might go to jail. But at his hearing in November, a magistrate merely slapped his wrist. As Page stood before him, the judge said, "Generally for a second offense of this nature you should go to prison. But I take the view that if a prison sentence is passed, it may well prevent you from pursuing your profession." Jimmy was fined £450. He was just too valuable as an artist and as an earner of American dollars to go to jail. Later that month, he announced that he and Paul Rodgers had formed a band called The Firm. An album and a tour were said to be imminent.

But by 1985, the pop world that Led Zeppelin once knew and dominated no longer existed. Young music fans were now spoon-fed a vapid diet of enforced trends and bad taste—Michael Jackson, Culture Club, the new young Metallists. Now narrowcasting video magnates and racist radio programmers ran pop music. Led Zeppelin had been bad-mouthed as gangsters for years, but now the *real* bullies had their way. Some fans felt that Led Zeppelin was better off dead than under their thumb.

A LED ZEPPELIN BIBLIOGRAPHY

Altman, Billy. "Front Page News." *Village Voice*, Dec. 18, 1983.

Atlantic Records. "Robert Plant" (publicity biography). 1982.

Barton, Geoff. "Rare Plant." *Sounds*, Aug. 13, 1983.

Blake, John. "Zeppelin's 'Black Magic' Mystery." *London Evening News*, Sept. 26, 1980.

———. "Page's Plan." *The Sun*, Jan. 6, 1984.

Bradley, S. A. J. *Anglo Saxon Poetry*. London: Dent, 1982.

Bronson, Harold. *The Yardbirds/Afternoon Tea*. Los Angeles: Rhino Records RNDF 253, 1982.

Burroughs, William S. "Rock Magic." *Crawdaddy*, June 1975.

Calta, Louis. "Led Zeppelin Ticket Sales Stir Crowds and Disorder." *The New York Times*, Jan. 1975.

Carr, Roy, and Howard Mylett. "Everything You Wanted to

Know about Led Zeppelin . . ." *New Musical Express*, May 17, 1975.

Coleman, Ray. "Zeppelin Over America." *Melody Maker*, June 25, 1977.

Colin, Jacques. "Vol Sans Escale" ("Nonstop Flight"). *Rock et Folk*, July 1980.

Considine, J. D. "Robert Plant." *Musician*, Dec. 1983.

Crowe, Cameron. *Fast Times at Ridgemont High.* New York: Simon & Schuster, 1981.

———. "Led Zeppelin" (interview). *Rolling Stone*, March 13, 1975.

———. "Secrets of the Object Revealed." *Rolling Stone*, June 3, 1976.

Davis, C. B. *Led Zeppelin Gothic—Rock in the Midwest.* Garden City, N.Y.: Herta, 1983.

———. *Presence—The Gods Go on Vacation.* Germantown: Wissahickon Press, 1983.

———. *A Rune with a View.* New York: New Goatish Library, 1983.

Delahunt, Jim. "Yardbird Jimmy Page Says, 'Open Your Minds.' " *Hit Parader*, March 1967.

Douglas, Alfred. *The Tarot.* New York: Penguin, 1973.

Flynn, Bob. "Robert Plant/Edinburgh Playhouse." *Melody Maker*, Dec. 3, 1983.

Gardiner, Diane. "Jimmy Page: Magic Music Man." *Hit Parader*, April 1970.

Gett, Steve. "Led Zeppelin Über Alles!" *Melody Maker*, July 12, 1980.

———. *Robert Plant.* London: Spotlight, 1983.

Gillett, Charlie. *The Sound of the City.* London: Souvenir Press, 1983.

Godwin, Robert. *The Illustrated Led Zeppelin Collection.* Kitchener, Ontario: Blue Flake Productions, 1984.

Gold, Mick. *Rock on the Road.* London: Futura, 1976.

Goldberg, Danny. "On Tour with Led Zeppelin." *Hit Parader*, Dec. 1973.

Green, Jim. "Simon Napier-Bell." *Trouser Press*, Oct. 1981.

Greenberg, Alan. *Love in Vain*. Garden City, N.Y.: Doubleday/Dolphin, 1983.

Gross, Michael. *Robert Plant*. New York: Popular Library, 1975.

Harper, Roy. *Harper 1970–1975* (album liner notes). London: Harvest/EMI Records SHSM 2025, 1976.

————. "Finger on the Pulse." *Melody Maker*, March 19, 1977.

Herr, Michael. "Rock Is Hell." *Crawdaddy*, January 1978.

Hodenfield, Jan. "Pursuit of a Zeppelin." *New York Post*, May 21, 1974.

Hollingsworth, Roy. "Zapped by Zeppelin." *Melody Maker*, Dec. 1971.

Huddleston, Henry. "Led Zeppelin/Kezar Stadium." *Rolling Stone*, July 1973.

Hutchinson, John. "Robert Plant: Into the Light." *Record*, Sept. 1983.

Jerome, Jim. "Led Zeppelin." *People*, Dec. 20, 1976.

————. "Robert Plant Is Flying Solo." *People*, Aug. 9, 1982.

Jones, Jerene. "Robert Plant and Led Zeppelin Have Risen Again." *People*, August 27, 1979.

Kane, Joseph. "Alcohol Blamed in Bonham's Death." *Rolling Stone*, Nov. 15, 1980.

Kendall, Paul. *Led Zeppelin in Their Own Words*. London: Omnibus Press, 1981.

————. *Led Zeppelin: A Visual Documentary*. London: Omnibus Press, 1982.

Kent, Nick. "Jimmy Page: The Roaring Silence." *New Musical Express*, Nov. 20, 1976.

————. "The Page Memoirs." *Creem*, May 1974.

Lammers, Tjerk. "Forging Ahead with Robert Plant." *Rock*, Feb. 1984.

Landau, Jon. *It's Too Late to Stop Now*. San Francisco: Straight Arrow Books, 1972.

Led Zeppelin. New York: Modern Day Periodicals, 1980.

Led Zeppelin. Birmingham: Creem Close-Up, 1981.

Led Zeppelin Complete. New York: Warner Bros., 1973.

Led Zeppelin: In Through the Out Door. New York: Swan Song/Flames of Albion/Warner Bros., 1980.

Lewis, Dave. *Led Zeppelin: The Final Acclaim*. Manchester: Babylon Books, 1983.

———, and Geoff Barton. "The Complete Led Zep." *Sounds*, Sept. 16, 25, 30, 1978.

Loder, Kurt, and Michael Goldberg. "Rock of Ages: Ronnie Lane & Co." *Rolling Stone*, Jan. 19, 1984.

Margouleff, Perry. "Beck, Clapton and Page." *Guitar Player*, Jan. 1984.

Marsh, Dave. *Before I Get Old*. New York: St. Martin's Press, 1983.

———. "Every Leaf Must Fall." *Record*, March 1984.

Mylett, Howard. *Jimmy Page: Tangents Within a Framework*. London: Omnibus Press, 1983.

———. *Led Zeppelin*. London: Granada, 1981.

———, and Richard Burton. *Led Zeppelin in the Light*. London: Proteus, 1981.

Newsweek. "American Graffiti" (on Zeppelin's supposed Satanism). May 17, 1982.

Owen, David. *High School*. New York: Viking, 1981.

Palmer, Miles. *The New Wave Explosion*. London: Proteus, 1981.

Palmer, Robert. *Deep Blues*. New York: Viking, 1981.

———. "Led Zeppelin Gone, Group Lives On." *New York Times*, July 7, 1982.

Palmer, Tony. "Stairway to Heaven." *The Observer Magazine*, May 18, 1975.

People. "Led Zeppelin." Aug. 20, 1973.

Platt, John, with Chris Dreja and Jim McCarty. *Yardbirds*. London: Sidgwick & Jackson, 1983.

Preston, Neal. *Led Zeppelin/Portraits*. Los Angeles: Mirage Books, 1983.

Pulver, Jeffrey. *Paganini, The Romantic Virtuoso*. New York: Da Capo Press, 1970.

Robinson, Douglas H. *The Zeppelin in Combat*. Seattle: University of Washington Press, 1980.

Robinson, Lisa. "The Led Zeppelin Circus Is Back." *Creem*, Sept. 1973.

———. "Led Zeppelin Dances on Air." *Creem*, May 1975.

———. "Led Zeppelin: The Hit Parader Interview." *Hit Parader*, April 1977

Rolling Stone, Editors of. *The Rolling Stone Record Review*. New York: Pocket Books, 1971.

———. *The Rolling Stone Record Review Vol. II*, New York: Pocket Books, 1974.

———. *The Rolling Stone Rock Almanac*. New York: Rolling Stone Press, 1983.

Rosen, Steve. "Jimmy Page." *Guitar Player*, July 1977.

———. "John Paul Jones." *Guitar Player*, July 1977.

Salewicz, Chris. "Smiling Men with Bad Reputations." *New Musical Express*, Aug. 1979.

Sander, Ellen. *Trips*. New York: Charles Scribner's Sons, 1973.

Schulps, Dave. "Jimmy Page" (three part interview). *Trouser Press*, Sept.–Nov. 1977.

Spence, Lewis. *Myth and Ritual in Dance, Game and Rhyme*. London: Watts, 1947.

Standish, David. "Missing Planks on the Stairway to Heaven." Unpublished manuscript, 1973.

Strick, Wesley. "Jimmy Page Files His Report." *Circus*, June 9, 1979.

Tobler, John, and Stuart Grundy. *The Guitar Greats*. New York: St. Martin's Press 1984.

———. *The Record Producers*. New York: St. Martin's Press, 1982.

Weinberg, Max, and Robert Santelli. *The Big Beat*. Chicago: Contemporary, 1984.

Welch, Chris. "Jimmy Page: Paganini of the Seventies." *Melody Maker* (three-part profile), Feb. 14, 21, 28, 1970.

———. *Jimmy Page, Sonny Boy Williamson, & Brian Auger* (album liner notes). London: Charly Records CR 30193, 1975.

———. "Led Zeppelin." *Melody Maker*, March 13, 1971.

————. "Page: It's a Massive Compromise Making Films." *Melody Maker*, Nov. 20, 1976.

————. "Plant: Converting the Blues." *Melody Maker*, March 19, 1977.

————. "Solved: The Great Zeppelin Mystery." *Melody Maker*, Jan. 1972.

————. "Why Led Zeppelin took off in America and not Britain." *Melody Maker*, March 1969.

————. "The Zeppelin Remains the Same." *Melody Maker*, Nov. 5, 1977.

Whitcomb, Ian. *Rock Odyssey*. Garden City, N.Y.: Doubleday/Dolphin, 1983.

Wilmer, Valerie. "Jimmy Page Talks about Led Zeppelin." *Hit Parader*, July 1969.

Wilson, Colin. *The Occult*. New York: Random House, 1972.

Yorke, Ritchie. *The Led Zeppelin Biography*. New York: Methuen, 1976.